CHURCH DOCTRINE AND PRACTICE

CHURCH DOCTRINE
AND
PRACTICE

selections of ministry from
Precious Seed

Edited by
J. Heading and C.E. Hocking

PRECIOUS SEED PUBLICATIONS

Precious Seed Publications
P.O. Box 8
Neath
West Glam., U.K.
SA11 1QB

ISBN 1 871642 13 2
© 1970 Precious Seed Publications
Reprinted 1971, 1975, 1984, 1999

Printed in Ireland by ColourBooks Ltd.

Preface to the 1970 Edition

In preparing this selection of ministry on "Church doctrine and practice" to mark the 25th anniversary of the publication of *Precious Seed*, the anniversary falling in September 1970, the Editors have worked in full fellowship with their brethren on the *Precious Seed* Committee, and in particular they acknowledge special help received from Messrs. Leonard Cave, Denis Clapham, H. Hobbs, W. J. Mansfield and J. Williamson.

The object of the selection was to secure as wide a range as possible of every aspect of what is commonly known as "church truth". In some sections, the subject matter of individual articles may overlap slightly, being expressed both in easily read prose style and in more detailed note form for careful study. Articles have been selected from the Young Believers' Section as well as from the main body of the magazine, ensuring that the book is suitable for every age group, both spiritual and natural. Four articles have been specially written for this book.

In editing the articles for republication, the Editors have touched as little as possible the original style and presentation. The layout has, however, been harmonized throughout, to gain complete uniformity with the magazine's present house-style. In reading the articles, the Editors have noticed here and there that a few authors' interpretations of certain words and phrases outwardly appear to be contradictory. Where such comments are *scripturally true*, the articles have been left untouched, with no imposition of editorial judgment as to which explanation more appropriately fits the particular context.

Some authors whose work is reprinted are now with the Lord, while others are still engaged in His service here; we are thankful to make their past writings available once more.

The Editors and the Committee trust that the Lord will use this selection of ministry "for doctrine, for reproof, for correction, for instruction in righteousness, that the man of God may be perfect, thoroughly furnished unto all good works", and that every reader may know "how thou oughtest to behave thyself in the house of God, which is the church of the living God".

JOHN HEADING
CYRIL HOCKING

Preface to the 1999 Edition

The reissuing of *Church Doctrine and Practice* in its original format is tribute to the value of its contents, and evidence of a continuing demand for scriptural teaching concerning the structure and operations of the church, universal and local.

There is a natural tendency to assume that passage of time must bring about regulated change in the affairs of institutions if they are to survive in a constantly changing world. To keep up with the times is judged to be essential, so that infusion of new ideas to promote change of practices is welcomed. In a general sense, as it is applied to ordinary institutions and social groups, few would challenge such an assumption: outdated practices hold little appeal, and even less relevance, for the people of today.

However, the certain logic that accepts that change is inevitable with the passage of time hardly applies in matters ordained by God. That which is established by God must always be acknowledged, whatever the time or place. That which He creates is unique, and is not subject to change according to the judgements of men in calculated adaptation to suit changes in their circumstances. How true this is of the church – planned in eternity past by God, brought about in time at infinite cost, and destined to be 'a glorious church' for all eternity to come!

We rest, with assurance, upon the promises of an unchanging God. Let us continue to obey the precepts of an unchanging God, conducting our affairs within the parameters He has established for all time. It is with such thoughts in mind that we commend this new edition to a new generation of readers.

IVAN STEEDS
January 1999

CONTENTS

Warnings and Exhortations

INTRODUCTION

"Precious Seed" 1945-1970

by C. GAHAN*

THIS BOOK is published as the magazine *Precious Seed* reaches its twenty-fifth anniversary of service, and we cannot let the occasion pass without recording our gratitude to God for enabling us throughout these years to publish a magazine devoted to the exposition of New Testament Church Principles. Many readers will be acquainted with the history and policy of the magazine, but this may be a fitting moment to explain the reasons for its inception in 1945. For some time before the second world war, there had been in many quarters a growing concern at the decline of clear teaching in matters of assembly life and order. The war with its inevitable aftermath only served the more to emphasize this downgrade trend. Prior to the first issue in September 1945, several meetings were held at Taunton, Somerset, for the consideration of this important matter, and a number of brethren reached the unanimous conclusion that the situation called for wider systematic instruction in Scriptural Principles of Gathering. It was the considered opinion of these brethren that the need could best be met by publishing an attractive magazine containing sound exposition of New Testament principles of worship and service, together with reliable information of Gospel work in connection with the above assemblies. These brethren did not overlook the fact that there were already a number of magazines in circulation among these assemblies, but they felt that from an assembly point of view these magazines left much to be desired; instruction in New Testament Church teaching was scanty in the extreme, and in

* This article has been specially written for this book.

these magazines there was a lack of information about the activities of the assemblies and the labours of God's servants in the work of the Gospel. In view of this and all the circumstances of the case, they were satisfied that a magazine with these special objects in view was amply justified. *Precious Seed*, therefore, was born out of a deep conviction that the great need of the moment was a reaffirmation of New Testament Church Principles in assembly life and service. Looking at these words afresh we can say that our experience over the years has only confirmed the above conviction. So much for the past, but –

What of the Future? For the future, the key-note of *Precious Seed* will remain the same. Firmly believing that there is a definite responsibility upon every Christian to avoid unscriptural systems of worship and service, we shall continue to emphasize the importance of divine principles of gathering. Just as every new generation of unbelievers must be won afresh for Christ, so each new generation of believers must be instructed afresh in God's pattern for "the churches of the saints". What we are trying to say here can be summed up in words that we wrote some years ago: "To give sane and balanced teaching along these lines is the policy of *Precious Seed*. How far we have succeeded in so doing we must leave our readers to judge. We have sought to avoid widening any existing differences; it is not our intention to swing from one extreme to the other, but rather to give a simple and sensible presentation of the teaching of Scripture. Nor have we forgotten the divine injunction to 'speak the truth in love', and this because we have little liking for controversy with, or criticism of, others. It has been well said that good tidings spoken harshly are no good tidings. To expound the truth of the Church in a harsh, bigoted and intolerant manner (and this is by no means uncommon) is no recommendation of it. Let us beware lest in our zeal for the truth we engender a narrow and ungracious spirit. The fact that this particular truth is unpopular with some, is but another reason for dealing with it in love. This will we continue to do in these pages; we shall constantly endeavour to preserve the divine equilibrium of 'truth in love' ".

Over the years we have counted it no small privilege to have been of some help to our magazine readers in emphasizing the importance of building up a strong and vigorous assembly-life, taking the Word of God as our guide. These readers are now numerous as our circulation figures clearly show; we are now reaching the twenty-thousand mark. If the magazine and this book have helped you, will you help us by making a special effort to make the magazine more widely known? To our many readers at home and abroad we send our Christian greetings, expressing the hope that you may all find increasing pleasure and profit in God, and that He may find increasing pleasure and profit in you.

The World Church

by A. E. PHILLIPS

WITH THE LAMP of prophecy in our hands, this "murky" world is seen to have dark shadows cast by coming events. The last days are to be times of apostasy from the truth of God, and the "itching ears" of the congregations will "accumulate for themselves teachers to suit their own likings", 2 Tim. 4. 3 R.S.V. The vapouring of such teachers would be "blasphemous", 1 Tim. 1. 20; "lies", 4. 2; "unwholesome", 6. 3; "gangrenous", 2 Tim. 2. 17; "devoid of spiritual discernment", 3. 8, marg.; and "unhealthy", 4. 3.

It is unnecessary to produce proof that we are living in such times, for error has now become organized. Most denominations have acquiesced in the dissolution of the truth, despite those in their midst who have taken a commendable stand for the basic beliefs of the gospel.

A hotch-potch of pseudo-Christianity will yet be formed and, abandoning distinctive truths of Christianity, will boast of its unity as well as its power. This Babylon – for such she is called – has her precursors, and we are right in expecting that she will prepare beforehand for her short time of Jezebel-like glory, Rev. 17. In view of this, it behoves those who look for the Day Star to assess present religious movements in the light of the Word of Truth, lest the winds of false teaching carry them along in the current of merely fashionable Christianity.

Now, the confused state of Christendom is apparent to all, and varied have been the attempts to bring harmony among the many factions. Most of these attempts have miserably failed, but we are now witnessing a new and far-reaching attempt to establish a universal church. To this end, major portions of many denominations have joined together with the purpose of establishing this "inclusivist" church. The Roman church,* so far, has superciliously drawn its garments tighter and frowned upon the new venture, yet it is showing more than a passing interest, for it has frequently been invited to become an essential part of the ecumenical

* This article was written in 1952.

church. The Greek church sometimes deigns to associate with the movement.

The movement already has attained to tremendous proportions, and has exerted no small power in some lands. Its platform includes all "Christian" creeds, whilst by mis-application the Lord's prayer "that they all may be one", John 17. 21, seems to have become a religious totem. Of course it often finds difficulty in expressing itself in terms of belief, and not all its member-groups feel at home in it (as an archbishop confessed), but its local councils often contrive to clear up such difficulties.

It should not be thought that an idea is just being toyed with. Rather is it being translated into action, and being aggressively pursued. Not a few theological colleges are doting on the idea, and courses in "Ecumenics" will soon be general. Some mission-fields have felt the pressure of this movement, resulting in some Missionary Societies feeling capitulation to be the safer course.

Yet, mere criticism of these associations is quite inadequate. What provision have we for such times of apostasy? Is there a workable plan for pure Christian testimony? Our spiritual instinct tells us there must be, for we rightly expect the Head of the Church to have left nothing to fortuitous circumstances. It is for just such a time that the word is prepared: "the foundation of God standeth sure, . . . *and*, let every one that nameth the name of Christ depart from iniquity", 2 Tim. 2. 19. To assert the fact of the first clause, whilst neglecting the warning of the second, is akin to confessing a fruitless creed.

The last days have their own characteristics, see 3. 1–5, but they should throw into better relief "the doctrine" *and* "manner of life" which have been found in the God-breathed Scriptures, vv. 10, 14 and 16. Let the reader collate references in the Epistles to Timothy regarding the inspiration, value, and authority of Holy Scripture for individual and church alike. It will prove more than interesting!

It is evident that in view of world developments, both religious and political, God's principles for church life are the most suitable, as well as authoritative. Under pressure of unfriendly governments, or the persecution of religious systems, it is found that God's way works. This does not mean that the cold blasts of earth are not felt by such churches, for they are exotic plants which are not in their native soil down here. Nevertheless, New Testament Christian vigour, testimony and "body-consciousness" are best perpetuated in such gatherings.

China is a good proving-ground, and it must be conceded that local churches, each directly responsible to the Lord and without central denominational authority, not only have the best possibility of survival, but also the best means of propagation. Other lands witness to the same truth, and if a world-survey were possible it would decisively and universally justify apostolic methods. How we should value them and encourage one another in God's ways!

Objections to these truths are due, we feel, to two weaknesses. Firstly, an ill-informed criticism, which wrongly equates bigotry with adherence to the pattern. Secondly, the attempt to use the Spirit's principles of gathering without the accompanying Spirit's power. But mists of doubt born of our weakness should not be allowed to becloud the pattern "shown in the mount".

It is good that we "measure the pattern", not just as a lifeless blue-print, but to lead to "shame" for our shortcomings, Ezek. 43. 10, 11. Then the glory of the Lord will fill the house. At such times as these, how necessary to be "taken up by the Spirit" into the "inner court" of God's purposes, v. 5, and then to allow no intruder into the gate which belongs to the Head alone, 44. 2, so that God may have "glory in the church", Eph. 3. 21.

The Church and The Churches

by JOHN HEADING*

Vocabulary, Profane and Spiritual. Every subject, whether spiritual, natural or academic, has its own specialized vocabulary, and the subject cannot be properly grasped if this vocabulary is not appreciated. Any process of "modern-

* This article has been specially written for this book.

ization" or of "simplification" by-passes the true nature and basis of a subject if the corresponding specialized vocabulary is discarded. Appreciation of a subject is also restricted if parts of this vocabulary are twisted and distorted in meaning, either by traditional development or by modernistic trends and heresies. The word "church" has suffered more than most in this direction.

If almost any person in the street were asked what "the church" or "a church" is, answers would essentially conform to the standard definitions found in any dictionary, namely "an organized Christian society at any time" such as the Established Church, or "building for public Christian worship". However, the English word "church" originates from the Greek word *kuriakos* which occurs in the New Testament twice only, namely in the expressions "the Lord's supper", 1 Cor. 11. 20, and "the Lord's day", Rev. 1. 10. The New Testament Greek word translated "church" is *ekklesia*, derived from a verb meaning "to summon forth". It is used of the congregation of the children of Israel, Acts 7. 38. In a profane sense, it is used of a popular assembly of town folk, as in Ephesus, Acts 19. 32, 39, 41. Translators such as Tyndale would use the word "congregation" consistently for this Greek word *ekklesia*, employing the actual word "church" in Acts 19. 37 to refer to a heathen temple. The Authorized Version retains this rendering "church" in Acts 19. 37, but unfortunately uses this same word for *ekklesia*, thereby introducing a perpetual confusion. In the New Testament, this Greek word *ekklesia* is never used of a building, and it is a great achievement of the powers of darkness, influencing the very thinking of people through the mistaken meanings of words, to direct attention to buildings rather than to the redeemed people of the Lord. The Lord's last public announcement regarding religious buildings is in Matthew 24. 2, when He said of the temple in Jerusalem that not one stone would be left upon another.

Spiritual Concepts and Affections. What, then, should be the spiritual appreciation of the Lord's people concerning the Church? Does it really matter, some would say, as long as the knowledge of salvation is firmly held? Let such realize that "God so loved the world", John 3. 16, and that "Christ also loved the church", Eph. 5. 25. Sinners to be saved by grace on the one hand, and the Church to be sanctified, washed and presented on the other, cannot be separated in the divine affections, and so young converts – yea, and more mature ones as well – who have no interest in the things of the Church, demonstrate a stunted growth, and like a plant, need to face the sun so as to grow in the direction of the light.

The Church. The Church is often designated by expressions such as "the universal Church" or "the mystical Church", though it must be realized that these are expressions not found in Scripture.

The Church in its universal or mystical form consists of believers in the Lord Jesus throughout all time from Pentecost to the rapture, from one end of the earth to the other. Most of its members are no longer on earth in the sphere of their testimony, but they are "absent from the body . . . present with the Lord", 2 Cor. 5. 8. The Church is eternal in its divine concept. In the *past* it was rooted in the eternal counsels of God in Christ. In the fulness of time, this Church has been purchased with the blood of the Son, Acts 20. 28; He gave Himself for it, Eph. 5. 25, as well as for individual believers, Gal. 2. 20. In the *present*, this Church is now for the pleasure of Christ its Living Head; it is unassailable, Matt. 16. 18, and it is the divine purpose that the mind and life of Christ should operate in and through His members. Moreover, in the *future* this Church is seen as the Bride of Christ, Rev. 19. 7–8, that shall be His complement throughout the eternal ages.

What a thrill such concepts should bring to every heart – truths unknown by the men of the world who can see nothing of this vast universal and age-long entity bringing pleasure to Christ. What deep affection it should form, what loyalty should be developed, what a separating influence such truth should have in the Christian life.

The Local Churches. In Acts 2, the initial stages of the building of the Church by the Lord Jesus corresponded with the initial development of the first local church, namely that at Jerusalem. The practice of those who had been baptized in one Spirit into one body corresponded with the practice of the local assembly. The zeal of the house of the Lord caused the early converts to be baptized in water, thereafter continuing "steadfastly in the apostles' doctrine and fellowship, and in breaking of bread, and in prayers", Acts 2. 42. This was no mere formal, mechanical service, neither was it based on tradition. Rather, the practice was maintained by a living, spiritual exercise; it was the manifestation of the power of the Spirit causing the local assembly to function in keeping with the revealed mind of the Lord.

The local churches, both individually and in numbers, grew through the gospel message spreading far and wide. We never find any other pattern in the New Testament. When evangelistic efforts in a new district were successful then the converts were gathered together as a local church as a normal spiritual conclusion to conversion. When such local churches had been formed, Paul ever continued to be exercised about them, in that there came upon him "daily, the care of all the churches", 2 Cor. 11. 28. For whereas the Church universal cannot be assailed since it depends upon the work of Christ alone, yet local churches can be disturbed and damaged in many ways, since their well-being depends on responsibility and obedience. In the New Testament, the churches in Galatia, the church at Corinth, the church at Colosse, and the seven churches in Revelation 2–3 give examples of local testimony in doctrine, service and conduct departing from the New Testament pattern. For the Church universal, the Lord Jesus is seen as Bridegroom, but for the local churches, He is seen walking among them with His eyes "as a flame of fire", and with a "sharp twoedged sword" proceeding from His mouth, Rev. 1. 14, 16. He walks as the corrective Discerner of the hearts and practices of the local churches, the extreme remedy being the removal of a local testimony, as in the case of Laodicea.

The Present Position. Present day weaknesses are indicative of a decline in the appreciation of local church doctrine, which is expounded at such length in the New Testament. The tendency to copy the systems erected by men, thereby to be "carnal, and walk as men", 1 Cor. 3. 3, and to abandon the holy things instituted by God, seems to be gathering momentum. The natural appetite for carnality, worldliness, academic theology and denominationalism is gaining the ascendency over the spiritual appetite for the things revealed by the Spirit. The remedy can only be repentance and a return to doing the first works, both hearts and hands being rectified, by practical resanctification towards the things of the Lord. The following pages develop in considerable detail these great concepts of the Church and the local churches.

THE CHURCH

❦❦❦❦❦❦

The Church Universal

by T. W. CARRON

WHEN MEN SPEAK of the Church they usually have in mind the mass of religious systems professing the Christian name, including, for example, the Church of Rome, the Eastern Orthodox Church, the Anglican, Lutheran, Presbyterian Churches, the Congregational, Baptist, Methodist, and many other bodies and fellowships. These systems and sects which compose Christendom are not however the Church described in the New Testament. Some contain obviously a very large proportion of persons who are Christian in name only, and many who deny the very foundations of the Christian faith. As foretold by the apostles, false teachers have entered the Christian profession, and they have gained many followers. In 2 Timothy 2. 19 the apostle Paul says: "The Lord knoweth them that are his", implying that man may not know. The Lord Himself, in the parable of the wheat and tares, said that among the wheat (whom He described as the children of the kingdom), the enemy would sow tares (whom He described as the children of the wicked one). He speaks of the field in which the wheat and tares are sown as the *world*, not as the Church. This is an important distinction which is often overlooked. The Church universal according to the New Testament is *not* a mixture of wheat and tares but Christ's own building, and it is unthinkable that He would build any spurious material into His Church. In Matthew 16. 18 we read: "upon this rock (referring to Peter's confession of Himself as the Christ, the Son of the Living God) I will build my church". Peter's confession was based on a supernatural revelation by God, the Father. This was the *rock*. The claim of the Roman Catholic Church that the Lord was proposing to build His Church on

Peter is utterly repugnant to the whole teaching of Scripture. Such a notion was not held by the early Church. The collateral idea that Peter was the first pope is also without historical foundation.

It may be well to point out at this stage that much is said about local churches but we shall deal with this later. Here we are dealing with the Church in its complete, age-long, or "universal" aspect, as composed only of born-again persons who have received the Holy Spirit. Such persons Peter calls living stones. All others are dead in trespasses and sins, whatever their religious or ecclesiastical profession may be.

It should be observed that most of the references to the Church "universal" are found in the Epistles to the Ephesians and Colossians. These references we now deal with. In Ephesians 1. 22-23 Christ is presented in all His glory as Head over all things, and the Church is said to be His body, the fulness (the counterpart or complement) of Him who fills all in all. It is impossible to conceive any greater role for the Church than this. He is the Head and the Church is His body. The body is the means of expression, and in the coming day of glory Christ will express Himself through the Church, His body. She is moreover His complement. As Adam, head over the physical creation, needed the woman as his complement, so it has pleased God in His wisdom to give Christ a complement – the Church, composed of all those who, through the ages, have been redeemed, and baptized by the Holy Spirit into *one body*. As Paul says in Ephesians 5. 32, "This is a great mystery". The same truth is presented in Revelation 21. 9 where the angel tells John "I will show thee the bride, the Lamb's wife" and proceeds to show him the holy city in which the glory of God shines in the coming age of glory. Such is the divine presentation of the *true* Church. The judgment of the *false* church is described in Revelation 17. The true Church is invisible as a united whole today. Many of those who compose it are with Christ and the members on earth are hidden in the mass of Christendom. However, while hidden in her completeness from human eyes, the true Church is known and recognized in heaven and even *now* through her is perceived by angelic beings the all-various wisdom of God. They see God at work in redemption. They witness joy in their presence when a sinner repents. They see God's ways as the living stones are formed for the great building which Christ is erecting – His Church, Eph. 3. 10.

In Ephesians 5 the apostle uses the relationship of husband and wife – the closest and most intimate relationship God has created – to illustrate the relationship of Christ and the Church. Christ "loved the church", he writes, "and gave himself up for her, that he might sanctify her, having cleansed her by the washing of water with the word, that he might present the church to himself in splendour, without spot or wrinkle or any such thing, that she might be holy and without blemish", vv. 25–27 R.S.V. Christ foresaw the Church in all her beauty as His bride-to-be when He gave Himself up for her in order to redeem those who were to form it. Doubtless this was in His mind when, in parable, He spoke of the merchantman seeking goodly pearls, who having found one pearl of great price, sold all He had to secure it. (A common misinterpretation of that parable makes Christ Himself the pearl. Sinners however cannot be compared to a merchantman seeking goodly pearls. Unregenerate men seek the evil things of this world. The prodigal son was not seeking goodly pearls when he wasted his substance in riotous living).

In Colossians, which brings before us the glory of Christ as the One by whom and for whom all things were created, it states that one of His glories is that He is the Head of the Church, 1. 18, and the Church is again said to be His body in 1. 24.

In Hebrews 12. 23 the Church is described as the Church of the first-born ones whose names are written in heaven. First-born here refers to pre-eminence, not order of time. The Church is composed of Christ's brethren. There can be no higher rank than this on earth or in heaven. Hence they are the Church of first-born ones.

These Scriptures demonstrate clearly the nature, status and destiny of the Church "universal" as presented in Scripture, and clearly distinguish it from the mass of sects which in men's eyes is the Church. It is hidden to-day, but it will be displayed in glory with Christ in that day described in Revelation 19. 6–7: "And I heard as it were the voice of a great multitude, and as the voice of many waters, and as the voice of mighty thunderings, saying, Alleluia: for the Lord God omnipotent reigneth. Let us be glad and rejoice, and give honour to him: for the marriage of the Lamb is come, and his wife hath made herself ready".

Ephesian Figures of the Church

by A. McD. Redwood

THE EPISTLE TO THE EPHESIANS is the great exposition of the doctrine of the Church considered as a spiritual organism. In this Epistle the Church universal is presented under three (perhaps four) different figures, and it is well to study these figures carefully.

These figures are

1. A Body, 1. 22–23; 4. 15, 16; 5. 23;
2. A Bride, 5. 30–32; (2 Cor. 11. 2–3, in its local aspect);
3. A Building, 2. 20–22;
4. A further figure seems to be hinted at, that of a Family or Brotherhood, 2. 19.

These four aspects of the Church may be examined separately, but here we shall look at them as a whole in order to notice certain things that they have in common.

The first thing is that each is under a

Divine Controlling Will. What we mean is this: the Body, having a Head, is controlled by that Head, and so in that sense is possessed by the Head. Without the Head, the Body is not merely useless but lifeless. Then the Bride has a Bridegroom, otherwise there would be no bride. The Bridegroom (or Husband) takes the Bride to Himself, thereby coming into possession of her. She is thenceforth called by His name. The Building has a Designer, a Builder and a Possessor who owns it. It may be that the same one who designed the Building owns the Building, and so Architect and Possessor may be one and the same Person. Finally, no Brotherhood is likely to realize its fullest expression without some Leader, inspiring in the best sense its life and activities. In all this we are reminded of the relationship and position of the Lord Jesus towards the Church: He is at once the Head of the Body, the Bridegroom of the Bride, the Fashioner, Builder and Possessor of the Building, and the Leader of the Brotherhood (see Hebrews 2. 10–12).

The second point is that in connection with each figure there is a

Unique Commencement, a starting point when each came into being. It was "before the foundation of the world" that we were chosen in Christ, Eph. 1. 4. We remember also that the purpose to form one Body out of Jew and Gentile "from the beginning of the world hath been hid in God", Eph. 3. 9. The choice and the purpose were therefore in the eternal past, but the choice became manifest and the purpose was fulfilled in time. There was a day when the Body came into being, when it became a fact. That day was the day of Pentecost, Acts 2. 4. There the foundation of the Building was laid, "Jesus Christ himself being the chief corner stone", Eph. 2. 20. There also believers were constituted the Bride for the Bridegroom, and the Bride began to be made aware of her high calling. There the hidden meaning of the words "my brethren" in John 20. 17 began to be experienced. Manifestly the choice of eternity was ratified there.

The third point is that the Church, viewed under each of these figures,

Pursues a Definite Course, a process of development and growth, in preparation for that great future day. This process continues today during what we call the dispensation of the Church. Today, if only we would see and understand, we shall find the Body in expansion, the Bride in preparation, the Building in construction, the Brotherhood in progressive and holy conspiration, invisible and silent though the process may be. We use the word conspiration purposely to bring out the thought of agreement or concurrence for some common end or purpose.

Then each of these aspects brings out and emphasizes a particular point. In regard to the Body, the emphasis is on the growth to maturity, Eph. 4. 16. In regard to the Bride, the emphasis is on adornment with the grace of the Spirit in preparation for the day of presentation as a "glorious church, not having spot, or wrinkle, or any such thing; but that it should be holy and without blemish", Eph. 5. 27. In regard to the Building, the emphasis is not only on growth in cohesion, but growth in extension – one "living stone" being added to another, being "builded together for an habitation of God through the Spirit", Eph. 2. 22. Newly saved souls are therefore "fitly framed together". In regard to the Brotherhood, the emphasis is on growth in fellowship and mutual comfort, a holy conspiracy to edification (see Gal. 6. 10; 1 Tim. 5. 8).

The final consideration is that each has a

Consummation. The Body comes to perfection, the Bride realizes the joy of her presentation, the Building reaches completion and the Brotherhood attains the climax of spiritual harmony. The last stone will have been added, the last jewel of grace and love will have been fitly set, the last stages of maturity will have completed a "body of glory", and the last disciplinings of love shall have crowned Love's own Fraternity. The Head will never have cause to be ashamed of the members, the Bride will never leave the presence of the Bridegroom, God will ever have a perfect habitation, nevermore shall love be baffled. "The Church we oft forget" shall become the Church by His side.

The New Testament is given over to the revelation, the exposition, the illustration and the application of these truths. If we read the New Testament without seeing these facts we lose immeasurably. In the Gospels we find the historical foundation; Christ is there seen paying the price of His own blood for the Possession, whereby He becomes the rightful Possessor. Again, historically in the Acts, we find the commencement of the visible fulfilment of the eternal purpose "hid in God" – the formation of the Church. In other words, Christ is seen entering into visible possession of that which He has purchased. In the Epistles, we have a body of doctrine brought together, through the instrumentality of which the

Holy Spirit is in this day perfecting, adorning, building up the Possession. In the book of the Revelation, a glimpse is given of the future when the Possession is glorified in bliss.

"The Riches of the Glory of this Mystery"

by C. GAHAN

"To whom God would make known what is the riches of the glory of this mystery among the Gentiles; which is Christ in you, the hope of glory", Colossians 1. 27.

IN VERSES 24 to 27 of this first chapter of the Epistle to the Colossians, a special aspect of Paul's ministry is brought before us. It has to do with the mystery. Of this mystery he was the chosen minister or administrator. "Whereof", he says in verse 25, "I am made a minister". We can understand, therefore, why this theme always fired and thrilled him. It was revealed to him by special revelation from heaven; he was a chosen vessel unto God to make it known. In this meditation we shall confine ourselves to the verse quoted above. With silvery words born out of glowing thought, the apostle speaks of "the riches of the glory of this mystery among the Gentiles; which is Christ in you, the hope of glory". And this is no mere rhetoric; for Paul, this wonderful mystery was pregnant with unsearchable riches and radiant with unspeakable glory. Three things require our consideration here: (1) The *mystery*, (2) The *glory* of the mystery, (3) The *riches* of the glory of the mystery.

THE MYSTERY

Here let it be noted that New Testament mysteries must never be confounded with that which is incomprehensible. With but one exception, that is never the sense of the word in the New Testament; the one exception being "the mystery of godliness . . .", the mystery of the Incarnation. With this one exception, the word "mystery" always means that which was hidden but is now revealed. There have been mysteries relating to the purposes of God which have been hidden from the foundation of the world. Prophets have inquired and searched diligently into these mysteries, and angels have desired to look into them, but from them all these mysteries were concealed. Why? Because the key to their solution was held by Him who was to come. That is why, when Paul speaks of these mysteries, he uses the words "the mystery of Christ". No one could reveal the hidden counsels of heaven but "he who came down from heaven". When, in the fulness of time, He came, the time had arrived to make them known. New Testament mysteries, therefore, are no longer mysteries in the sense of being hidden; they reveal truth, and no longer conceal it. Such a mystery is the one now before us.

What It Is. What is this mystery of which the apostle is here thinking? The answer is to be found in the words, "among the Gentiles". He identifies this mystery with the Gentiles; the mystery being that Gentiles should be admitted to the blessings of salvation on equal terms with Jews. The old distinction between Jews and Gentiles was to be abolished, and an entirely new system of things was to be introduced. The state of Jew and Gentile, dispensationally, was to be brought to an end. Thus a new milestone was reached in the purposes of God. He Himself had instituted the distinction between Jews and Gentiles. The Jews were a chosen nation, a people set apart for God; between them and the nations of the earth God had set a wall of partition. But now, having fulfilled its purpose, the wall was to be taken down, and Jews and Gentiles were to be brought on to a new platform before God. In this new structure the Jew was to cease to be a Jew, and the Gentile was to cease to be a Gentile; both were to be welded into "one new man", Eph. 2. 15. This, then, was "the mystery which from the beginning of the world hath been hid in God", 3. 9. The mystery was not merely that Jew and Gentile should be blessed – that had been long foretold – the mystery was that the age-old line of demarcation between Jew and Gentile was to be removed, and "that the Gentiles should be fellow-heirs (with Israel), and of

the same body, and partakers of his promise in Christ by the
gospel", 3. 6. Of this mystery, as we have seen, the apostle
Paul was the chief exponent. In him as the apostle of the
Gentiles the ages-old silence of heaven is broken, and through
him the long-kept secret is revealed. Not only believing Jews,
but believing Gentiles were to be brought into the fulness
of the blessing of the gospel of Christ.

What It Does. It produces a new thing on the earth, a
new division among mankind. We have already seen that the
human race was regarded as being divided into two classes,
Jews and Gentiles. So it had been since the time of Israel's
exodus from the land of Egypt. All inside the nation of Israel
were Jews, all outside – outside Jewish worship, privilege, and
blessing – were Gentiles. These two classes embraced the
whole human family on earth. But with the advent of the
truth of the mystery a new division appeared. It was no
longer just Jews and Gentiles, now it was "Jews, . . .
the Gentiles, . . ., the church of God", 1 Cor. 10. 32. It was
no longer two, but three distinct divisions; the Jew out of the
nation of Israel, the Gentile out of the nations of the earth,
and the Church of God out of both. Here was something
altogether new; this was the secret "which in other ages was
not made known to the sons of men", Eph. 3. 5. It was something that had not existed before. Saints there had been,
but they were not the Church; Old Testament saints were
never constituted the Church or Assembly of God. The
Church was not Israel; the Jews were a people separated
unto God, but they were not the Church. The Church is
essentially a New Testament truth. Our Lord Himself, in one
of His most weighty sayings, effectually disposes of the
possibility of there being any Church prior to the New
Testament. Of Himself, He says to Peter, "Upon this rock
I *will* build my church". In this momentous utterance we
have the first mention of the Church in the Bible; until we
come to this passage in Matthew 16. 18, the Church is conspicuous by its absence. Even here it is not yet an established
fact. Speaking in the future tense, our Lord says, "Upon this
rock *I will build* my church". He Himself was the rock-

foundation of the Church; but not yet was the foundation laid, and you cannot raise the structure until the foundation has been laid. When was the foundation laid? It was laid when the Lord Jesus died and rose again, the wonderful event being sealed and certified by God Himself when the Holy Spirit came down from heaven. When the Lord Jesus ascended, the Holy Spirit descended, and with the coming of the Holy Spirit the Church was now a reality.

What It Implies. This wonderful mystery implies something greater and grander than any Israelite ever dreamed. Just as the Church is not Israel, so the Church is distinct from Israel. The Church was chosen in Christ from before the foundation of the world; Israel was chosen in Abraham after the worlds were made. The Church is heavenly in its hope and calling, whilst the hope and calling of Israel is of the earth. The hope of the Church is the glory of heaven; the hope of Israel is the sovereignty of the earth. The Church will share the throne of Christ; Israel, the throne of David. The Church, unified and glorified, will reign *over* the nations of them that are saved; Israel, converted and restored, will reign *among* the nations of the saved. Awaiting the Church is the New Jerusalem in the glorified heavens; awaiting Israel is the restored Jerusalem in the restored earth. The New Jerusalem above will overshadow the restored Jerusalem below, and beneath the glory of that Holy City, that New Jerusalem, converted Israel and saved nations will walk in the light of the Lord. That Israel will be glorified in a coming day is beyond question. She will be God's light in the earth, and nations will come to that light, and kings to the brightness of its rising. Unprecedented glory and blessing is awaiting both the Church and Israel, but for the Church it will be "a far more exceeding and eternal weight of glory". Whilst Israel will be exalted among the nations, the Church is to be exalted "far above all principality, and power". God is calling the Church out of the world "that in the ages to come he might show the exceeding riches of his grace, in his kindness toward us through Christ Jesus", Eph. 2. 7. In future ages the Church, and not Israel, will be the greatest triumph of redeeming grace.

Israel rests on earthly promise,
   Israel's heart is on "the land",
There, for God Himself hath said it,
   Israel shall in triumph stand.
But the Church, with eyes uplifted,
   Sees her all in heaven above;
Waits her blessed Bridegroom's coming,
   As the object of her love.

THE GLORY OF THE MYSTERY

According to the apostle Paul in the magnificent fifteenth chapter of his first Epistle to the Corinthians, "there is one glory of the sun, and another glory of the moon, and another glory of the stars". And according to this same apostle there is a glory of the mystery. The word "glory" in this verse under consideration is no mere ornament or embellishment. A special and peculiar glory attaches to the mystery. What constitutes the glory of sun and moon and stars? Just this: They never talk about themselves; they talk about the great God who made them. It is not their beauty, it is not their harmony, it is not their profundity, it is not their multiplicity, it is their *testimony* which constitutes their chief glory. "The heavens declare the glory of God (literally, the heavens are recounting the glory of God); and the firmament sheweth His handywork", Psa. 19. 1. They are

For ever singing as they shine,
The hand that made us is divine.

A similar, and at the same time, grander glory belongs to the mystery. Of that mystery it is recorded: "To the intent that now unto the principalities and powers in heavenly places might be (made) known by the church the manifold wisdom of God", Eph. 3. 10. This constitutes the greater, grander glory of the mystery. "The glory of the celestial is one, and the glory of the terrestrial is another", 1 Cor. 15. 40. The glory of creation is one thing, the glory of redemption is another thing. Creation, magnificent as it is, is but the platform for the display of the manifold wisdom of God in the greater work of redemption. The Church is a witness to the redemptive work and purpose of God. And here she is a spectacle not only to men, but to angels. The dispensational purpose of God was the revelation of the mystery; the dispensational work of the Church is to make known to heavenly intelligences the wisdom of God in the glorious economy of redemption. For the Church this is a dispensation of testimony.

The Subject of this Testimony. The grand subject of this testimony is, as we have just intimated, "the manifold wisdom of God". A transcendent subject indeed! Who can doubt the wisdom of God!

> The heavens declare Thy glory Lord,
> In every star Thy wisdom shines.

None but a wise God could have contrived so great and wondrous a universe. Every star that glitters, every flower that grows, every bird that sings, every river and stream, every wood and hedge-row, every rolling sea and placid lake, every lofty mountain and high hill, and all things great and small in nature's vast and glorious panorama, bears constant testimony to "the manifold wisdom of God". "O Lord, how manifold are thy works! in wisdom hast thou made them all", Psa. 104. 24. And if this is true of creation, much more is it true of redemption. Redemption is the great masterpiece of God's wisdom.

What a masterpiece of divine wisdom is God's remedy for human ruin! How can sin be condemned, yet the sinner freed from condemnation? How can God so save sinful men, that, at the same time His honour shall remain untarnished and the righteous claims of His throne be fully met? How can God be just, and yet justify every sinner who believes? How can God be just and good? How can God temper justice with mercy? It was here that the wisdom of God came in. A way was contrived whereby every problem was solved, every question answered, and every claim fully met. Justice and mercy found a suitable meeting-place in Christ crucified.

The Son of God took our place; He the just One suffered for the unjust; He the sinless One died for the sinful. In the obedience unto death of God's dear Son, the claims of both justice and mercy have been met, the one in punishment and the other in pardon. The law which says that the sinner must die, has been so fulfilled that it can now say: "Let him live". Well might we say with the apostle, "O the depth of the riches both of the wisdom and knowledge of God"! Mercy pitied us, love wept over us, and grace sought us; but the contriving of a way to happiness between the justice of God and the sin of man, was the rich discovery of wisdom. Thus the Church is both a monument and a testimony to "the manifold wisdom of God".

> Oh, loving wisdom of our God!
> When all was sin and shame,
> A second Adam to the fight
> And to the rescue came.

The Objects of this Testimony. According to the verse already quoted in Ephesians, the special objects of this testimony are "principalities and powers in heavenly places". In the first chapter of the first Epistle of Peter, the apostle tells us that angels desire to look into these things; and the apostle Paul in chapter four of his first Epistle to the Corinthians, reminds us that we are a spectacle to angels. From these and other Scriptures, it is very evident that the angels contemplate with holy curiosity the beautiful house that wisdom has built out of redemption's precious and enduring materials. Clearly, "the house of God, which is the church of the living God" is of very deep interest to them.

Have we considered the implications of this sufficiently? We are accustomed to think of the angels as encamping round the godly, and ministering well-being to those who are the heirs of salvation. All of which is blessedly true. How tenderly the angels watch over us! They protect us from countless dangers, and lead us into the enjoyment of unnumbered blessings. A great deal of what we call providence is really the ministry of angels. How much we owe to their watchful care! On the other hand it is our privilege, not only to receive contributions *from* the angels, but to make contributions *to* the angels. "To the intent that now unto the principalities and powers in heavenly places might be *made known by the church* the manifold wisdom of God". What a dignity is ours! We are called to minister instruction to angels. Every redeemed soul is intended to be an object-lesson to angels. The call of the Church, involving as it did the marvellous scheme of redemption, was no afterthought with God. It was all part of an eternal plan which is of deepest interest to angels. In this gracious arrangement, purposed in God before time was, not only were Jews and Gentiles to be brought into one body – made into "one new man" – but angels, and principalities and powers, were to be enlightened in "the manifold wisdom of God".

The Vessel of this Testimony. The Church is the chosen vessel of this special testimony. We have already seen something of this. The Church is constituted a holy and beautiful vessel for the display of the manifold wisdom of God in the greatest and grandest of all His works, the work of redemption. Both in the universe of nature and the universe of grace, God is the great Workman. In that wonderful universe of wisdom, love, and power which we call creation, God has fashioned the most amazing instruments for His use and service. From the highest archangel to the creeping worm, from the loftiest mountain to the smallest grain of dust, all are intended to minister to God's pleasure. Every created thing and being in heaven, earth and sea is intended to be, in its measure, an expression of the glory of the invisible God.

So, too, in the universe of grace. Here, also, everything is intended to minister to God's glory. Thus the Son of God became incarnate, that in Him the glory of the invisible God might shine forth. He was "the brightness of his (God's) glory, and the express image (or substance) of his person", Heb. 1. 3. All that is of the essence of God was embodied in the Person of the Lord Jesus. His brightness was not the reflected brightness of His Father's glory, but the very brightness of that glory itself. In Him God is revealed to us in all the perfections of His uncreated light and glory. Such an unveiling of the glory of God there never had been before. Truly:

> God in the person of His Son,
> Hath all His mightiest works outdone.

But He who was the effulgence of His Father's glory is no longer here. He is now in heaven. Where is the glory of God resting now? It is resting on the Church. With the coming of the Holy Spirit, this beautiful vessel was formed, and upon it the glory of God is now resting, and through it the manifold wisdom of God is being made known. What honour God has heaped upon us! It is not through angels, principalities, and powers; it is not through heavens, worlds, and systems; it is not through sun, moon, and stars – it is largely through the Church that God is now revealing His perfections to the universe. Just as we give active expression to ourselves through the medium of our bodies, so, today, God is giving active expression to Himself through the medium of His body, the Church.

Such is the glory of the mystery. The Church is God's vessel of testimony on earth. It is both her privilege and responsibility to make known to men and angels the many-coloured glories of the manifold wisdom of God.

THE RICHES OF THE GLORY
OF THE MYSTERY

The word "riches" here is no mere instrument of rhetoric. For Paul, this wonderful mystery was overflowing with riches. All riches are attractive, but what riches could be more attractive to a spiritual mind than "the riches of the glory of the mystery"! What boundless wealth is intimated here! Elsewhere the apostle speaks of "the weak and beggarly elements" of Judaism. A striking contrast this to "the riches of the glory of the mystery". To be brought into the truth of the mystery is to be rich indeed. Power, not weakness; wealth, not poverty; is the keynote of the mystery. The word "riches", therefore, well describes that mystery, the revelation of which has conferred such unspeakable blessings on Jews and Gentiles. What constitutes "the *riches* of the glory of the mystery"? The apostle tells us: "which is Christ in you, the hope of glory". These riches are here comprehended in three things: "Christ", "hope", and "glory"; riches of Christ, riches of hope, and riches of glory.

Riches of Christ. "Christ in you", says the apostle. Christ in whom? Christ in you Gentiles. That was the wonderful thing. These sinners of the Gentiles not only received like precious privileges and like precious blessings with the heirs of the promises, Acts 11. 17, they also received a like precious Christ. Christ was among them, Christ was with them, Christ was for them, and, wonder of wonders, Christ was *in* them. Sinners they had been. In times past they had walked according to the course of this world, fulfilling the desires of the flesh and mind; but now, washed and sanctified, they were temples of the Holy Ghost. Christ was in them – in them saving them; in them separating them; in them transforming them; in them educating them; in them comforting them; in them both to will and to do His good pleasure.

And such a Christ, and such a privilege, is ours. He is not only among us, He is not only with us, He is not only for us, He is *in* us! What a heart-searching, soul-thrilling truth this is! Christ *in* us! Christ brought into our hearts by the Holy Ghost! That He should save us; that He should remove our transgressions as far as the east is from the west, is wonderful. But the greatest wonder is that He should take up His abode *in* us; that we should become the temples of His Presence. May it be ours to be temples in deed and in truth; temples of love, light, and power.

> Make me a temple O my God,
> Set apart for Thyself alone;
> A temple cleansed, a temple radiant,
> With Thee as Lord upon the throne.

Riches of Hope. To sinners of the Gentiles this wonderful mystery not only brings riches of Christ, it brings riches of hope. They had been without Christ and without hope; the mystery, therefore, brings a Christ to the Christless, and hope to the hopeless. Well might the apostle speak of "the *riches* of the glory of the mystery"; overflowing all barriers, it dispenses its wealth even to despised Gentiles.

Be it noted: Christ first, then hope. What is hope? Hope is the expectation of future good. But what expectation of future good could there have been for any child of Adam's fallen race but for the down-stooping of the Son of God? He is Himself the hope of every contrite heart. He is the fountain from whence all the streams of hope flow. He is the "Lord Jesus Christ, which is our hope", 1 Tim. 1. 1. He is Christian hope personified; the beautiful grace of hope is the fruit of which He is the root. This fruitful tree springs from the rich and fertile soil of His death and resurrection. God, "according to his abundant mercy hath begotten us again unto a living hope by the resurrection of Jesus Christ from the dead", 1 Pet. 1. 3. Natural hope sometimes dies, Christian hope never; it is bound up with Him who lives in the power of an endless life. While He lives Christian hope can never die. From whence comes this living hope? It arises from God's abundant mercy. Upon what does it rest? It rests on the basis of the resurrection of Jesus Christ from the dead.

> Hope is a living act
>   Of Jesus' life within;
> 'Tis founded on the Gospel fact,
>   That Jesus died for sin.

Riches of Glory. To sinners of the Gentiles this wonderful mystery not only brings riches of Christ and riches of hope, it brings riches of glory. The hope here is the hope of glory. What is hope? Hope is the joyful anticipation of glory. What is glory? Glory is the crown and consummation of hope. Two glories are mentioned in this verse under consideration; one is connected with the mystery, the other with the riches. The one is present, the other future; the one is here, the other is something outside of this scene altogether. The one is on earth, the other in heaven.

And what is true of hope, is true of glory. It is "Christ

in you, the hope of glory". Christ must be in me here, if I am to share His glory hereafter. Does not the apostle speak of salvation "in Christ Jesus with eternal glory"?, 2 Tim. 2. 10. There can be no eternal glory without salvation in Christ Jesus, and there can be no salvation in Christ Jesus without eternal glory. He who is the Christ of hope and glory will not fail to bring many sons to eternal glory. Such is His gracious purpose, such will be the consummation of "the mystery".

> A purpose, wondrous fair!
> Of hope and glory, too,
> Hope in time; the glory
> When He maketh all things new.

THE LOCAL CHURCH

❦❦❦❦❦❦

The Church Local

by T. W. CARRON

AS POINTED OUT in our previous paper,* the Church universal is presented in Scripture as Christ's building, as His body and as His bride. It is never addressed as a responsible entity. On the other hand the local church *is* viewed as a responsible body. Moreover *man's building* enters into it. Paul says to the Corinthians, "I have laid the foundation". That refers to his preaching in Corinth which laid the basis of the local church. Paul clearly did *not* lay the foundation of the Church universal. It existed before he came into it. With regard to the foundation that he had laid however at Corinth, he says, "another buildeth thereon", 1 Cor. 3. 10. Then he warns against building in spurious material – wood, hay, and stubble.

All in Every Place. The New Testament churches comprised all the believers in a locality. Thus, the first Epistle to the Corinthians is addressed to the church of God existing in Corinth, to the sanctified in Christ Jesus, called saints (i.e. saints by divine calling), with all those calling upon the name of our Lord Jesus Christ (theirs and ours) in every place, 1. 2. Note the words *all in every place*. Paul planted churches in many cities and towns. When he wrote to the Christians in a region such as Galatia, he addressed them as the *churches* of Galatia. There was no regional church in the New Testament. Likewise John in sending the Lord's messages to the seven churches, addressed "the seven churches which are in Asia". They are named specifically. There were other churches in Asia which are not addressed. There is no exception to this pattern in the New Testament.

* See page 21.

Responsibility of the Local Church. It is absolutely clear that each local church is held responsible to the Lord alone. Subject to His authority and the guidance of the Holy Spirit, each church was an autonomous body. No church had any jurisdiction over any other church. There were no regional or national authorities, no synods, no diocesan bishops. The only church council (if it may be so called) was that held at Jerusalem and this consisted of the apostles and elders of the church in Jerusalem to whom Paul and Barnabas went from Antioch for consultation. It was not a council of churches such as developed in later days. When Paul the apostle, and founder of the Corinthian church, wrote his second Epistle, he says: "Not that we have dominion over you and lord it over your faith, but rather that we work with you as fellow labourers", 2 Cor. 1. 24 AMPLIFIED VERSION. Even the great apostle did not claim such an authority as grew up in later years. The responsibility of the local church to the Lord alone is most clearly brought out in the Lord's messages in Revelation chapters 2 and 3 to the seven assemblies in Asia. Each is addressed specifically, and is warned by Him. *He* calls to repentance. *He* threatens the removal of the candlestick where there is no repentance. Each assembly is held responsible to *Himself* alone.

Failure in the Local Church. Unlike the Church universal as the body of Christ, unbelievers and false teachers may be found in the local church. Sinning saints may also be present. The local church is held responsible to deal with these in discipline. In the message to Ephesus, Rev. 2, the Lord commends that church for their intolerance of wicked men and for having tried false apostles, whilst He charges Pergamos with harbouring those who hold the doctrine of Balaam, and Thyatira for tolerating the false prophetess Jezebel. Paul calls for the excommunication of the incestuous brother and any person who is a fornicator or covetous or an idolater or a railer or a drunkard or an extortioner, 1 Cor. 5. 9–13. Failure to exercise discipline in the local churches is the cause of nearly all the evil that has marred the Christian testimony down the ages.

Local Church Government. In the New Testament the only form of church government to be found is that of local elders. These elders are also referred to as overseers. Two Greek words are used, *presbyteros* ("elder" is a precise translation) and *episcopos* for which "overseer" is an accurate equivalent. The situation is brought out clearly in Acts 20. 17, 28 R.V. "And from Miletus he (Paul) sent to Ephesus, and called to him the *elders* of the church . . . Take heed unto yourselves, and to all the flock, *in the which the Holy Ghost* hath made you bishops (overseers), to feed the Church of God". They were made overseers by the Holy Spirit. This same word is sometimes translated *bishop* elsewhere, e.g. Titus 1. 7, bishop being simply an anglicized form of the word *episcopos*. But the term bishop today usually means a man who supervises a diocese covering many places. Such an office did not exist in New Testament times and it infringes the New Testament principle of local responsibility. Titus was told, as the apostle's delegate, to appoint overseers (elders) in every city in the island of Crete – not an overseer (bishop) for the whole island – small though it was. In Titus 1. 6–9 the qualifications for local church elders are specified. They are quite rigorous. Similar qualifications are insisted on in 1 Timothy 3. 1–7, a passage which should be read carefully. A plurality of elders (overseers) marked the local churches of the New Testament, and from 1 Timothy 5. 17 we learn that some laboured especially in teaching – indeed aptitude for teaching was a necessary qualification for all. When we compare the New Testament pattern with what we see around us today, the extent of the departure is evident. Some would say it is development. To us it looks more like confusion, and God is not the author of confusion. In closing, it may be remarked that the recognition of a single overseer or bishop began in Antioch with Ignatius (martyred A.D. 107). Afterwards the custom of one local church with one bishop gradually developed into one bishop over many churches, until the bishop of Rome ruled over most of Christendom. This move was thus a fatal step in the history of the professing Church. Church history shows that it opened the door to the rule of man in the Church of Christ. It formed the basis of popery.

The New Testament pattern is clear enough: one church in every place, governed by elders qualified by blameless lives and ability to teach, whose work is to feed and shepherd God's flock.

Gathering In His Name

by C. GAHAN

IF WE RIGHTLY APPREHEND the implications of our Lord's death and resurrection, we shall have little difficulty in understanding the truth connected with His Name. That truth He Himself has set before us in one of His most striking sayings: "For where two or three are gathered together in my name, there am I in the midst of them", Matt. 18. 20. Few of our Lord's sayings are so well known, and so little understood as this one. Because it follows a reference to prayer we are apt to overlook its significance and importance; it has a much wider reference than to prayer only. To confine the context to verse 19 is to miss the point and force of these verses; the context is to be found, not in the words about prayer of verse 19, but in the words about the church of verse 17. In this chapter and in verse 18 of chapter 16 of this Gospel, we have the first mention of the Church in the New Testament. The words "I will build my church" of chapter 16 intimate the whole Church, the Church in its totality; the words "tell it unto the church" of chapter 18 have in view the local church – the local church exercising its authority in a matter of discipline. Thus in this first mention of the Church a distinction is drawn between the Church and the churches – between the Church in its aggregate and local companies of believers. From this it will be seen that our Lord was contemplating the advent of the local church or assembly, when He said, "For where two or three are gathered together in my name, there am I in the midst of them". In his Reference Bible, Dr. C. I. Scofield speaks of this verse as setting forth "the simplest form of a local church"; the fact is, here we have the only form of church constitution envisaged in the New Testament. Rowland C. Edwards in his book *New Testament Churches*, repre-

sents this passage, Matt. 18. 15-20, as being the basis of all
New Testament teaching about "the churches of the saints".
Certain it is that, in the words of the Lord Jesus now before us,
we have the seed-kernel of the Christian assembly. This
great saying of our Lord constitutes the foundation on which
the glorious structure of local churches is built.

The corner-stone of this structure is set forth in three
words: "For where two or three are gathered together IN
MY NAME, there am I in the midst of them". The name of the
Lord Jesus is the corner-stone of New Testament churches,
and it is important to a proper understanding of this passage
that we keep this in view. The Lord's presence and blessing
in the local assemblies of His people is conditional on the
place given to His Name. Indeed, it is difficult to see how
local churches can be churches in the scriptural sense of the
word, if there is no recognition of the claims due to His
Name. Nor is this a new thing; long before the advent of the
Church it was written: "In all places WHERE I RECORD MY
NAME I will come unto thee, and I will bless thee", Exod. 20.
24. God's presence and blessing in the collective testimony of
His people always have been conditioned by what was due
to His Name. In the days of Israel the very first of "the statutes
and ordinances which ye shall take heed to " had to do with
the place where God would "set his name", Deut. 12. 4-6.
There was to be but one place where God would "record his
name", and it was only in this place – "in the place where the
Lord thy God hath chosen to place his name there" – that
Israel could meet with God and God with them. There was
no choice or option about this, every solemn assembly had
to be in the place of God's choosing – the place where He
had "set his name". This is equally true today; the Church
has superseded Israel, the outward form has changed, but
God's principles of gathering remain the same. Viewed in
the light of this context, Matthew 18. 20 ceases to be merely
a promise, it assumes all the force of an absolute decree. God
has a people today, and for their holy convocations He still
has a chosen place and Name. If believers are to be gathered
together according to the thoughts and will of God, it must
be in the place and Name of God's choosing. This is not a
matter of personal choice or private judgment, it is not for us

to choose the principles on which we come together in church fellowship; like Israel we are called to worship, not in a place of our own choosing, but in the place where God "has set his name". It was this place our Lord had in mind when He said: "For where two or three are gathered together in my name, there am I in the midst of them"; to be gathered together in His Name, is to be in the place of God's choosing. Thus local churches after the order and constitution of the New Testament now answer to the place where God has "chosen to record his name".

With what significance and far-reaching importance does this invest the name of the Lord Jesus! His Name is THE GATHERING NAME. Believers are rightly gathered, gathered that is in a scriptural way, when they are gathered simply and solely in the name of the Lord Jesus. Paul rebuked the church at Corinth because they were permitting party names to creep in: "Every one of you saith, I am of Paul; and I of Apollos; and I of Cephas; and I of Christ. Is Christ divided? was Paul crucified for you? or were ye baptized in the name of Paul?". Let us beware of becoming men and party followers, rather than followers of Christ! His Name and not the name of preachers and teachers, no matter how gifted they may be, is the great gathering name of the Church. If it was wrong for believers at Corinth to take sectarian names, it cannot be right for believers to do so today. His Name is THE UNIFYING NAME. In His Name we are "gathered together", gathered together or knit together into one living unity. Be it noted: it is not "where two or three gather together", it is "where two or three *are gathered* together". It is not we who gather ourselves together; this "togetherness" is not of the will of man, it is the work of the Holy Spirit. He it is who gathers us around the Lord Jesus as witnesses to His Name and Word. Local churches or assemblies after the pattern of the Scriptures are formed by the Spirit of God. Such assemblies are indwelt by Him, and are the sphere of His operations in bestowing spiritual gifts and making known the truth of God. His Name is THE RULING NAME. In the days of Israel the name of God was a symbol of authority, and to be in the place where God had "recorded his name" was to be under His direction and control. This is no less true today: to be gathered together in the name of the Lord Jesus means that we are to be subject to His authority and control. The implications of this are all too often overlooked. How can believers be said to be gathered together in the name of the Lord Jesus, if in their assembly gatherings they set aside His ordinances and disregard His commands! How can that be a church after the New Testament pattern, where the authority of the Lord Jesus and the guidance of the Holy Spirit have been displaced by human arrangements! For the believer, here as elsewhere "One is your Master, even Christ", to which our Lord adds by way of emphasis, "And call no man your father upon the earth: for one is your Father, which is in heaven", Matt. 23. 8, 9. Theological masters and ecclesiastical fathers were never prescribed for the Church, and for the offices of such men there is no authority in Scripture. We have one God and Father and one Master and Lord; to be gathered together, therefore, in the Name of the Lord Jesus involves, in all matters pertaining to doctrine and practice, subjection to His authority and control. His Name is THE DISPLACING NAME. It abolishes and displaces the "carnal ordinances" of ritualism, and reduces to a blessed simplicity all our approaches to God. God is no longer with His people symbolically and ceremonially; priestly pomp and Jewish ritual have been for ever done away.

> Ritual and ceremonial passed away,
> When dawned the Church's glorious day.

The church or assembly of God is to be marked by unworldly simplicity. A striking contrast this to the huge, highly organized religious systems of Christendom today! How slow we are to learn that truth is more simple, beautiful and divine, than the most magnificent ritual, wood and stone, of any earthly shrine. Nor must we forget THE HOLINESS OF HIS NAME. The mere fact of gathering according to the teaching of Scripture is not sufficient; if we are to know the presence of the Lord when we come together there must be a state and condition of things agreeable to His Name. Outward correctness is not enough, there must be inward holiness. When we come together everything we say and do should come under the sanctity of His Name.

From the foregoing it will be seen that there is more in gathering in the name of the Lord Jesus than many suppose. His Name is not merely a designation to distinguish Him from others, but that which sets forth the essential characteristics of local churches as originally constituted. May it be said of us what was said of the church of Philadelphia, "Thou hast kept my word, and hast not denied my name", Rev. 3. 8.

Is the Scriptural Assembly Possible Today?

by W. E. VINE

The Finality of Scripture. In 2 Timothy 3. 16, 17, the apostle Paul declares that the Scriptures are God-breathed, and are "profitable for doctrine, for reproof, for correction, for instruction in righteousness: that the man of God may be perfect, throughly furnished unto all good works". This provision "for every good work" stamps the Scriptures with completeness and finality. "Those things", he says to the church at Philippi, "which ye have both learned, and received, and heard, and seen in me, do", Phil. 4. 9, and to Timothy: "Continue thou in the things which thou hast learned". Timothy was to charge certain men "not to teach a different doctrine", 1. 3. He was to commit what he had learned from the apostle among many witnesses "to faithful men who shall be able to teach others also", a plain intimation that apostolic teaching was to be handed on from one generation of Christians to another, indefinitely. Jude states that Scripture comprises "that faith once for all (*hapax*) delivered to the saints", Jude 3 R.V. The word *hapax* is noticeable; it is to be distinguished from *pote* "once upon a time", and this the Revisers had in view when they substituted the phrase "once for all" for the A.V. "once". How can that which is given "once for all" necessitate or allow of modification, readjustment, or addition?

The Permanent Requirements of 1 Corinthians. Certain instructions given in 1 Corinthians as to the conduct, worship, and testimony of a local church, are regarded by some as having been applicable merely to the church at Corinth. But the Epistle is addressed not only to that church but to "all that in every place call upon the name of Jesus Christ our Lord", 1. 2. Many of its teachings are foundations of the faith, e.g., 15. 3-5, and what was of local application contains principles and injunctions essential for individual believers and for churches at all times.

What has been said thus far is sufficient of itself to show not only that it is possible to carry out apostolic teachings in these respects but that they are obligations for all true followers of Christ.

In view of the absolute claim of the Scriptures upon the obedience of God's people, many at different times and in various places throughout the present age, have been enabled to conform to the scriptural mode of gathering, in contrast to the variety of methods prevalent throughout apostate Christendom from early post-apostolic times onward.

Apostasy and Inadequate Recovery. It does not lie within the scope of this article to record the history of the apostasy by reason of which popery became dominant, or to set forth the incomplete character of the work of the Protestant Reformation. The latter, while it effected in great measure the overthrow of the papal system in certain countries, failed to lead back fully to the truth of the Scripture those who were freed from that system. Amidst the various sects that resulted there remained in general the prevalence of clericalism, and with it to a large extent the teaching of baptismal regeneration, and other errors.

A Significant Movement. Notwithstanding this, owing to the spread of the Scriptures, the light they afford, and the power of the Holy Spirit, there was in the early part of last century a widespread movement by which large numbers of God's people were able to free themselves from the shackles of human tradition and to meet together in conformity to those principles which the Scriptures set forth. That movement arose, not in one locality, nor from a single centre from which it spread. On the contrary, in various places Christians met together under the guidance of the Word of God, independently of any knowledge of what was simultaneously going on in other places, itself an evidence of the work of the Spirit of God, and of the absence of human propaganda and organization.

It is always possible for people to conform to the truth; and a deep significance lies in the fact that owing to the world-wide circulation of the Bible, companies of believers in different lands have been led by the Scriptures to return to apostolic teaching apart from human agency and instruction.

What the New Testament Sets Forth. The New Testament makes clear that under apostolic teaching no single minister was appointed to conduct the worship of God's people, or to administer the sacraments. Such things are conspicuous by their absence. According to 1 Corinthians 10. 16 it is "the bread which we break . . . the cup of blessing which we bless". There is no such paradoxical arrangement as the communion rail, no such ritual as the reception of the elements from a minister or priest. The Spirit of God acted in the churches to provide spiritual gifts of elders or overseers in a single gathering, to exercise oversight, Acts 20. 17, 28, and other spiritual gifts. The work of the Holy Spirit in this respect is set forth clearly in 1 Corinthians 12. 4–11. He divides "to each one severally even as he will".

The teaching of 1 Corinthians 14. 26–33 shows how a gathering should be opened for one and another to lead in praise or to edify the company under the direction of the Spirit of God. To this the ministerial system is definitely opposed and constitutes a quenching of the Spirit. Many gifts which might edify the Church are rendered inactive. Numbers of believers are shut up in their pews week by week listening to sermons, and are like paralysed members of a body. A veritable return to obedience to the revealed will of God would constitute a reformation that would revolutionize the denominations of Christendom.

The Question Answered. That there are failures, imperfections, and delinquencies among those who are seeking to follow the Word of God affords no grounds for the supposition that it is impossible to get back to its teaching. The existence of evil only affords a ground for humiliation before God, and for a rectification according to the revealed mind of the Lord.

To endeavour to counteract failure by following the traditions of men is only to turn from one evil to another. Two blacks do not make a white. One error cannot be corrected by the pursuit of another.

FIGURES OF THE CHURCH

⊗⊙⊗⊙⊗⊙

The Place of My Throne
THE ASSEMBLY THE SPHERE
OF CHRIST'S LORDSHIP
by WILLIAM TREW

THE TRUTH of the Lordship of Christ in the assembly should be kept prominently before the saints in ministry as giving character to the assembly life and witness. The apostle labours to emphasize this in the first Epistle to the Corinthians. His object in writing was to set in order details of assembly life, according to an order that was divine, of which God was author, 14. 33. The Saviour's title of authority is used in the Epistle 68 times, for the saints have been brought by the grace of God under theocratic rule, and the Lord dwells in the midst of His redeemed to govern and guide, working out His Own will in those who are gladly surrendered to His authority. The churches of God are characterized as "all that in every place call upon the name of Jesus Christ our *Lord*", 1. 2.

When pleading for unity, which had been disturbed as the result of their carnality, the apostle beseeches "by the name of our *Lord* Jesus Christ", 1. 10.

As Balaam observed it, the camp of Israel was a beautiful picture of perfect order and unity, each tent pitched by its own standard, and each tribe encamped in relation to the sanctuary in the midst. So that he was constrained to say, "How goodly are thy tents, O Jacob, and thy tabernacles, O Israel". The secret of that orderliness was the one principle of rule acknowledged there. In the practical acknowledgment of the *Lordship* of Christ in the assembly by every member of it, lies the secret of unity today.

The remembrance meeting is the very heart of assembly

life and testimony. The instructions that govern the observance of the Lord's supper were given to Paul by special revelation from the *Lord*. It was the *Lord* Jesus who instituted it; the loaf speaks of the body of the *Lord*, the cup symbolizes the blood of the *Lord*; and "as often as ye eat this bread, and drink this cup, ye do show the *Lord's* death till he come", 11. 23-26. The constant recurrence of His title of Lordship in the passage shows that the Lord's supper is spread in that which is the sphere of His *Lordship* and rule. Because of this we must be prepared to judge everything in our lives that compromises His glory, and if we bring defilement into such a holy place, the *Lord's* hand will be upon us in chastisement, 11. 27-32.

The Epistle has displayed the pattern of divine order, and now, as if anticipating cavillers, the apostle says, "What! came the word of God out from you? or came it unto you only? If any man think himself to be a prophet, or spiritual, let him acknowledge that the things that I write unto you are the commandments of the Lord", 14. 36, 37.

When God would dwell in the midst of His people in the wilderness, He gave them the privilege of building His sanctuary saying, "Let them make me a sanctuary; that I may dwell among them", Exod. 25. 8. But He denied them the privilege of being the architects of His dwelling, saying, "According to all that I show thee, after the pattern of the tabernacle . . . even so shall ye make it", 25. 9. That pattern was afterwards detailed, and, significantly, the first thing that God did was to describe the ark and mercy seat; then followed everything around it and in relation to it. The ark with its mercy seat was God's throne in the midst of His people. He issued His commands for the guidance of every step of their path, 25. 22. The throne of God was given the central place in the service of "The tent of meeting" – "The sanctuary of God".

The glory of the millennial house is thus described: "Behold, the glory of the Lord filled the house . . . and he said unto me, Son of man, the place of my throne, and the place of the soles of my feet, where I will dwell in the midst of the children of Israel for ever, and my holy name, shall the house of Israel no more defile", Ezek. 43. 5-7.

In this dispensation the assembly, God's spiritual house, answers to the material house in which God dwelt in old times. These titles of dignity and privilege, making such tremendous practical demands upon us, describe the character of the assembly. It is intended to be, "The place of my throne, and the place of the soles of my feet". The first of these emphasizes His claim upon us as our absolute Lord. The second expresses our loving response to His claims, as we gladly bow at His feet with worship and homage and unreserved surrender, henceforth to serve His pleasure in obeying His Word, seeking His glory in giving practical form to His will.

So shall the presence of God be manifested in power and blessing in our midst, and "the glory of the Lord" will fill the house.

The Temple of God

I CORINTHIANS 3. 16

by J. H. LARGE

THIS EXPRESSION was applied to the company of believers at Corinth, and not to the individual believer. True, a similar expression, "the temple of the Holy Ghost", is applied to the body of the individual and a powerful plea for personal sanctification is based upon that solemn truth. But the expression we are now considering is applied to the assembly as such.

In Christendom, great importance is attached to the buildings which have been erected for the worship of God, and it is probable that the impressiveness of some religious services owes a great deal to the sensuous effects of massive architecture. There can be little doubt that the immense expenditure of skill and labour and wealth involved in the erection of these temples was often due to genuine devotion and a sense of what was due to the majesty of God, but the effect has frequently been to draw attention away from the fact that, in this age, the true temple of God is the assembly of His people and not the building in which they gather.

Human nature being what it is, it is not a matter of great surprise that some who have grasped this truth have swung to the other extreme; and because they have seen that no material building can be the temple of God, they have acted as though the building they use is of no consequence. We believe that a proper sense of what is due to God would lead to the assembly's building being made as suitable as possible for its purpose, and of a character likely to commend itself to the public. It indicates a spurious spirituality when saints live in exceptionally well-appointed houses, but are content to meet in a shack.

Nevertheless, we must stress that the temple is not the material building but the saints who gather together in the name of the Lord Jesus for the worship and service of God.

There are, we suggest, two leading lessons we may learn from the truth that the assembly of the saints is the temple of God.

The First Lesson is "Privilege". It would not make very great demands on the least imaginative of us, to realize how a young priest would have felt when he was first privileged to enter into the holy place in the temple of old. Such is the infirmity of human nature, that it is at least possible that with the passage of years he would become accustomed to his privileges and gradually take them as a matter of course, but there can be no reasonable doubt that the young priest would be acutely conscious of a sacred joy and thankfulness as he was admitted to the ministry of the sanctuary. It might be argued that in some respects it was easier for him than for us, because he was surrounded with so much that would appeal to his senses; but surely it does not demand a super-spirituality to realize that, as the temple of old was but a shadow and we have the substance, our privileges spiritually are greater than his.

Each believer helps to form this temple, just as each stone in a material building goes to make up the complete structure. In this temple every believer, even the youngest, is a holy priest, 1 Pet. 2. 5, whose sacred function it is to offer up spiritual sacrifices of worship and praise. This does not necessarily involve taking some audible part – it is fully time we realized that far more depends on the state of heart of the believers than upon the ability of those who may lead the congregation.

It is quite a mistake to confine the idea of worship to the gathering specially convened for the remembrance of the Lord at the Lord's supper – *every* meeting should be a worship meeting. All our service should be undertaken in a worshipping spirit, and where this is true of a company of Christians the whole tone of the gathering is raised and the Holy Spirit is able to move amongst them with greater freedom and power. Of course, it is only natural that when we come to meetings we hope to receive blessing, but there is a nobler motive than this – remember how the Greatest Giver said, "It is more blessed to give than to receive". When the saints wend their way to meetings with hearts dancing for joy and overflowing with praise, at the realization that they are to be privileged to join in heart with their fellow-priests to worship God, they will prove the truth of these words.

The Second Lesson is "Reverence". We have already suggested that there is the danger that in freeing ourselves of the artificial thraldom generated by massive architecture and ornate ritual, we may become too casual in our attitude. God is greatly to be feared in the assembly of His saints and to be had in reverence of all that are about Him, Psa. 89. 7, but we fear that those who are fond of claiming God's presence do not always give evidence of the reality of their convictions by a reverent manner. God, of course, knoweth the heart and it is not for us to judge, but we wonder whether it has not often been the case that devout though poorly-instructed believers, who have been attracted to the principles we profess to hold, have been stumbled by a deportment inconsistent with our profession.

This is not to be interpreted as a plea for a formal manner – true reverence is not at all inconsistent with all that would properly flow from the warmth of Christian love and genuine interest in each other and pleasure in one another's company.

How often it has been the case that as our hearts have been kindled by the warmth of Christian fellowship, God's presence has been made all the more real – it is difficult to imagine this stumbling any but the most inveterate ritualists. Nevertheless there can be no excuse for the unconcerned and careless air.

Maybe, however, more irreverence springs from long familiarity with the various forms of assembly-meetings than from almost any other cause – and irreverence which is not always recognized as such. To take but one example: when we lead the assembly in prayer, do we *really* believe that we are actually addressing the Most High God? Do we? Here again, God is the only Judge of the heart but it is sometimes difficult to resist the conclusion that prayer is used as an opportunity, not of speaking to God, but of imparting news or exhortation to others. This might be done with the very best of intentions, and simply as a habit unconsciously acquired over the years – possibly from the example of others – but it at least raises the question whether such a one has really paused, before rising to his feet, to consider the implications of professing to draw nigh to God. If we honestly believe that certain news should be imparted to our brethren, let us do the plain and honest thing and tell them, but do not let us use the cover of prayer for this purpose.

The same considerations would deter us from *reliance* upon well-worn phrases, either picked up from others or which were once used by us in freshness but have now worn a track in our minds from which it is difficult to deviate. There are limits to the vocabulary of the most accomplished, and there is no advantage in forsaking an expression which beautifully clothes an important idea, so long as we are watchful to resist the tendency to repeat the expression when it no longer answers to the feeling of the heart. Surely if we love God and really believe we are approaching Him on matters of vital and ever-fresh importance, we shall not be content to repeat a string of phrases which may be more like shackles than aids to warm and reverent expression of our spirits? It would be a thousand pities if drawing attention to these things quenched the spirit of prayer – we are not suggesting that there is any necessary virtue in novelty of expression. Striving after novelty might be the greater of two evils – all we plead for is exercise of heart so that forms of words are ever kept as the servants, and not the masters, of our hearts and minds.

It is a great comfort to know that God knoweth our frame and remembers that we are but dust, and we may reverently believe that He graciously makes allowances for that frailty of human nature which finds it exceedingly difficult to resist the cramping power of habit. Even so we may well exercise our hearts, to learn the tremendous lesson which brought Isaiah down in humiliation before the Lord, Isa. 6. Here were the seraphim, who for ages had served God before His very throne, yet were so filled with awe that they covered their faces and cried, "Holy, holy, holy is the Lord of hosts". When it fell to the lot of one of them to apply a live coal to the prophet's lips, he felt the things of God to be so sacred that, though no flame could have hurt his hand, he took the tongs. Is there the danger of becoming so accustomed to ministry in the sacred things that at last we get used to handling the things of God and cease to exercise our hearts to maintain a due sense of their solemnity?

From this state of heart it is but a step to that more serious form of irreverence – self-will. How much damage has been caused by a determination to have one's own way. This is always disastrous for the Christian, but never more so than when self-will intrudes into the church of God. To this sin, more perhaps than to most forms of irreverence in the assembly, the solemn warning is apt, "If any man defile (mar) the temple of God, him shall God destroy".

What must angels think, awed as they still are with the holiness of God, when they see puny man, redeemed at infinite cost from well-deserved doom, acting carelessly in the presence of his Redeemer God?

It is a comfort to know that God never despises a contrite heart and if we have been guilty of conduct unbecoming His presence, there is grace available for us which will enable us to retrieve our mistakes and learn to serve God acceptably with reverence and godly fear.

This spirit will not rob the gatherings of the saints of any of their warmth and joy – on the contrary it will so raise the spiritual level and give such reality to our worship, that all occasions of church fellowship will deepen our appreciation of the things of God. And since these occasions will normally take place in the assembly hall, that building, whilst never being confused with the real temple of God, will nevertheless be a place permeated with fragrant and sacred memories.

The House of God

THE CHURCH OF THE LIVING GOD

by T. E. WILSON

THE KEY VERSE of the first Epistle to Timothy, and indeed one of the basic statements in the New Testament concerning the local church, is found in chapter 3. 15. Paul says that he is writing these things to Timothy so that men might know how they ought to behave themselves in the house of God, which is the church of the living God, the pillar and ground (stay, buttress) of the truth; (see R.V.). Here he makes four great statements concerning a local company of believers.

1. **It is the House of God.** This is a term which occurs frequently throughout the Scriptures. The first reference to it is in Genesis 28. 17. After Jacob's dream of the ladder set up and reaching from earth to heaven, and the divine confirmation of the covenant made with Abraham and Isaac, he says "How dreadful is this place! this is none other but the house of God, and this is the gate of heaven". He called this sacred spot *Bethel*, meaning "the house of God". There he raised his pillar and it was to Bethel that he returned after his twenty years of discipline in Padan-Aram. We believe that this is the passage that Paul has in mind; he mentions the house, the pillar and the angels in 1 Timothy 3. 15–16.

The house of God is where God dwells. In the Old Testament He dwelt among His people in the tabernacle. The overshadowing Shekinah cloud of glory was the visible evidence of the presence of God among His people. Moses was the servant in this house, Heb. 3. 1–5. It was built according to divine instructions and followed a divine pattern. Such also was the case with the temple built by Solomon centuries later. But the house of God today is the local church, 1 Cor. 3. 16–17. Over this house Christ is both Son and Head; He is the Master of the house.

The two chief characteristics of the house are *discipline* and *love*. In 1 Corinthians especially Paul gives detailed instructions as to the order and discipline in the house of God. The reasons he gives for this are twofold. First of all the temple of God is holy, 1 Cor. 3. 17; the house must be clean. Secondly sin is like leaven; it works in the dark and has the tendency to spread, 1 Cor. 5. 6–8. Its activity can only be arrested by the counteraction of salt and fire. Then again, on the human level, a man builds a house as a haven of rest where his affections and love are given expression. Discipline can be difficult and painful but love must be all pervading and the very atmosphere of the house. It is the air conditioning which keeps all things sweet and happy, cf. 1 Cor. 13.

2. It is the Church of the Living God. The expression "the church of the living God" is reminiscent of Matthew 16. 16–18. Peter's confession was "Thou art the Christ, the Son of the living God". Then he was given the tremendous revelation of the church, the *ecclesia*. Granted that in Matthew 16 the reference goes far beyond the local church, but in Matthew 18 where the church is mentioned twice it obviously refers to the local church, 18. 17. But some might say that local churches were not in existence when our Lord spoke. Like the institution of the Lord's supper recorded in Matthew 26. 26–30, the instructions were given in anticipation of the church age commencing at Pentecost. If the question be asked "what is a local church?", the simplest answer would be one definition given by the Lord Himself in the context where He first mentions it. He said "For where two or three are gathered together in my name, there am I in the midst of them", 18. 20. The Acts of the Apostles and the Epistles generally describe the foundation and features of these local churches. They often met in private homes, carried out the ordinances of baptism and the Lord's supper, and had a recognized eldership. In their worship and service they gave room for the exercise of the priesthood of all believers and the use of divinely given gifts. As colonies of heaven they used every opportunity to spread the Gospel where they lived, Phil. 1. 27.

Paul uses the word "church" three times in 1 Timothy. In chapter 3. 5. we are taught that one of the functions of an elder is to take care of the church of God. In chapter 3. 15 we learn that the instructions Paul has written to Timothy are related to behaviour in the house of God, which is the church of the living God. In chapter 5. 16 the apostle speaks of the responsibility of the believers to care for widows in their own family, a practical evidence of godliness, so that the church could devote its resources to the widows who had no one to provide for them. It is clear that in each case he is referring to the local gathering of believers. It has been suggested that "the house of God" emphasizes what we have been *brought into* whilst "the church of God" also indicates that we have been *called out from* the world to gather to His Name.

3. The Pillar. This is an obvious reference to Jacob's pillar. The stone on which he had rested his weary head as a pillow, he finally raised up as a pillar. Four times in his life, of which this is the first occasion, he did this. Sometimes he poured oil upon the pillar. It was a testimony to God's grace and faithfulness. The local church is a pillar of the truth. It is both a golden lampstand, Rev. 1. 20, and a pillar of testimony.

The tabernacle had 69 pillars supporting the court, the door and the veil. They all speak of Christ in His mediatorial glory. The temple of Solomon had two pillars, Jachin and Boaz, situated at the porch. In Ephesus where Timothy was living, was the temple of Artemis, said to be one of the seven wonders of the world. It was reputed to have 127 pillars, every one the gift of a king. All were made of marble, some were studded with jewels and overlaid with gold.

A pillar has at least four functions in modern life.

i. To support a building.
ii. To spread a light, like a lighthouse to guide the storm-tossed.
iii. To glorify a man, such as Nelson's pillar in Trafalgar Square.

iv. To honour a name, as Washington's monument in Washington, D.C.

The church has all these functions in relation to the truth.

4. The Ground of the Truth. Here we have the base of the pillar. The word *hedraioma* means "a stay, support or buttress". A pillar often has three parts; the base, the column and the capital on the top. On the base there is sometimes an inscription and inside a receptacle where documents are placed for posterity. The church is not only the testimony to the truth for all to see, but it is also the stay, support and depository of the truth.

God's Husbandry

by WILLIAM TREW

THE CONDITION of the saints in Corinth was such, that when the apostle wrote his first Epistle to them, he felt the need of repeated warning. In 8. 9, he warns against the spirit of inconsiderateness so prevalent among them, and encourages the spirit of selfless love. In 10. 12, he warns against the spirit of self-sufficiency and self-confidence, and encourages humility and dependence upon God. He sounds a note of warning in 3. 10 when showing the havoc caused by their carnality, and encourages to spirituality in exercise and energy.

The whole of chapter 3 is a warning against allowing the workings of the flesh. These saints were not spiritual but carnal, and their carnality evidenced itself in three ways:

1. Carnality dwarfs: vv. 1, 2;
2.   „   divides: vv. 3–15;
3.   „   defiles: vv. 16, 17.

The remedy is a spiritual apprehension and appreciation of the divine constitution of the assembly. Therefore the apostle does what Ezekiel did at the command of God in an effort to arouse the consciences of the people of God in his day, to bring them to conviction and confession, and so to restoration and complete recovery – he "shows them the house", Ezek. 43. 10.

Divisions among the saints practically deny God's supreme claims upon His own. Servants of Christ, such as those mentioned in this passage, are instruments through whom we believed. The giver of faith in every case is the Lord. They plant and they water, but "God giveth the increase". They are "labourers together of God" NEWBERRY, but no more than that. The assembly is not "of Paul", or "of Apollos", or "of Cephas", or of any other. "Ye are God's husbandry", "Ye are God's building". "Ye are the temple of God", vv. 9, 16.

The use of these three designations of the local assembly lays upon us the responsibility to preserve—

a. The *fruitfulness* of that which is *God's Husbandry*;
b. The *unity* of that which is *God's Building*;
c. The *sanctity* of that which is the *Temple of God*.

Some might excuse a turning away from what is called "Church truth" on the plea that it is not practical. No phase of truth is more practical, if only the teaching of the Scriptures as to the divine constitution of the local assembly is apprehended in a spiritual way.

Let us think of the first of these figures. The assembly is compared to cultivated soil – a garden – and the responsibility is ours to preserve its fruitfulness. Paul and his fellow labourers had gone to Corinth while yet it was wholly heathen. The soil was virgin. These servants of Christ had sown the good seed of the Word in many hearts. They had planted and watered, and God gave the increase. In that city God now had a garden producing beauty, fragrance and fruit, for His glory and the delight of His heart. The figure is a lovely one, but it lays on us a responsibility to preserve that fruitfulness for His pleasure and praise. For this two things are necessary – *wells and walls*.

The Living Waters of the Well. The first of these necessities is the presence of the Spirit of God in the midst of the assembly, and His sweet ministrations to our hearts. This is beautifully illustrated in the Song of Solomon, 4. 12–16, where the bridegroom compares the one on whom he has lavished his love and in whom is all his delight, to a garden. That garden produces fruit and fragrance of such a kind that it is likened to a "paradise" (NEWBERRY), and the secret of its fruitfulness is the fact that the soil is richly nourished by "the well of living waters". John 4 assures us that "the well of living waters" is *the energy of the Spirit of God in our spirits*, leading us to the enjoyment of God in holy, intimate communion.

Three things in John 4 are before us in the divine order of experience:

   a. The well of communion, v. 14;
   b. The sanctuary of worship, vv. 21–24;
   c. The harvest fields of service, vv. 35–38.

The value and character of our service in the harvest fields depend upon our sanctuary experience. It is the outward expression in relation to men, of our worship in the sanctuary of the presence of God. Our spirits will never be thrilled with the ecstasy of worship apart from the daily experience of the well of communion – our spirits satisfied in God. The streams of Lebanon too, surely have their message, Song 4. 12–16. Lebanon means "white". Here are pure streams that constantly flow, nourishing the soil that produces the fruit and fragrance to delight the heart of the one to whom the garden belongs. They speak of those streams of holy life that evidence the workings in us of the Spirit of holiness. The assembly is made up of individuals, and just as tributary streams feed the main river, so streams of holy life supplied by each individual become a concentration of holiness in the assembly. In that way the fruitfulness of the assembly garden is preserved.

Enclosing Wall of Separation is the second necessity. This also is illustrated in the same passage. "A garden enclosed is my sister, my spouse". If the well is the *secret* of fruitfulness, the wall is the *safeguard* of fruitfulness. The very opposite is seen in Proverbs 24. 30–34. "The field of the slothful" had once been productive of fruit. Now nature was producing itself without restraint! The man was too lazy to give the necessary labour to the uprooting of weeds and to keep the wall unbreached. His poverty came slowly but surely, as a man that travels. It was his worst enemy, and difficult to throw off, as an armed man. Such will be our lives, such will be the assembly, if the enclosing walls are broken down.

This is precisely what was wrong in Corinth. (a) The wells of spiritual nourishment were choked, and (b) the walls of separation were breached. Heathen life had made inroads, and there was foulness and stench where there should have been the beauty and fragrance of Christ. Therefore the apostle wrote those two Epistles. In the first he *clears the choked wells* of spiritual nourishment – see chapter 12. In the second, he *rebuilds the enclosing walls* – see chapter 6. 11–18. We are living in a day of carnality and compromise. Let not "the field of the slothful" be the picture of our assembly. Worldliness will come in if the walls are broken down and as a consequence the wells will become choked. In the measure in which the walls of separation are kept intact and the streams of spiritual nourishment flow, in that measure will the assembly be the garden of the Lord, for the delight of His heart.

A Body

by J. H. Large

THE HUMAN BODY is a wonderful unity, not merely because of the physical connection of its parts, but by the presence in all parts of

One Pervading Life. This may be less obvious in relation to a company of believers, but it is equally true – in fact the unity between member and member is far more wonderful, by reason of the fact that here the pervading life is the Spirit of Christ – "*by (in) one Spirit are we all baptized into one body*", 1 Cor. 12. 13. The objection that this refers to the church universal does nothing to destroy the local application, for "*now ye are the body of Christ*", v. 27, implies that an assembly should be the expression of what is universal. In any case since the Spirit of Christ is in all believers, they have a corporate spiritual life in one all-pervading and unifying element.

To injure a member, then, is to injure the body. To injure one is to injure all. *"We are . . . members one of another"*, Rom. 12. 5. More solemn still, when we injure a member of the body we injure the Head. Saul of Tarsus learned this never-forgotten lesson when challenged by the Risen Lord, not with persecuting *"my* people", but "why persecutest thou *me?"*. We should as little think of insulting or slighting a fellow-believer as we would of insulting Christ – it is the same thing. *"When ye sin so against the brethren, and wound their weak conscience, ye sin against Christ"*, 1 Cor. 8. 12. This sobering truth has its other side – a service rendered to a member of the body is also rendered to Christ.

Turning from responsibility to privilege, we next note that in the body

Each Member Has His Place. *"Now hath God set the members every one of them in the body, as it hath pleased him"*, 1 Cor. 12. 18.

Few would venture to suggest any improvement in the arrangement of the physical body – most admire the divine wisdom which has placed the members where they can function with maximum efficiency for the benefit of the whole organism. So in the spiritual body, there is a divinely-appointed sphere for each believer, and we may be quite sure what pleases God is wisest and happiest for us all. An assembly can function at its highest spiritual efficiency when each member is able to discern his appointed sphere, and is willing to fill it cheerfully and devotedly for the glory of God and the blessing of his fellows.

If one does with his whole heart what lies nearest to his hand, it will not be long before he reaches conviction as to his niche, and discovers that for his niche

Each Member Has His Gift. The importance of this point may be judged from the fact that it is made clear in all of the three principal passages which take up the figure of the body:

"According as God hath dealt to every man *the measure of faith"*, Rom. 12. 3; *"The manifestation of the Spirit is given to* every man *to profit withal . . . dividing to* every man *severally as He will"*, 1 Cor. 12. 7, 11; *"Unto* every one *of us is given grace according to the measure of the gift of Christ"*, Eph. 4. 7.

The gifts are bestowed by the Risen Christ but they are distributed according to the Spirit's will. This is something more than natural ability – it is spiritual equipment to enable one to fill his appointed sphere. In these gifts there are diversities, but they are all divided out by the one Spirit, so that it is not a question of human attainment, although we have a responsibility to exercise them properly – not to "neglect" them, but to "stir them up". God is a God of unity but not uniformity – perhaps we would like our brethren to conform to little patterns of our devising, but God prefers to give each his distinctive individuality and endow him with his own gift.

Nevertheless, "diversities of gifts" might lead to confusion were it not that

Each Member Has His Function. *"There are differences of administrations"; "There are diversities of operations"; "All members have not the same office"*, 1 Cor. 12. 5, 6; Rom. 12. 4.

It is foolish to ape someone else. By attempting to mould ourselves upon another's pattern, we are not only attempting the impossible, but what, if we could succeed, would merely duplicate what God did not want duplicated, whilst at the same time depriving the body of something necessary to its completion. Even greater harm is done when a dissatisfied member attempts to usurp the proper function of another – it results in confusion and unhappiness. In the natural body our ears render a unique service which no other members can, or attempt to, perform. If the eyes abandoned their office to serve as ears, the body would be rendered blind without any corresponding improvement in hearing. On the other hand the body has amazing powers of adaptability, and, to some extent at least, organs seem to have the ability to compensate, by increased sensibility or skill, for the failure of another, but the process involves a strain upon the unfortunate individual. Similarly some assemblies are afflicted with those whose determination to occupy a sphere to which they are not called (and therefore not fitted) renders them unwilling and unfit to perform their true function, and so there is imposed upon others the strain of trying to make up the deficiency.

It would be interesting to consider in what respects individuals can be to the assembly what the members mentioned in 1 Corinthians 12. 15–17 (feet, hands, ears, eyes, etc.) are to the body, but we must pass on to the fact that

No One Member Is Sufficient. The most gifted member, albeit the most godly, can never be adequate to the need – a member he can be, an important member no doubt, but no more. The eye is an invaluable organ in the body but *"if the whole body were an eye, where were the hearing?"*; *"And if they were all one member, where were the body?"*, 1 Cor. 12. 17, 19.

The most prominent, and, indeed, what we might regard as the most useful members are not the most vital. Arms and legs, eyes and ears, are invaluable to us and we could regard the loss of any one only with dismay, but the body can survive the loss of them, whilst the loss of other hidden and forgotten organs would spell death. An assembly can get on without gifted men, but it cannot survive without spiritual men.

However feeble some may appear,

Each Member Is Necessary. *"Those members of the body, which seem to be more feeble, are necessary"*; *"The eye cannot say unto the hand, I have no need of thee"*, 1 Cor. 12. 22, 21.

We used to be told that certain organs in the body were redundant and now performed no useful function, but medical science – impressed by the marvels of anatomy, revealed by intensive research – is far less ready than formerly, to dismiss any organ as useless. Although their purpose may still remain obscure, the conviction is growing that greater knowledge will reveal the contribution they make to the body's health. Are we to judge a person's value to the assembly merely by the degree of prominence his gift secures him? Is no value to be put upon the gracious, perhaps indefinable, influence exerted by an obscure saint who brings the spirit of Christ to the gathering? It may well be that his is the greater contribution. Are we not safe in believing that many a humble soul who, alas, may come and go almost unnoticed, renders the assembly a signal service by his (or, more likely, her) prayerful support? Such may not "enjoy" the dubious honour given to more prominent individuals, but if we were wise enough to discern their worth we would "bestow more abundant honour" upon them.

Members Are Inter-dependent. Hands and feet are dependent upon *"The whole body fitly joined together and compacted by that which every joint supplieth"*, Eph. 4. 16, never forgetting, of course, that, even so, everything depends upon "holding the Head", Col. 2. 19.

The successful evangelist will gladly own that, in the battle for the souls of men, much depends upon saints who kneel in the closet before he stands on the platform. The busy teacher, who thanks God for the refreshment of spirit often granted in his ministry, knows full well that his word had power because he was supported by unknown inter-cessors. Much time, money, effort and efficiency are lost by *overlapping*, but there can only be untold gain from that loyal co-operation which *supplements* the efforts of one another. We have chosen as our illustrations the more obvious cases, but who does not know how the assembly becomes happy and vigorous when all are able to bring their distinctive contribu-tions to its life and service?

Surely the truths we have been considering make it clear that there is

No Occasion For Jealousy. *"There are diversities of gifts, but the* same Spirit. *There are differences of administrations, but the* same Lord. *And there are diversities of operations, but it is the* same God", 1 Cor. 12. 4–6.

This impressive suggestion of the unity of the Holy Trinity in the operations of the assembly should create that atmosphere of awe and reverence where jealousy would be unable to raise its ugly head, but we cannot afford to ignore the wickedness of our deceitful hearts. But why be jealous of your brother? True – he has a place and a gift you have not;

but, equally so, you have a place and a gift he has not. The same Spirit which imparted to him his gift, imparted yours, and seeing it is according to His will, and neither yours nor your brother's, your part is cheerfully to embrace the Spirit's purpose, so that by the operation of the same God in you both, the Lord may be glorified and His people blessed. What higher privilege could there be? Guard your own gift as a · sacred deposit and "wait on" your ministry. If your brother's gift involves him in greater prominence, it also involves him in greater danger and, instead of envying his seemingly greater responsibility, you should fear for him as one who "shall receive the greater condemnation" if, alas, he should fail. Whilst you foolishly envy him, perhaps he would be thankful if he could with a clear conscience accept a less perilous sphere. Give him your prayerful co-operation and earn the Lord's commendation.

But if there is no occasion for jealousy, there is certainly

No Occasion For Pride in one's own gift. If you are conscious of having been entrusted with a gift, how foolish to boast as though it were your own doing. "*What hast thou that thou didst not receive?*", I Cor. 4. 7.

Paul did not meet the Corinthians' foolish boasting by denying or belittling their gifts – rather he thanked God that they came "behind in no gift". What he did say was, "*now if thou didst receive it, why dost thou glory, as if thou hadst not received it?*", v. 7.

A man is not to ape mock modesty and deny that he can be of any help, but a man is "not to think of himself more highly than he ought to think". It is no credit to a man who, for the number of years he has known the Lord, should have reached something approaching spiritual maturity, if he cannot discern in what way the Lord is pleased to use him, but he must "*think soberly, according as God hath dealt to every man the measure of faith*", Rom. 12. 3. Humble thankfulness for the exquisite privilege? Yes! A due sense of accountability? Yes! But pride? There is no surer way of destroying the usefulness of the very gift in which he glories!

To what end is all this?

(a). **The Welfare Of The Body.** The communion of the body of Christ should express itself in a wholesome regard for fellow-members, "*there should be no schism in the body . . . the members should have the same care one for another . . . whether one member suffer, all the members suffer with it*", I Cor. 12. 25–26. How often have tried and troubled saints found their sorrows easier to bear because the love of Christ has been expressed to them in the sympathy of their fellows. There is no need to descend to unwholesome sentimentality, but the virile love of Christ can be shown in being "kindly affectioned one to another with brotherly love".

But we are exhorted to something even harder than suffering with those who suffer – we are to rejoice with those who are singularly blessed. If "*one member be honoured, all the members rejoice with it*", v. 26. Can we thank God and rejoice with a brother when his prayers are answered and ours seem not to be? If his service is blest and we seem to toil in vain, do we so recognize the oneness we have in the body that we feel we have been honoured because a fellow-member has been?

(b). **Usefulness To Christ.** "*Now ye (the assembly) are the body of Christ*", I Cor. 12. 27.

Have we lost the vision of what the local assembly could be, as an organism through which Christ could express Himself? If your assembly were a healthy body, every member energized and controlled by the one all-pervading Spirit, its many gifts in gracious exercise, its activities all co-ordinated to the master-plan, its operations under one divine super-vision ("*all these worketh that one and the selfsame Spirit*"), could it not be a wonderful body which Christ would be glad to use for the blessing of your neighbourhood? Paul's desire for the Philippians was that they should "*stand fast in one spirit, with one mind striving together for the faith of the gospel*", Phil. I. 27. The idea here is that the church in its service for Christ should present such an appearance of unity in its various operations as to suggest that all were possessed of but one soul.

Instead of lamenting that so few show promise of rising to this height, let each of us resolve that we, "holding the Head", should at least be a channel of "nourishment" to the body, that it may be "knit together" and "increase with the increase of God".

A School

by J. H. LARGE

WE ARE IN DANGER of falling into a quite unjustifiable complacency with our level of spiritual knowledge and intelligence. It might not be difficult to suggest causes for this unwarrantable frame of mind, but it will be more profitable to turn our attention to what may help to dispel it. A comparison with New Testament standards is all that is necessary.

For example, whilst it is extremely unlikely that the recent converts at Colosse enjoyed anything approaching the privileges and opportunities which we accept as a matter of course, the fact remains that immediately Paul learned of their conversion he was moved by the Spirit of God to pray unceasingly that they "might be filled with the knowledge of his will in all wisdom and spiritual understanding", Col. 1. 9. If the Holy Spirit prompted this prayer, who will dare say that it was impossible of accomplishment? Does the Holy Spirit prompt prayers which cannot be answered? Certainly Epaphras, who was himself a Colossian, did not accept this view, for in hearty association with Paul's desire he laboured fervently in prayer for them that they might "stand perfect and complete in all the will of God", 4. 12.

If two teachers like Barnabas and Paul felt justified in devoting a whole year to the instruction of believers at Antioch, we shall be foolish to suppose that a few special ministry meetings at considerable intervals are likely to meet our needs. The pathetic thing is that, whilst the great worthies of old earnestly desired to know the things which have been revealed for our benefit, and although their earnestness in diligently seeking puts our poor zeal to shame, we too often lightly esteem the privileges they would have valued so highly but were not permitted to enjoy. Peter tells us that even the angels "desire to look into" these things, and it would seem that God is in fact allowing them to learn "the manifold wisdom of God". Shall we not be ashamed if, later, we discover that those whose function it was to serve the heirs of salvation, had learned more than those they served? Heirs of God, and yet not sufficiently interested in our inheritance to "gird up the loins" of our minds to explore the riches and glories of those secrets which God kept locked in His mind and heart until they were revealed through His holy apostles and prophets!

Teachers. We are without excuse because we have the Holy Scriptures and the indwelling Spirit of God to lead us into the truth. Moreover the Risen Lord saw fit to give teachers to the church and the spurious spirituality which affects independence of the help which God-given teachers can render, impugns the wisdom of the exalted Christ. There is, however, cause for thankfulness in the evidence there is of an awakening as to the need for more reverent and more exact study of the teachings of Holy Scripture, but we are rather disquieted at the tendency to look to professional theological seminaries for the meeting of the undoubted need. We should have thought that the history of denominationalism would have proved a sufficient warning in this respect. We are glad to know that there are many Bible Colleges which are sound in the faith, and we are not going to undervalue their efforts to give young men a grounding in theology, but it is our conviction that the Lord desires men to be trained in the fellowship of the local church, learning to know God in the experiences of every day life, and acquiring a practical knowledge of the Word and mind of God under the guidance of older men whom the Lord has given as teachers in the church. When a successor for Elijah was needed, he was found, not in any of the various schools of the prophets, but on the farm following the plough. With God-given discernment the old prophet saw the potentialities in the young man and took him under his wing and, under his tuition and the power of his example, what was potential in the young man became actual. But Elijahs are needed if we are going to have Elishas.

To this some readers may object that, in their assembly, at least, there are no such teachers. If this is the fact it should not be difficult to secure the help of godly and competent teachers; where there is an eagerness to learn, suitable men can be invited to minister the Word. Barnabas took energetic steps to get the need at Antioch met, even though it meant a considerable journey to reach Paul and bring him back. But are you *sure* that there are no teachers in your midst? If this *is* so, it may be worth while to inquire whether the reason is, either that though you once had them the Lord removed them because they were not appreciated, or whether it is that there is not that earnest desire which would prompt the Lord to supply them. "He satisfieth the longing soul" and we may believe that a church gets the teachers it deserves. The likelihood is that there are potential teachers available, but unchanging human nature still has its eyes in the ends of the earth and is unable to believe that a brother, who lives round the corner and whom we have known all our lives, can be a gift to the church.

Such liberty is allowed amongst us, that we may get into the way of accepting ministry in a very casual manner. It is high time that Christians realized that it is a solemn responsibility to minister God's Word and, realizing this, were more ready to support in prayer those whose responsibility it is. It is quite likely that if your local brother, whose help you undervalue, were made conscious of your prayerful interest and appreciation, he would be much freer in spirit, and his ministry would be correspondingly more effective. May it not be that the attitude we have been deploring helps to explain the dearth of real teachers? A contributory factor may be that in rightly rejecting the principle of a one-man ministry we have wrongly swung to the other extreme until we tolerate any man's attempt at ministry. Every man has his proper sphere and if he fills that sphere with grace and devotion he can be an immense benefit to the church, but it is a complete mistake to suppose that every man is called upon to minister the Word of God. How often an unsuitable man is given the platform under the seemingly disarming plea that he will be hurt if he is not given the opportunity. If he is a godly man, sincerely desirous of pleasing the Lord and not himself, he will not seek a position to which he has not been called, and for which he is therefore not fitted, and he would certainly not be offended because it was not thrust upon him. If a man takes offence because he is not asked to speak, he is simply confirming the judgment of his brethren in not entrusting ministry to him. Is it more important that one self-seeking man should not be offended than that scores of saints be offended by being obliged to endure unprofitable ministry? Is this at least one reason why interest in the regular ministry meeting often leaves much to be desired?

If this attitude were corrected it is probable not only that the Lord would raise up more men, but that those men would be encouraged to addict themselves to their ministry. It might not be out of place here to offer some suggestions to young men who may feel called upon to equip themselves as teachers. The Scriptures indicate, what is often forgotten, that among the gifts given to the church are exhorters and comforters, and we cannot be too thankful for men who can stir us up when we are in danger of getting apathetic or encourage us when we are down-hearted. But teachers have a different task—to instruct the saints in the deeper things of God, into those broad principles of truth which, once grasped, enable those so taught to make progress for themselves. Hence the solemnity of the work, because, whilst an exhorter or a comforter aims at meeting a temporary need, the teacher is laying a foundation on which the future is to rest, and woe betide him if his foundation is faulty. Consequently this is not a task to be entered upon lightly—indeed James might almost be thought to discourage too great a readiness to assume this responsibility, by reason of the severer standards by which such service will be judged in a day to come, James 3. 1.

Training of Teachers. If resort to theological seminaries has been questioned, it is not because training is regarded as unnecessary. If the State is right in demanding that those who educate the mind in secular things should undergo proper training and prove their ability, how should it be thought that the souls of God's people can be entrusted to unqualified men? But the training and qualifications are different. It calls for an experimental knowledge of God so that spiritual growth keeps pace with increasing apprehension of truth, and a submission of heart and mind to the moulding influence of the Spirit of God, who ever strives to produce Christlikeness of character. Teachers need to be men of character who "do and teach". The ability to impart truth clearly and logically to the minds of others is valuable, but it is by no means enough. Paul emphasizes that his speech and preaching were not with enticing words of man's wisdom but in demonstration of the Spirit and of power; the result was that he spoke the wisdom of God in the words which the Holy Ghost taught, imparting spiritual things by spiritual power, 1 Cor. 2.

The teacher must have a clear conception of the aim of true teaching. It is not the impartation of mere knowledge, which will tend to puff up both speaker and hearers; the gifts enumerated in Ephesians 4 are for the maturing of the saints with a view to each discovering his appointed sphere in the church, where he can make his individual contribution to the edifying of the body of Christ so that spiritual progress toward the ideal is achieved.

Since there never will be any substitute for such growth, every generation will need to develop by the same processes. No man or body of men can provide ministry for future generations except by the true apostolic succession enjoined on Timothy, "the things that thou hast heard of me among many witnesses, the same commit thou to faithful men, who shall be able to teach others also", 2 Tim. 2. 2. Here surely is an indication that true elders need to be on the look out for young men of spiritual promise, who by their godliness and earnestness, coupled with the ability to absorb and impart, seem to be marked out by the Lord as teachers for the coming generation. True elders will put these young men in the way of acquiring an accurate and all-round knowledge of the Holy Scriptures, and they in turn will need to be ready for the sacrifices involved in meditating upon these things and giving themselves wholly to them. Half-hearted men will never make teachers.

A Hospital

by J. H. LARGE

IN THIS HIGHLY-MECHANIZED AGE there is a tendency to sacrifice everything to the idol of efficiency—higher and higher production is the cry. When people live in this atmosphere day by day it is not altogether surprising if this mentality, invading the spiritual realm, leads them to regard the assembly as though it were little more than a spiritual workshop, where the amount of work accomplished is the sole test of its success. Activities must be organized, people must be regimented, the machinery must be kept revolving at high speed, and everything must run smoothly according to schedule. It might be well to pause and inquire whether all this activity is producing any commensurate spiritual result. No reader will suppose that we are opposed to things being done decently and in order; it is no credit to servants of Christ if they are more careful about business affairs than about the Lord's service. It would be foolish to frown on efficiency, but let us beware of the danger of looking upon believers simply as "hands" whose claim to consideration depends solely upon their ability to contribute to the "effectiveness" of the assembly. Certainly the assembly should be effective, but the above attitude breeds a spirit of impatience towards those who, for some reason or other, cannot throw their weight into whatever enterprise may be on hand at the moment. In industry this concentration on "results", to the ruthless exclusion of all else, came perilously near to robbing business of the little soul it once possessed, until it was realized that even the most amazing advances of technology could not eliminate the human factor. It is all very well to have industry highly organized and geared to all-out efficiency, but life is not so accommodating as machinery, and men and women cannot be treated as mere units. However exasperating hindrances may be to production-experts, human personalities do not appreciate being pressed into one mould, and the sheer march of events has compelled the recognition of an obligation to care for personnel. Welfare schemes are now regarded as indispensable auxiliaries and a great deal is done to help the worker to accommodate himself to his environment, with what success others must judge. Even so, people still have accidents or fall sick. Is industry the modern Amalekite who throws out the sick Egyptian to die? No, there are hospitals to care for the injured and the ill, and in an age which tends to grow increasingly impersonal it is greatly to the credit of these admirable institutions that they succeed in retaining, to a surprising degree, the human touch.

Surely all this has an obvious lesson for those whose ideal assembly is comparable to a hive of busy bees, a community organized for the highest efficiency, with scant mercy for the drones. However well an assembly may be run, no matter what standard of ministry is maintained (and let us have the best, if by "best" is meant the most spiritual), the uncomfortable fact demands recognition that believers fall sick, they succumb to temptation, they become discouraged by trial and difficulty, take offence at slights (real or imagined), or perhaps fall victims to unsound teaching. Many have been bruised and crushed by experiences which we have been mercifully spared, and those who can be guilty of making efficiency the only criterion betray a complete absence of the spirit of their Master, who loved to heal the broken-hearted and give rest to the heavy-laden.

Suitable spiritual ministry may perform the useful function of a clinic, but very often more is needed – the assembly needs to have a special ward of grace where souls can receive personal treatment as "in-patients".

Commentators have long likened the inn in the parable of the Good Samaritan to the church to whom Christ entrusts the care of those who have been robbed and battered by spiritual foes, and whom He has rescued from death. The innkeeper was not told to find the unfortunate man a job, but was given the wherewithal to look after him. If some object that this is not the point of the parable, it matters little for our present purpose because our application of the figure of a hospital to the assembly is amply justified in other parts of the New Testament. "Him that is weak in the faith receive ye", Rom. 14. 1, may not be very acceptable advice to those whose restricted ideas of the many-sided aspects of assembly life would prompt them to receive only those who are as strong as they imagine themselves to be and who promise to be an asset instead of a liability. This may be a sound enough policy for a factory, but a hospital takes the opposite line and caters for the sick and injured, fulfilling in the physical realm the exhortation given to the Romans – "We then that are strong ought to bear the infirmities of the weak, and not to please ourselves", 15. 1. It would be strange if a hospital imposed a test of health, or ability to work, as a condition of admission. We must be willing to accept the burden of caring for those who show no present prospect of being able to make any useful contribution to the service of the assembly, having always in mind the transformation grace can accomplish. So long as life remains, the hospital will receive a man in the hope of nursing him back to health, and what amazing success often crowns the skilled and patient efforts made on his behalf.

Because for the moment we are confining our thoughts to the hospital aspect of the assembly, we refrain from going into the question of "reception" in its broader sense – for example, "receiving the weak" does not imply the reception of those who hold erroneous doctrine, although even here we need to discriminate between one who has definitely embraced error and one who is the unsuspecting victim of false teachers. On such we must have compassion, making a difference, with a view to delivering such victims.

Paul's exhortations to the Thessalonians clearly show that he expected them to adopt a "hospital" attitude to some. Whilst we do not overlook the fact that he instructed them to "warn the unruly", he urged them to comfort the feeble-minded. He did not have mental defectives in mind, but those who were faint-hearted, small-souled, who lacked robust confidence and, seeing difficulties or dangers in every situation, shrank from any enterprise for Christ; nor did he mean the Thessalonians to comfort them in the sense of pampering them, which would but aggravate their frailty. He meant that such were to be encouraged, an effort was to be made to put fresh heart into them. Moreover they were to support the weak and to be patient to all. Patient – how like a nurse! "Patients" do not usually live up to their strange misnomer, they are more often querulous and nervous – those who wait on them manifest such admirable patience. And so would we if, thankful for our measure of spiritual health, we recognized difficult or dispirited saints as being sick and in need of sympathetic and wise treatment.

Casualties sometimes occur among the saints, and some get overtaken in a fault. Here we have nothing to say about cases where Scripture calls for solemn discipline for the sake of the Lord's name and for the sinner's own good. Perhaps we might think of such cases in the light of painful surgical operations, which have sometimes to be resorted to when the trouble is too grave to admit of ordinary curative methods. We are thinking not of cases where a deliberate course of wickedness has been pursued by a believer, but where a believer has been pursued and overtaken by a fault. The spiritual may be able to restore such an one – surely a hospital function. Note – *the spiritual*. Much as we admired the humanity and patience of hospital staffs we would have grave misgiving about their ministrations were we not assured of their qualification, of their knowledge and skill acquired by training and experience. Similarly, how can men discharge the solemn responsibility of caring for souls unless they have learnt the art in communion with the Great Shepherd, as He has revealed to them, first of all, the secrets and the sicknesses of their own hearts, and His gracious skill in His treatment of them? Only as the healthy and strong imbibe, and then manifest, something of His Own Spirit of understanding and patient kindness, can the confidence of troubled souls be gained – and how important this is! A doctor who commands the respect and confidence of his patient has gone a long way towards curing him even before treatment has begun, and if he can spare the time to listen sympathetically while the patient unburdens his trouble, the cure is sometimes automatic. What a wonderful gift is the art of listening aright. How eager we are to give advice, when often enough if we could only listen and listen, we could help our brother to discover his own cure.

No doubt the true reward of a born doctor or nurse is not the salary received but the consciousness of a high duty well done – the satisfaction of seeing a man, once weak and ill, restored, by skilful attention, to health and strength. The man may be sufficiently dense not to recognize his indebtedness, or so inexcusably thoughtless as not to express his gratitude, but the doctor who follows his noble profession with a strong sense of vocation can look beyond the thoughtless individual, to the high ideal which animates his work.

The servant of Christ who cares for souls has neglected the plain lessons of Scripture if he looks for his brethren's appreciation as his reward. He may, by prayer and unostentatious but skilful ministrations, render a service of untold value to troubled souls without those souls ever recognizing their debt. It will be joy enough to the one who seeks only the Lord's glory and His people's blessing, to see the development of spiritual vigour in those once sickly and weak. He serves not merely an ideal, though he has the noblest, but a personal Master, who is quick to note with approval those who are ready to spend and be spent for the saints' sake, and will give the grace needed to look forward with joy to the fulfilment of the promise "and whatsoever thou spendest more, when I come again, I will repay thee", Luke 10. 35. Splendid recompense!

Meanwhile let "him know, that he which converteth the sinner from the error of his way shall save a soul from death, and shall hide a multitude of sins", James 5. 20.

CHURCH UNITY

⊰⊱⊰⊱⊰⊱

The Holy Spirit and the Church

by ERNEST E. HOLLOWAY

ONE INDISPENSABLE TEXT BOOK for this subject is The Acts of the Apostles which, Dr. A. T. Pierson somewhere remarks, might aptly be named "The Acts of the Holy Ghost". This book, besides informing us of the activities of the Holy Spirit, introduces a new community – the Church. These two – the Holy Spirit and the Church – are indissolubly linked and, as will be apparent, the Church came into being by the operation of the Holy Spirit. The Spirit is invisible, but the manifestations of the Spirit are patent to those with spiritual discernment, and such manifestations are observable in the life and activities of the Church in a number of ways. A word or so must then first be said about this body.

One gains an impression from Scripture that in the creation of man God sought thereby for communion and fellowship, but for such fellowship in its highest form there must be like-mindedness. (Note an illustration of the converse when James and John would have called down fire from heaven upon the Samaritans, a spirit which met with severe rebuke, Luke 9. 55). So God formed man in His Own image and likeness, breathing into his nostrils the breath of life, Gen. 1. 26; 2. 7, and the record in Genesis 3. 8 of the Lord seeking man in the garden in the cool of the day is suggestive of the fellowship which God desired. Alas, sin dissolved that intimacy and God chose a nation – Israel – for His peculiar treasure, Psa. 135. 4. Of this nation it is declared by God, "I will walk among you . . . and ye shall be my people", and "my spirit remaineth among you", Lev. 26. 12; Hag. 2. 5. This time the nation failed, and Paul shows, Rom. 9 – 11, how for the time being Israel has been set aside in favour of a

new community knowing no racial barriers. This new body –
the Church – is composed of believers in our Lord Jesus
Christ, a holy nation, a people for God's own possession,
1 Pet. 2. 9. How came this body (in which the Spirit of God
would dwell, and through which He would manifest Himself)
into being?

The Holy Spirit was Active in the Birth of the Church.
Just as the Spirit of God was instrumental in the creation of
Adam, in the conception of the Lord Jesus Christ, and in the
new birth of the individual believer, so He was instrumental
in the birth of the Church. The story is given in Acts 2. The
circumstances of the time were grim. The authorities and
people generally were hostile or indifferent to Jesus Christ,
who in their eyes had been discredited by His death upon the
cross. The material for the Church was meagre. The disciples
and their company seemed ill-fitted to launch a campaign
that proclaimed Jesus alive and still the Head of His followers.
But whatever the weaknesses of this company, there were
certain things to the good:

a. They continued stedfastly in prayer, Acts 1. 14, and it
   may be reasonably conjectured that they were praying
   for the Power promised by the Lord, 1. 8;
b. They recognized that, whatever the future held out for
   them, their witness must be of the resurrection, 1. 22;
c. They were a united body – "all with one accord in one
   place", 2. 1.

It was upon that company the Holy Spirit came, and
the Church was born. The members at once went into
action inspired by this new Power, so that many of the
crowd hearing their message were convicted, convinced
and converted, to the tune of about 3,000, Acts 2. 41. This
gathering of believers was fused into a vital body and continued in the fellowship and practices of the apostles, Acts
2. 42. This body having been created, it must not be expected
that there should be a continual and exact repetition of the
phenomena accompanying the initial outpouring of the
Spirit, but wherever a true Christian church is formed it is

because of the operation of the Holy Spirit. So the church of the Thessalonians came into being through the message of the gospel in the power of the Holy Ghost, 1 Thess. 1. 5, 6.

The story in Acts 2 continues and day by day other believers were added, who were "sealed with that holy Spirit of promise", Eph. 1. 13. From this beginning in Jerusalem the Church spread and believers were gathered in from the Jews, and Samaritans, and Gentiles. God's desire to have a dwelling-place among men had been achieved in the formation of His Church, for

The Holy Spirit Dwells Within the Church. An old-time writer has said, "the presence of the Holy Ghost (in the Church) is a fact, not merely a doctrine", and it is simple faith that is needed to appreciate the fact. Paul, writing largely to a Gentile church, or churches, shows how Jew and Gentile through a common faith in our Lord Jesus Christ are "builded together for an habitation of God through the Spirit", Eph. 2. 22. This "habitation" is described in the previous verse as a "holy sanctuary in the Lord", R.V. marg. Jewish members would be reminded of that most holy place wherein dwelt the ark of God, symbol of His presence. The approach thereto demanded the strictest care. Holiness was essential. It is well to be reminded that the Holy Spirit dwells within the Church and, therefore, holiness is required of us as individual members of that body; see 1 Cor. 3. 16, 17; 2 Cor. 6. 16. The figure of the body, 1 Cor. 12. 27, emphasizes how that the ill-being of one member can affect the whole. There is a tragic example of failure in the early days, in the case of Ananias and Sapphira. By their action they thought only to hoodwink the church, but the words of Peter's condemnation are noteworthy – ". . . why hath Satan filled thine heart to lie to the Holy Ghost . . . to tempt the Spirit of the Lord?", Acts 5. 3, 9. Deceiving the church is lying to the Holy Ghost who dwells therein.

The whole progress of the Church depends upon the Holy Spirit, so that, when following the conversion of Saul there was a temporary cessation of active persecution, Luke wrote that the church had peace, being edified; and walking in the fear of the Lord, and in the comfort of the Holy Ghost was multiplied, Acts 9. 31. Now in the life of this new body it was obvious that a difficulty would arise. Jew, Samaritan and Gentile had largely held aloof one from the other. Now, they were gathered into one company. Could the old disagreements be resolved so that these one-time irreconcilables would henceforth live together in harmony and unity? The answer is that

The Indwelling Holy Spirit is the Bond of Unity in the Church. In this connection the following Scriptures should be noted – 1 Cor. 12. 12, 13 (by one Spirit baptized into one body); Eph. 2. 18 (both have access by one Spirit); 4. 2-4 (one body and one Spirit). There is emphasized the "one Spirit" and it has been remarked by a certain writer that the common bond in the Church was "not only an allegiance to Christ but common participation in His Spirit". How do these truths work out in the life of the Church? The book of Acts provides illustrations which may be supplemented by information in the Epistles. Hence to maintain this unity:

a. *The Holy Spirit directs the policy of the Church.* This is clear from the record of the expansion of the Church from Antioch, Acts 13. 1-4. The Holy Ghost instructs the church as to the choice of Barnabas and Saul for special work, and sends them forth. The church concurs. Further, the very important matter of the reception of the Gentiles arose. What should be the course of action? The decision was with the Holy Ghost, so that James wrote, "it seemed good to the Holy Ghost, and to us . . .", Acts 15. 28, 29. But for the carrying out of a policy executives are needed, so

b. *The Holy Spirit fitted men for particular tasks.* This is clear from Paul's words to the elders of the church at Ephesus (the Holy Spirit hath made you overseers, Acts 20. 28-32); and earlier in the history of the church seven men are chosen and fitted to deal with an especial financial problem – Stephen, one of the seven, is "a man full of faith and of the Holy Ghost", Acts 6. 3, 5. It is the Spirit who prompts Philip to speak to the eunuch of Ethiopia, Acts 8. 29, and informs Peter concerning the three men from Cornelius, Acts 10. 19. But executives – personnel – without supplies would be a poor business, so

c. *The Holy Spirit makes full provision for the Church.* The great need was power, for the Church was faced with mighty foes. In the pronouncement of the Lord concerning the Church, Peter and those with him had been assured that the gates of Hades should not prevail against it", Matt. 16. 18. Peter therefore refuses to be intimidated, Acts 4. 19, and saw in the persecution they were suffering a fulfilment of Psalm 2. The oppression of the authorities led them to prayer, and again there was a manifestation of the Holy Spirit, so that "they were all filled with the Holy Ghost, and they spake the word of God with boldness", Acts 4. 31. This power was so evident in the activities of Paul and Silas at Thessalonica, that the critics declared that they had turned the world upside down, Acts 17. 6. That was power, but, more than that, the Holy Spirit provided gifts to the Church and so enabled its members to use the power to advantage. Paul in his letter to the Corinthian church gives a clear statement concerning the provision and use of gifts, 1 Cor. 12. 4–11, "diversities of gifts, but the same Spirit . . . all these worketh that one and the selfsame Spirit, dividing to every man severally as he will"; and there are somewhat similar passages in Romans 12. 6–8 (gifts differing according to grace given) and Ephesians 4. 4–12 (unity in body; diversity of gifts). The Holy Spirit has dispensed the different gifts, and it is the responsibility of the recipients to use these gifts for the edification of the Church. Then

d. *The Holy Spirit inspires the worship of the Church.* Ephesians 5. 18–20 ("be filled with the Spirit") is in the first place addressed to the individual, but if the individual is "filled with the Spirit" he will be able to contribute to the praises and worship of the church. Paul expands this thought in 1 Corinthians 11. 17 and chs. 12, 13 and 14, explaining how the various gifts help in the corporate worship. Perhaps the climax can be seen in 14. 25, where there is visualized an unbeliever, coming into the church and being so impressed with the Spirit operating in and through the members' that, "falling down on his face he will worship God, and report that God is in you of a truth".

Thus the subject comes round again to the opening thought – God dwelling among His people – and if the Church would experience such a consummation there is a word, oft repeated in The Revelation, "He that hath an ear, let him hear what the Spirit saith unto the churches".

The Unity of The Spirit

by W. E. VINE

All references are from the Revised Version

AT THE BEGINNING of the fourth chapter of Ephesians believers are exhorted to walk "worthily of the calling" wherewith they were called, a walk to be characterized by "all lowliness and meekness, with longsuffering, forbearing one another in love". For this it is necessary to give diligence (not merely to endeavour, but to make it their business) "to keep the unity of the Spirit in the bond of peace".

Unity can exist only where we have a right estimate of ourselves, a realization of our own littleness and demerit, and that unassuming self-abasement which is a reflection of the lowliness of Christ; when, too, we exercise that spirit of glad submissiveness to God's dealings which produces considerateness towards others even when under provocation, the "invincible might of meekness", which reflects the meekness of Christ and overcomes evil with good. To these is to be added the longsuffering which patiently bears with unreasonableness and meets disappointments with quiet fortitude. Only so can we forbear one another in love. That kind of forbearance is not studied courtesy or frigid endurance, but is characterized by the holy attachment which binds believers together in the bonds of Christian love.

The unity is there; it is not for us to make it. The Church is one, a divine entity. The Spirit of God makes it so. As the presence of the Holy Spirit imparts to the Church its fitness to be God's temple, Eph. 2. 22, so His power imparts its unity to it. That unity is not formed by man, nor by any ecclesiastical organization on earth. Human arrangements and institutions may devise, and have devised, something which possesses a show of uniformity from the natural point of view, but the unity of the true Body of Christ of which Scripture speaks is spiritual in its course of development and heavenly in its position and character, its design and destiny.

There is no hint here or anywhere else in the New Testament, of anything like unity consisting of the combination of a number of communities, or assemblies, delimited by geographical conditions, or formed into earthly associations or circles of fellowship, nor is there any hint of a number of churches bound together by the bonds either of formulated religious creeds or of human tradition. No matter whether such communities are organized by mutual consent or under a church council or any form of ecclesiastical authority centralized in a given locality, all such combinations are a distinct departure from the plain teaching of Christ and His apostles. They do not constitute the unity spoken of in this passage or any other in the Word of God. They satisfy the aspirations of men but are contrary to the mind of the Lord.

All bitterness, and wrath, and anger, and clamour and railing, and all malice are to be put away from us; we are to be kind one to another, tenderhearted, forgiving each other, even as God also in Christ forgave us, 4. 31, 32. In maintaining unity thus in the local church, our harmonious conduct would be in conformity with the unity of the Spirit which pervades the whole spiritual Body.

The Risen and glorified Head has made provision for the spiritual direction and care of each local assembly. The traditions of men and the bondage, or confusion, which has been brought about by them, have naught to do with the unity formed by the Holy Spirit. Where a local church acts in conformity with the teaching of the Word of God, it is thereby an expression of the unity of the Spirit.

There are elements of unity which characterize the whole. These are enumerated in verses 4 to 6: "There is one body, and one Spirit, even as also ye were called in one hope of your calling; one Lord, one faith, one baptism, one God and Father of all, who is over all, and through all, and in all". The mention of the Trinity, "one Spirit", "one Lord", "one God and Father of all", is significant. The Spirit is put first, for the immediate subject dealt with is the unity of the Spirit. Associated with Him are the spiritual and heavenly unities of the Body and the hope of our calling.

The next three unities are associated with Christ. They have to do with public witness; firstly, the acknowledgment of Christ as Lord. Secondly, the one faith, the complete divine revelation, which testifies of Christ; he who holds it confesses Him. Thirdly, the one baptism, an ordinance involving the public recognition of, and identification with, Christ as Lord. Then, to crown all, "there is one God and Father of all, who is over all" (His transcendence and supremacy), "and through all" (His pervading and controlling power), "and in all" (His indwelling and sustaining presence).

All these constitute "the unity of the Spirit", v. 3, and they are enumerated as inducements for us to give diligence to keep this unity in the bond of peace. They have to do with the one Church, the body of Christ, in which all believers are thus united to Him. Its unity is not yet visible, for the Head is not visible, but it will become so when He is manifested and His saints with Him.

God's Principles of Unity

by JOHN R. CALDWELL

THE TENDENCY of all sects has always been to consolidate themselves on the principle of confederation. Each sect, as it extended, sought the amalgamation with it of all who adopted the same views or principles. Then arose the necessity for a constitution and rules, and a definite membership. These might be largely, or not at all, Scriptural; but compliance with such rules became the bond of union, and thus, practically, the way is barred in each community or sect against further knowledge of many truths.

Outside of all such we have been led, in order to be where one authority only is owned, that of the Lord Jesus Christ; where one final standard is appealed to – namely, the Word of God; and where there is liberty for the Spirit of God to minister by those whom He has qualified and set in the body for the edification of the whole. Whatever be our relationships as individuals with the children of God in the various denominations or sects of Christendom (and these must never be ignored), relationships with the sects as such we can have none. The truth that demanded separation at first, demands that the separation be maintained; otherwise the sacrifice of the truth will surely follow. The results of all attempts

To Form a Unity of Assemblies have been so sad and dishonouring to the Lord, that many have naturally recoiled to the other extreme, and the consequence is that attempts at united action and fellowship among assemblies, which are perfectly right and Scriptural, are opposed and suspected of being a beginning to drift back into organized sectarianism.

If unity be made an object instead of Christ, then the end must be disaster. Some have made it the object, and have taken the exclusive position, and God has blown upon it. Others have made it an object, and have in their zeal for the union of all Christians consented to sacrifice their testimony as to distinctive truth, thus purchasing the wider fellowship at the expense of unfaithfulness to that which God has taught them. Thus, whether it be the rallying cry of the "unity of the body" or "fellowship with all saints" (both truths of the highest importance if rightly understood) it is equally making unity an object, and the result is disaster to the truth. Properly, unity is a result, not an object.

In building the wall of Jerusalem, each man with his family built opposite his own house, and built upon the old foundation, Neh. 3. Thus acting, there was no need

to be concerned about unity. When the building advanced
far enough, each portion would meet with and join on to the
next. Thus in time, unity was the result.

That saints are all redeemed by the same precious blood,
and all indwelt by one Spirit, and all members of one body,
are precious truths. But these do not suffice to secure practical
unity or practical fellowship.

The Object Must be Christ Alone, the exaltation of His
name, as the name that claims the allegiance of every heart,
the subjection of every will; the exaltation of His Word as
the only statute-book whereby His will is made known; the
unhindered liberty for His Spirit to unfold its treasures and
put each individual in possession of the mind of Christ. Those
who were of one heart to make David king were able to keep
rank, 1 Chron. 12. 38. There was no wavering purpose, no
double heart; therefore, unity was the result.

It mattered not that few at first identified themselves
with the cause of the rejected king; the host increased in
numbers and in fervour, and in effectual unity, for David
was its centre and its object. Let Christ be our Centre and
our Object, and subjection to Him in all things our rule, and
unity will surely be the manifest result.

Let each assembly exalt Him and build upon the old foundation, and according to the divine pattern and plan, and then,
like the walls of Jerusalem, there will come in time to be a
joining together of all that are so acting out the will of God.
Fellowship between assemblies will be the natural outcome
of individual and united subjection to the will and Word of the
Lord.

The Word that separates some practice from one assembly
will separate from all, not because all are confederate, but
because all acknowledge the one authority. The Word that
introduces to one, will introduce to all, not because one is
bound by the action of another, but because each is acting in
obedience to the same Word and will.

Unity

by FRANK HOLMES

UNITY IS A SUBJECT on which there is a great deal of misunderstanding and confusion of thought. Sentimentality, worldly wisdom and deliberate evil intent all contribute to the beclouding of the issue. The only safe course is to adhere to the position clearly set out in the Scriptures.

We must begin with a clear perception of the difference between the Church and Christendom. The Church consists of all who are truly born again. Christendom is a mixture of saved and unsaved. Divisions between Christians may well grieve us but the unity of Christendom is not the answer, and when it is achieved it will not be the work of God. A Christian is well advised to have nothing to do with a World Council of Churches, which is simply an attempt to unite Christendom.

A great deal of the talk about unity today concerns a series of compromises which will result in the formation of bigger groups dominated by unsaved people. Rome is observing this carefully. She is only interested in swallowing other systems.

The unity of the church is a much simpler matter. It already exists in the spiritual realm, and has to be recognized and maintained. It is, in fact, the oneness of all believers, produced by the Holy Spirit. As the members of a family are one because of a common relationship to their father and mother (though in practice they may become disunited) so believers are one because of a common relationship to the three persons of the Trinity, Eph. 4. 4–6.

If I know that my sins are forgiven, and you know that your sins are forgiven, it is the same Holy Spirit who gives us each this assurance. He unites us. If I know that Christ died for me, and you know that Christ died for you, we both trust the same Lord. He unites us. If I know that God loves me, and you know that God loves you, we both thank the same Father. He unites us. So Christians are spiritually one because of their relationship to one Spirit, one Lord, and one Father. This marks them off from the world. They compose one body.

"There is one body." The unity is there. They do not have to create it.

That believers are fundamentally one is an experience, shared by the saved of all denominations. In this respect it is a grievous sin to think only of those saints who meet as we do.

> Oft we forget that we are one
> With every saint that loves Thy Name.

We should be ashamed of such miserable sectarianism. The attitude which unchurches all others and casts doubt upon the conversion of true children of God is a product of the flesh.

It is the duty of every Christian to give local expression to this unity. This is where difficulty is encountered. Believers have a deep sense of their oneness so long as they are with other believers, but often they go back to a sphere where saints and sinners are mixed up together, and where they are outnumbered and outvoted by unregenerate "church members".

Our business is to provide a local church life where true believers are received, but where unbelievers are excluded. We have no unity with the unregenerate. This explains why spiritual dangers are encountered, and serious problems arise, if we try to organize united efforts with mixed companies. The unity of the Spirit is then lacking and a man-made unity has to take its place.

Many believers involved in unsatisfactory religious systems are aware of the difficulty caused by the admission into membership of the unsaved. Clear teaching as to the unity of the Spirit recommends itself to them. It is the actual condition of affairs in the local assembly that puts them off in some cases. Giving local expression to the unity of the Spirit means exercising great love and patience towards our brothers and sisters in the assembly.

We must remember that the average person is unimpressed by a theory of the unity of all believers, but is immediately moved by the unusual spectacle of believers living, worshipping and working harmoniously together. Some of the factors which most commonly undermine this harmony are:

1. Differences of temperament. The reserved man tends to

be contemptuous of the bright and breezy brother. He tends to think himself more mature and godly, but this is not necessarily true.

2. Difference of interpretation. As we are only finite beings, and not spiritually perfect, we shall always find that genuine differences exist. But they need not be grounds for ill-feeling between godly men. It may, however, be necessary for those who cannot agree, to meet separately, if the only alternative is silence on some point of doctrine.

3. Jealousy of the gifts of others. This is common, but it is hard to confess that we are guilty of such a childish fault, and we easily delude ourselves into thinking that our motives are quite different.

4. Unwillingness to meet those whom we think have offended against us. Sores are allowed to run for years until they eventually eat into the life of the assembly. The observance of Matthew 18. 15 is a great preserver of unity.

5. Confusion between what is really vital and what is merely traditional. If a brother is not too clear on such matters he will often put up a fight for non-essentials, and may even obstruct the clear will of God. Real spirituality includes discernment and willingness to admit one's mistakes.

6. A love of change and a fear of reproach. Disunity is sometimes caused by men who have a desire for novelty and dislike being out of the prevailing religious fashion. They do not understand their own motives, and think that they are solely concerned about the salvation of souls. One test to apply to ourselves in this respect is, how much real blessing has come out of our past plans?

7. Family differences. These can creep into assembly affairs with terrible consequences. A willingness to discuss the matter after Scripture reading and prayer together, with

a real sense of the Lord's presence, is the solution here as in so much else.

Disunity is forced at a great pace in the frame of partisanship. When believers start to take sides, and range themselves with personalities, complete disruption of assembly life is very near. If the energy spent on this were spent on bringing the two parties together before the Lord, the unity of the Spirit would often be maintained. Our unity is a spiritual fact, and its realization always depends upon our spiritual condition.

Unity

by W. E. VINE

UNITY IN LOCAL CHURCH life is formed and maintained by the Holy Spirit. Unity is not uniformity. Human regulations may achieve uniformity, but they do not produce unity. The unity effected by the Holy Spirit is characterized by variety, but it is a variety maintained in harmony. Harmony is the effect of the blending of differing sounds into concord. Variety itself may produce discord, and in the spiritual sphere this is inevitably the result of carnal efforts to combine differing elements into a spiritual unity.

The basic idea of the word "harmony" is that which is fitted. So in church capacity, saints are designed to be fitted together as the joints of a healthy human frame. This is true of the whole Church, the Body of Christ; "There is one body, and one Spirit, even as also ye were called in one hope of your calling; one Lord, one faith, one baptism, one God and Father of all, who is over all, and through all, and in all", Eph. 4. 4–6 R.V. Of that body, Christ is the Head.

A Distinction in the Symbolism. The same figure of the human frame is applied to the local assembly in 1 Corinthians 12, but with this important difference, that some members are there spoken of as an ear, an eye, and these are parts of the head; so that in this application of the figure the head is not described as distinct from the body, as in the Epistle to the Ephesians. Concerning the local aspect, the apostle says to the saints at Corinth, "Now ye are the body of Christ, and members in particular", v. 27. There is no definite article before the word "body" in the original. This indicates that each local assembly is viewed as a body of Christ. Each assembly therefore is designed to be an expression of unity formed locally by the Spirit of God, Christ Himself acting in each member, including those represented by parts of the head. In this aspect of the local assembly as presented in 1 Corinthians, the divine purpose is that the members "should have the same care one for another", v. 25. This is significantly and beautifully appropriate to local assembly conditions.

Whilst spiritual unity is the work of the Holy Spirit, the keeping of the unity is dependent upon the diligent response of those who are subject to His power. We are to give diligence "to keep the unity of the Spirit in the bond of peace". This can be done only as we behave towards one another "with all lowliness and meekness, with long-suffering, forbearing one another in love", so walking worthily of the calling wherewith we were called, Eph. 4. 1–3.

Local Membership. A change of locality on the part of the believer does not affect his membership of the whole body of Christ, the complete Church as mentioned in Ephesians 1. 23, but a removal from one town to another does affect his membership locally. All that is involved in his membership of the body of which Christ is the Head remains true for him in every place where he may go. The changing circumstances of earth cannot affect that membership, for it will continue for ever when heaven and earth have passed away. To regard him, however, as a member of an assembly in two places because he is a member of the whole body of Christ is to confound things which differ. If a believer moved from Ephesus to Corinth, he would not have been a member of the local body in both places. The fact that, in addressing the church of God at Corinth, the apostle adds "called to be saints, with all that in every place call upon the name of Jesus Christ our Lord, both theirs and ours" is not contradictory to this. There are certain facts and features which are essentially common to all the assemblies of God's people, but local conditions involve the necessity of care to maintain the testimony of unity locally.

There is to be, for instance, the recognition of spiritual gifts as provided by the Lord in each assembly; the believers who form it are to fulfil the exhortation, "to know them which labour among you, and are over you in the Lord, and admonish you; and to esteem them very highly in love for their work's sake", 1 Thess. 5. 12–13. Obedience to the connected commands to be at peace with one another, to exhort one another and build each other up, vv. 11–13, concern the circumstances of a local assembly.

These circumstances involve the functioning of spiritual gifts locally, in subjection to the prerogatives and guidance of the Spirit of God, and, above all, the exercise of the love as described in 1 Corinthians 13. These and other similar exhortations show what the maintenance of unity in each assembly means, and what is the application of the figure of a body to local conditions, conditions which could not be fulfilled by believers in one assembly towards those of another assembly, say, in another land.

Differences of Opinion. The unity of the Spirit, which is most precious in God's sight, Psa. 133, is something which we are to give diligence to keep. Detailed instructions as to its maintenance are given in Colossians 3. 12–14 R.V.: "Put on therefore, as God's elect, holy and beloved, a heart of compassion, kindness, humility, meekness, long-suffering; forbearing one another, and forgiving each other, if any man have a complaint against any; even as the Lord forgave you, so also do ye: and above all these things put on love, which is the bond of perfectness". Where these things are fulfilled there is sure to be unity. Where differences of opinion or judgment arise (and such differences may not be unexpected while we are subject to the limitations of our present state), yet they should not be allowed to issue in division. It is not necessarily wrong to have different ways of looking at things. What is needed is the exercise of patience. No decision should be arrived at, no step should be taken, till oneness of view has been granted, and it will be granted in due time if we wait upon the Lord and seek His mind in the spirit of brotherly forbearance and mutual esteem. To attempt to lay down regulations where no specific commands are given in the Word of God, is to act in self-will and mar the unity which should be maintained. It is easy to lay down laws as a result of our inferences from certain texts, but that cannot meet the approval of God.

The passage just quoted from Colossians depicts love as the binding outer cloak. It is "the bond of perfectness". Following this we are exhorted to let the "peace of Christ rule", or rather arbitrate, "in your hearts". His peace should be the deciding factor in all our differences. If Christ's peace dwells in our hearts individually, it will find its expression in producing harmony of thought and action. To this peace we have been called "in one body", and here, again, its exercise is obviously to be put into practice in the local assembly. Moreover, where the benign power of His peace is at work, it will produce that spirit which is inculcated in the immediately following command, "be ye thankful".

BAPTISM

On Baptism – a Discussion

by E. L. LOVERING

All quotations are from the Revised Version

A GROUP OF YOUNG PEOPLE is discussing the subject of Baptism, and we are surprised to hear how varied are the views expressed.

"When I was an infant, I was baptized in the church and became a member of Christ, a child of God and an inheritor of the kingdom of heaven", said one young man quite firmly. To this came a sharp reply from one of the company who, though he too claimed to be a Christian had never been baptized. "I see no reason", said he, "why baptism is necessary, for surely neither the sprinkling of water on the head of an infant nor the complete immersion of a person in water can make any difference to the soul". "This is most strange and conflicting", rejoined a third member, "for one of you believes that water baptism is the gateway to the kingdom of God, while the other dismisses the act as unessential and unnecessary".

Meanwhile, a fourth person, while listening intently to the views already expressed, had been "thumbing" the leaves of his Bible and very sensibly suggested that, as the whole subject was dealt with in the New Testament, they might quietly and reverently refer to some relevant passages. Let us join them now and with a humble spirit and ready mind endeavour to find the answers to their problems.

What saith the Scriptures? Our first authority must surely be the Lord Jesus Christ Himself, who in His great commission to the disciples said, "Go ye therefore, and make disciples of all the nations, baptizing them into the name of the Father and of the Son and of the Holy Ghost: teaching them to observe all things whatsoever I commanded you: and lo, I am with you alway, even unto the consummation of the age", Matt. 28. 19, 20 marg. Similar verses were read in Mark 16. 15, 16 and special reference made to the fact that, "He that believeth and is baptized shall be saved; but he that disbelieveth shall be condemned". From these verses our Bible friend indicated to his companions that only disciples and believers were baptized.

This did not meet with immediate and wholehearted agreement, so he proceeded to refer them to the practice and example of the apostles in the early church. They turned to the book of the Acts and read such verses as the following: "*They then that received* his word were baptized: and there were added unto them in that day about three thousand souls", 2. 41. "But *when they believed* Philip preaching good tidings concerning the kingdom of God and the name of Jesus Christ, they were baptized, both men and women", 8. 12.

Our friend then reminded them of the story of the Ethiopian chancellor who, having been up to Jerusalem to worship, was returning homewards and was reading from the prophet Isaiah chapter 53. 7, 8. Arriving at the place where there was water, the eunuch asked to be baptized and Philip went down into the water with him and baptized him, 8. 36–38. Reading further in the book he told of a ruler of the synagogue named Crispus who had "believed in the Lord with all his house; and many of the Corinthians hearing believed, and were baptized", 18. 8.

Important Conclusions. After further discussion on these scriptures they concluded that on *the authority of the Saviour* Himself and *the example of the early church* there was certainly a valid reason for baptism.

It was also very apparent that in every case *baptism* followed *believing* and that the only proper subjects for baptism were believers in the Lord Jesus Christ.

Further Queries. Someone remarked, however, that there had been a reference in the Acts to *households* being baptized and that when the gaoler at Philippi had believed on the Lord Jesus Christ, he "was baptized, he and all his, immediately", 16. 33. It was pointed out that to assume that infants were included in these households was quite unjustified, as in fact, it was clearly stated that they that heard the word, believed and rejoiced in salvation, 16. 34.

"What then happens", said one of the company, "if as an infant I was sprinkled at my christening or immersed; do I need to be baptized again?". Our Bible friend said, "we shall find some help in that connection if we read Acts 19. 4, 5". Paul had come to Ephesus and found some disciples who had been baptized unto John's baptism of repentance. Having now heard the full gospel of the Lord's death and resurrection, "they were baptized into the name of the Lord Jesus". One should be baptized in obedience to the express command of the Lord subsequent to salvation whatever one's previous background may have been.

The discussion now turned upon the *mode of baptism*. Reference was made to John 3. 23 where we read that "John also was baptizing in Aenon near to Salim, because there was *much* water there", and to Acts 8. 38 where both Philip and the eunuch "went down into the water". These verses certainly seemed to indicate that much water was required and pointed to baptism by immersion. It was also pointed out that baptism was *in* water not *with* water.

Consideration was then given to the *spiritual significance of baptism*. Turning now his Bible to Romans 6. 3–4, our Bible friend noted that the believer who had been baptized was said to have been "baptized into his (Christ's) death". Hence baptism was a symbolic act of our identification with Christ in death, burial and resurrection, being raised to "walk in newness of life". In Christ the believer is "a new creation", 2 Cor. 5. 17 marg., the old Adam-nature has been judged, condemned and buried and it is his privilege and responsibility to live as one who is raised and seated with Christ in the heavenlies.

This thought provoked deep exercise of heart and conscience among the little company there gathered and we can only desire that those amongst them who had previously doubted the relevance of baptism in their Christian experience were led to follow their Lord and Saviour through the waters of baptism, with the resulting joy of obedience to His words. Could you have been one of that company?

Baptism

by A. G. CLARKE*

THE LORD JESUS appointed *two ordinances* only for His Church, namely Baptism and the Lord's Supper. Rome has added five others (confirmation, penance, extreme unction, holy orders and matrimony) without the least warrant from Scripture. We observe the last not because it is specifically of the church order but of the creation order, whereas Rome refuses to recognize marriage outside her "church".

Divine Authority. Christ's clear command in the great commission, Matt. 28. 19, 20; Mark 16. 15, 16. Making disciples, baptizing and teaching, form a composite charge, no part of which must be disregarded.

Apostolic Practice. Trace in the Book of Acts the invariable order following our Lord's mandate; see especially 2. 41; 8. 12, 36–38; 18. 8. (For "making-disciples" see Acts 14. 21). Unbaptized believers are never contemplated in the New Testament.

Proper Subjects. *All* believers in the Lord Jesus Christ were baptized and *no others*. In present-day circumstances it is generally advisable to have confirmatory evidence that a person is a true believer before baptizing him. In many mission-fields this procedure has been proved absolutely necessary. A too-hurried acceptance of a "candidate" may be a definite hindrance to his own spiritual welfare.

---

* After publication in *Precious Seed*, the complete set of articles by Mr. A. G. Clarke was first republished by the author in booklet form, and then by John Ritchie Ltd., Kilmarnock, under the title *New Testament Church Principles*.

Appointed Method. This is clearly manifest from (a) the meaning of the word, and (b) the significance of the rite.

(a) *Meaning of the Word* – a transliteration of the Greek, not a translation – from "bapto", to dip, Luke 16. 24; John 13. 26; Rev. 19. 13, "baptizo", an intensive form, to dip thoroughly. These words never mean to sprinkle or to pour – all standard lexicons give meaning indicated – Scripture use confirms; (see Acts 8. 38; carefully note procedure, John 3. 23).

(b) *Significance of the rite* – Romans 6. 4. Burial and resurrection of the believer with Christ is set forth – involving immersion and emersion. Sprinkling a few grains of earth upon a body, cannot by any reason be called a burial!

Question of formula. Matthew 28. 19 in force until "the end of the age", v. 20. Apostolic practice (Acts) in no case gives the formula – fact recorded that they baptized converts by the command of the Lord Jesus. Where preposition "eis" used, it indicates "into association with" Christ, 8. 16; 19. 5, and necessarily involves doctrine of Matthew 28. 19, so no discrepancy. Finally, there is but *one* baptism, Eph. 4. 5; neither different modes, nor one for Jew and another for Gentile, recognized in Scripture.

Doctrinal Import. Basic teaching – identification with Christ. The believer's standing before God is "in Christ", a new creation, 2 Cor. 5. 17. God reckons him therefore to have shared Christ's death, burial and resurrection, appropriately symbolized by water-baptism. The "old man" (Adam nature) with all its deeds has been judged, sentenced and executed in the cross of Christ, buried out of God's sight, and the believer is viewed as a "new man" introduced into the sphere of resurrection – life with Christ, Eph. 2. 5, 6. He is therefore responsible henceforth to walk in "newness of life", reckoning himself to have died unto sin and to be alive unto God, Rom. 6. 3–11. In submitting to the rite of baptism, the believer publicly confesses his acceptance of God's viewpoint and faith's resolve to live accordingly. For further teaching on the practical side of this truth, see Eph. 4. 2–25 ff; Col.

3. 8–10; Rom. 13. 14, etc. (In baptism we proclaim our death with Christ; in the Lord's supper, Christ's death for us).

Prevalent Malpractices. (a) *Infant Sprinkling.* Not only is this not "baptism", but it is associated with the destructive heresy of "baptismal regeneration", which teaches that the child thereby becomes "a child of God", "a member of Christ" and an "inheritor of the kingdom of heaven". It leads people to trust in a ceremony instead of Christ for salvation.

(b) *Household Baptism.* This error inculcates the idea that persons so baptized are brought into a place of special privilege and blessing. It is compared to the Jewish rite of circumcision, but the true analogy is that as natural birth determined the Jew's nationality and was followed by the distinctive sign in declaration of the fact, just so the new birth determines the believer's heavenly citizenship and baptism is the appointed public sign. In neither case does the rite itself procure the coveted privilege – circumcision does not make a Jew for it was practised by certain other peoples of the East, and baptism does not make a Christian, Acts 8. 13; cf. 1 Cor. 10. 1–6. Examples of households baptized, Acts 10. 44–48; 16. 14, 15; 16. 29–34; 18. 8; 1 Cor. 1. 16 with 16. 15. That infants are included is a wholly-unjustified assumption, for note Acts 16. 32, 34 and 18. 8. If old enough to "hear the Word", "believe" and "rejoice" in salvation, then old enough for baptism.

(c) *Baptism Ignored.* Certain sects teach that water-baptism is wholly unnecessary, and that the Spirit's baptism alone is essential. These surely forget that the Lord specifically enjoined the rite. See also Acts 10. 45–47 – reception of the Spirit followed by water-baptism.

(d) *Re-baptizing Unnecessary.* After conversion if the person has been previously sprinkled or immersed, some hold that re-baptizing is not necessary. See however, Acts 19. 4, 5 – pertinent question "Unto what . . . baptized?". Paul's words supplemented John's incomplete teaching concerning

Christ, which could not have included the facts of His death, resurrection, and consequent giving of the Holy Spirit. Now believing the full gospel, these men were baptized "into the name of the Lord Jesus".

Misunderstood Texts. (a) John 3. 5. Baptism is never connected with the new birth in the New Testament. The Lord is referring to Ezekiel 36. 24–27; 37. 1–14; which Nicodemus as a "teacher of Israel" should immediately have perceived.

(b) Acts 2. 38. Read with emphasis upon "repentance" not on "baptism", in accord with Luke 24. 47 R.V. marg. Repentance prominent in message to these Jews, for they were called upon "to change mind" with regard to Jesus whom they had crucified. In a similar message to Gentiles, prominence is given to faith, Acts 10. 43. Repentance and faith are like the two sides of one coin, Acts 20. 21.

(c) Acts 22. 16. Water cannot wash away sins, Saul is called upon publicly to repudiate his past life, especially deeds of opposition to Christ. Same word and same idea present, I Cor. 6. 11; see R.V. marg.

(d) I Cor. 1. 13–17. In evangelizing the city of Corinth, Paul refrained from several legitimate things on the score that they were not expedient (profitable to hearers) as events proved. It is apparent that the apostle usually left the baptizing to others, lest a party spirit and pride be engendered. The converts were not Paul's but Christ's, cf. John 4. 2.

(e) I Cor. 15. 29. One of the concluding arguments in the chapter for the truth of the resurrection – if no resurrection, then the rite of baptism is reduced to sheer absurdity – a ceremony in the interests of a lot of dead people, now dead spiritually and soon to be dead physically, with no hope beyond the grave. This would justify the attitude expressed at end of verse 32. (In the view of Dr. J. W. Thirtle and one or two other commentators, this verse is to be understood in reference to newly-baptized converts. Such are looked upon as being like courageous young soldiers eagerly pressing forward to take the place of warriors fallen on the battle-front – the martyred believers. They are baptized in the place of, or in succession to them. If there be no resurrection, such courage is exhibited in vain; nothing is to be gained by it now or here-after. This line of argument is thus closely linked with that in the next verse).

(f) 1 Pet. 3. 20, 21. Noah's ark in the Old Testament and baptism in the New Testament are corresponding figures of God's way of salvation through faith alone – committing oneself wholly to the Saviour, as Noah committed himself to the ark and so was borne safely through the judgment. Noah and his family were separated from the older creation and stepped out on a new world with new covenant terms.

Other Baptisms. These must be distinguished from Christian baptism dealt with above.

(a) *Ceremonial Purifications.* Another Greek word generally used ("baptismos"), Mark 7. 4, 8; Heb. 6. 2; 9. 10; but the verb "baptizo" is used in Mark 7. 4 and Luke 11. 38.

(b) *John's Baptism.* This was "unto repentance" and a confessing of sins, Matt. 3. 6, 11, preparatory to the advent of Messiah through whose blood-shedding alone could come remission of sins – a unique commission, John 1. 33, and apparently new in history.

(c) *Christ's Own Baptism,* Matt. 3. 13–17; identified Him as the true Messiah, John 1. 31–34 – the cross finally established His claims, 1 John 5. 6.

(d) *Disciples' Baptism,* John 3. 22, 26 with 4. 1, 2. This involved adherence to Jesus as Messiah, but not all these disciples "continued", 6. 66; 7. 31 ff.

(e) *Baptism of Suffering,* Mark 10. 38, 39; Luke 12. 50. Christ's, as being immersed in the deep soul-experience of the cross, overwhelmed by the billows of divine judgment vicariously endured on behalf of His people – James' and

John's not vicariously but as granted the privilege of suffering in fellowship with their Lord.

(f) *Baptism of the Holy Spirit,* John 1. 33; Mark 1. 8; Acts 1. 5; 1 Cor. 12. 13 – fulfilled at Pentecost, Acts 2, – believers incorporated into a spiritual entity – a "body" able to make increase of itself until reaching full maturity, Eph. 4. 13, 16. After initial act at conversion, no such thing as a later or second *baptism* of the Spirit known in Scripture.

(g) *Baptism of Fire,* Matt. 3. 11; Luke 3. 16. Not Pentecost but future judgment, as following verses show.

(Note that (e), (f) and (g) exhibit a metaphorical sense of the word "baptism").

Brief Summary. Baptism is an

(a) *Act of Submission* – obedience to the Lord's command;

(b) *Act of Confession* – owning the Lordship of Christ, Rom. 10. 9; cf. Gal. 3. 27 – a public confession, like a soldier who dons the queen's uniform upon enlistment – the uniform does not make him a soldier but it makes his calling evident;

(c) *Act of Identification* – symbolizing death, burial and resurrection with Christ, to walk with and serve the Lord in a new sphere, the "heavenlies", Eph. 2. 6;

(d) *Act of Proclamation,* in that it clearly sets forth the gospel message through "eyegate", 1 Cor. 15. 3, 4.

RECEPTION AND FELLOWSHIP

Fellowship – Recognition and Reception

by A. G. Clarke

Definition. The word signifies a mutual sharing, a common interest in anything, a partnership. The New Testament Greek "koinonia" is variously translated "fellowship", "communion", "communication", and cognates by allied words.

Basis. Christian fellowship is shown in Scripture to be based upon a common (shared-by-all) interest in the Person and work of Christ; not racial affinity or social status, not cultural aims or political creed, as with world "fellowships", "brotherhoods", and "unions". *The* Christian fellowship is composed of all who are sanctified (set apart) in Christ Jesus, 1 Cor. 1. 2; sanctified by faith in Him, Acts 26. 18, and thus called into the fellowship of God's Son, 1 Cor. 1. 9. Sharing a common faith, Titus 1. 4, they enjoy a salvation common to all, Jude 3. For a short period in the beginning they even held their possessions in the common interest, Acts 2. 44, 45; 4. 32. This was not communism (as some allege), for it was an entirely free contribution by happy mutual arrangement, whereas communism compulsorily takes from one to distribute to another, an appropriation by the State of the property, power and even persons of the people. Community of interest drew the Christians together into one holy fellowship, 1 John 3. 14, 16, 17, united in worship, in well-doing and in witness.

Nature. This fellowship established by God is eternal in character, though enjoyment of it depends upon the spiritual state of the individual believer. It is active not passive, an outworking of faith, James 2. 20ff, in serving the Lord and His people, Philemon 4, 7. In some businesses there are "sleeping partners", who draw a share of profits but do no work therein. The Christian fellowship is not so. Neither is it simply "pew-sitting" or merely sharing the Lord's supper. Moreover it negatives both "isolationism", Heb. 10. 24, 25; Acts 2. 42, and a "butterfly" procedure of flitting from one company of Christians to another, Acts 4. 23; Col. 4. 12 ("one of you"). This fellowship is:

1. A Fellowship with God, 1 John 1. 1-7. (a) *Privileged Communion* – (i) With the Father, v. 3, who shares His Beloved Son with us; (ii) With the Son, who shares the Father with us, John 1. 18; (iii) Of the Holy Spirit, 2 Cor. 13. 14, the unifying Power. We share possession of the indwelling Spirit, who enables us to commune with God and with one another.

(b) *Essential Condition*, vv. 5-7, walking in the light, cf. Eph. 5. 6-14; Rom. 13. 12; John 3. 20. Fellowship is disrupted by sin but the way of its restoration is indicated, 1 John 1. 9 to 2. 2.

(c) *Blessed Consequence*, 2 Pet. 1. 3, 4. Lit. "*become* partakers of divine nature*". It is not new birth here, but progressive likeness to Him, hence the exhortation, vv. 5ff. A child is not only born of its parents but grows in likeness to them, 1 Pet. 1. 3 with 15, 16 (lit. "*become* ye holy, for *I am* holy").

2. A Fellowship with the Apostles, 1 John 1. 3. They shared with us their personal knowledge of Christ and His work, vv. 1-4. The doctrine of Christ, 2 John 9-11, is that which embodies these facts, and is the apostolic doctrine referred to in Acts 2. 42, which formed the basis of the Christian fellowship; see John chs. 17, 18, 20-21; 1 Pet. 1. 25.

3. A Fellowship with the Saints. The Philippian Epistle brings this out most beautifully. It is the Epistle of joyful fellowship.

(a) *A Fellowship of Salvation*, Phil. 1. 7 – "partakers of grace" covers the whole range of spiritual blessings, Titus 1. 4; Rom. 11. 17.

(b) *A Fellowship of Service*, Phil. 1. 5 – examples Phil. 4. 3; Philemon 17; 2 Cor. 8. 23; Acts 13. 14 with 14. 26–28; Gal. 2. 9.

(c) *A Fellowship of Spirit*, Phil. 2. 1. Here it would seem better to read "spirit" with small "s" as denoting the Christian's spirit; see context, especially the exhortation of next verse. Harmony of spirit does not mean uniformity of disposition or of action (cf. the apostles themselves).

(d) *A Fellowship of Suffering*, Phil. 3. 10; 1. 29, 30. See also Heb. 10. 33; Rev. 1. 9. This suffering is (i) *with Christ*, 1 Pet. 4. 14 (not His vicarious sufferings as sin-bearer at the hand of God, which He endured alone, but malicious sufferings endured at the hands of men in persecution for righteousness' sake); (ii) *with saints*, 2 Cor. 1. 5–7 (present solace); 1 Pet. 5. 9, 10 (future splendour).

(e) *A Fellowship of Substance*, Phil. 4. 14ff; cf. Heb. 13. 16, in the necessities of (i) *Saints of God*, Rom. 12. 13; 15. 26, 27; 2 Cor. 8. 4; 9. 13; 1 Tim. 6. 18; (ii) *Servants of God*, Phil. 4. 14, 15; Gal. 6. 6.

THE LORD'S TABLE has been called "the focal point" of the Christian fellowship, 1 Cor. 10. 16, 17. Neither it, nor its sister-ordinance baptism, creates the fellowship; but they both express it, especially the former. Note the reversed order ("cup . . . loaf"), which is the order of our experience; (a) a common interest in that which was effected by the blood of Christ (His death), followed by (b) fellow-membership in the Body of Christ (His Church). This involves a responsibility of true separation from all contrary to Him, vv. 20–22. The Christian fellowship, then, negatives:

(i) *Fellowship with demons* such as in idolatry, spiritism, error-cults, etc. 1 Cor. 10. 18–22; 2 John 9–11.

(ii) *Fellowship with the world*, 1 John 5. 19 R.V. "world" – Greek "kosmos", the whole organized world-system, social, political and religious, 2 Cor. 6. 14 to 7. 1; Eph. 5. 10, 11; 1 John 2. 15; Rom. 12. 2; James 4. 4.

(iii) *Fellowship with sins* – of the flesh, 1 Pet. 2. 11; 1 Tim. 5. 22; Rom. 13. 14; of the harlot church and her daughters, Rev. 18. 4 with 14. 8 and 17. 3–6.

Reception. "Receiving into fellowship" is a much-used and much-abused phrase. Its only possible Scriptural meaning is the acknowledgment of a fellowship already existing between the individual and God. God's reception of necessity precedes man's, Rom. 14. 3, and we should receive all whom God has received. A local assembly is not like a man-organized fellowship, into which a person may be introduced and elected by fellow-members. Reception of a believer is in the name of Christ, as one who belongs to Him, Rom. 15. 7, not in the name of the church or upon any other ground.

Two classes of Christians are recognized, the "*strong*" and the "*weak*", Rom. 15. 1; 14. 1ff. Strong ones must support the weak not stumble them, which is a serious matter in the sight of the Lord, 1 Thess. 5. 14; Rom. 14. 21; 1 Cor. 8. 11–13. The "weak" one is to be received, and that not to the "criticizing of (his) thoughts", Rom. 14. 1. The "weak", be it noted, are those who hold sincere scruples about matters of no real importance. These include the legalistically-minded, who impose unnecessary restrictions upon themselves and others. How often such consider themselves to be the "strong ones"! Physical weakness may arise from (a) tenderness in age; (b) infirmity of constitution; so is it in the spiritual sphere. The assembly should be a nursery for "babes in Christ", a nursing-home for the "weak", and a training-home for all. In God's family there are various states of spiritual growth, 1 John 2. 12–14. There is room for all in happy fellowship, but no room for an intolerant spirit towards any member thereof. Weakness (infirmity) must not be confused with sins. The latter are to be dealt with, the former borne with, Rom. 15. 1–3. There is often "weakness" in those who have "grown up" from childhood in the assembly, converted but not fully taught through failure maybe on the part of elders to see that balanced ministry is afforded, or because of heedlessness of such ministry when given. A similar state of things is frequently found among Christians brought up in denominations. They find it difficult to throw off all at once wrong ideas and practices taught them in the past. When such are received, wise and gracious handling is needed, that they may be instructed in the way of God more perfectly, Acts 18. 25ff; Rom. 14. 19; 1 Cor. 12. 21, 25, 26; 13. 1–8.

Believers are received as –

(1) New Converts. Converted persons were "added to the Lord", Acts 2. 41; 5. 14; 11. 24, then "added to the assembly", Acts 2. 47 J. N. D. note. On being baptized they were immediately introduced to the fellowship of local believers, which included all the privileges and responsibilities connected therewith, Acts 2. 41, 42.

(2) Christian New-comers. Their reception may be by –

(a) *Letters of Commendation.* This is according to the Scriptural order, 2 Cor. 3. 1, 2; Acts 18. 27; Rom. 16. 1; Col. 4. 10; Philemon 12, 17. The principle was fully recognized by Paul though he personally did not need such a letter. To demand a letter of commendation in the case of a well-known servant of God is arbitrary and unwarranted, 3 John 5–8; Acts 21. 17. With an unknown believer it gives confidence as an endorsement from those who are acquainted with him. The Lord Himself, unrecognized in the world, presented His credentials, John 5. 30–37.

(b) *Personal Introduction,* i.e. by one in the assembly who can vouch for the *bona fides* of the new-comer, Acts 9. 27.

(c) *Satisfactory Evidence.* It is not possible in all circumstances for a letter of commendation to be produced. In such cases there is great danger of unwittingly doing harm to a dear child of God by refusing to receive him merely for the sake of upholding a rule locally made. It is then expedient for elders to make a few enquiries, which no right-minded Christian will resent if conducted in a gracious spirit. He will surely see the importance of maintaining godly order in the assembly. If enquiries are satisfactory it would seem well for the person's name to be brought forward in the assembly (i) to afford opportunity for possible objection, which must be upon valid (Scriptural) grounds, and (ii) that the person may become known to, and be accorded a welcome by, all in local fellowship. Elders do well to enquire of one coming from another assembly without a letter, if he or she be under discipline, for none in this position should be received, at least until full investigation has been made. A better way then is to seek a reconciliation with that assembly. Experience shows that few having ulterior motives will attempt to associate themselves with a Scripturally-conducted assembly. Exceptions should be dealt with as need arises, i.e. when moral or doctrinal evil manifests itself, Acts 8. 21. 1 Timothy 5. 24 shows that a man's reputation for good or evil often precedes his coming, in other cases it follows after, i.e. is shown up later. Elders are responsible to guard the assembly from erroneous teaching and moral evil, but must not go beyond this to impose restrictions upon a Christian's liberty to act as he believes the Word of God allows in matters of expediency. Though elders are to take the lead they must remember it is not they who receive or put away, but the assembly as a whole. Diotrephes' arbitrary action was a virtual denial of the Lordship of Christ, 3 John 9.

For assembly fellowship there should be evidence of salvation, soundness of doctrine (essential truth), and consistency in life. Baptism alone is no test. An unbaptized believer is as much a child of God and a member of the Body of Christ as a baptized one; a baptized unbeliever is neither. Baptism is no more essential to fellowship than to salvation, though necessary to obedience in common with other of our Lord's commands. Over-eagerness to partake of the Lord's supper, with reluctance to do His will in regard to baptism, should not be encouraged. Except in special circumstances the Scriptural order is not to be upset, Acts 2. 41, 42. It should be obvious that one who himself declines to obey the Lord in the matter of baptism is hardly qualified to be an instructor of others, especially as to Christian duties.

Disruption. Fellowship in the assembly is –

(a) *disrupted by sin*. The offence must be brought to light, judged and dealt with according to procedure indicated in God's Word.

(b) *disturbed by friction*. There are many causes for this and they are often petty and mean. He that sows discord is called a "worthless person" and if that discord be sown among brethren, that disturber (brother or sister) is strongly disapproved by the Lord, Prov. 6. 14, 16, 19; contrast Philippians 4. 5 where "moderation" (gentleness, yieldingness, sweet reasonableness that does not stand upon "rights") is enjoined.

Fellowship

by ANDREW STENHOUSE

What Fellowship is. Are you in fellowship? To such a question many would reply, "Oh yes, I belong to this or that assembly". But to be in fellowship is never, in Scripture, synonymous with belonging to an assembly. One may have belonged to an assembly for a long time and have attended all its meetings with regularity without being *truly* in fellowship. Fellowship has to do, not with physical presence, but with spiritual participation.

There is a certain confederation or "circle" of assemblies with clearly-defined limits, and, in the language of a periodical circulating amongst the believers in those assemblies, "the fellowship" means the visible association of those assemblies with one another without regard to their spiritual condition or that of the believers who compose them. Fellowship in this sense is nominal and sectarian.

In the Word of God, the term "fellowship" is employed in a much more elevated and worthy sense. True Christian fellowship is regarded as a spiritual link created first of all between us and God, and then between us and fellow-believers. It is essentially a spiritual, and not a nominal or official link. It is something that God Himself has created, and one of the choicest fruits of Calvary. It is a new attitude, a sympathy, an affinity, a harmony, a sharing, an agreement, a companionship and a co-operation – a living heart-warming experience that worldly or carnal men could never know. It is a merging of human spirits in the enjoyment of God-given privileges, and a sharing of the experiences of Christ Himself.

The Fellowship of God's Son. There was a great deal at fault in the fellowship of the saints at Corinth: a great deal of carnality and much else that the apostle needed to correct. How did he proceed? He began by reminding them that they had been "called unto the fellowship of His Son, Jesus Christ our Lord", 1 Cor. 1. 9. The appreciation of the fulness of the meaning of this one wonderful divinely-inspired statement would doubtless have proved a sufficient remedy for the carnality, sectarianism and all the ills of the Corinthian assembly. And doubtless it would be the cure also for many of the ills that afflict assemblies today.

The fellowship of God's Son, Jesus Christ our Lord, must not be construed to mean merely our fellowship with one another based upon what He has done for us. While including that doubtless, it is primarily fellowship with Himself – agreement, sympathy, harmony and companionship with Him. Only as we are in the enjoyment of this fellowship with Him are we truly in Christian fellowship with one another. Mere links of friendship or the spending of pleasant hours in one another's company is not fellowship, except there be the sharing of spiritual thoughts and privileges relating to the Lord and His interests: and this sharing, this true fellowship should exist between all Christians, everywhere, for all have been called to it, and the basis for it exists in the relationship that God has created. All Christians, having a living link with Christ, have also for the same reason, a living link with one another. However, there are practical difficulties today, more than ever in the Church's history, which make the enjoyment of this fellowship restricted and sometimes impossible. Many Christians find themselves torn between a desire to be faithful to God and the principles of His Word and an equally strong desire to enjoy and express the fellowship that is the blood-bought heritage of all true believers. Many of them are looking for guidance in this important matter, for there appears to be a great deal of confusion of thought.

Degrees of Fellowship. Fellowship is a thing of degrees. With some I may have *no* fellowship. I am told, e.g., by Scripture, to have no fellowship with unbelievers or with the unfruitful works of darkness. I have no spiritual affinity with these, and any associations with unbelievers, in marriage, in business or in religion, would constitute an unequal yoke. Light cannot have fellowship with darkness, and righteousness with lawlessness has nothing in common.

But I have *something* in common with all believers. When I read Pilgrim's Progress and accompany John Bunyan out by the wicket-gate and through the Slough of Despond, past Vanity Fair and the chained lions, I am in fellowship with him. I share the same experiences and have the same reactions. When I sing the hymns of Toplady or Horatius Bonar, I have fellowship with these men. I cannot avoid it. It is the linking of soul with soul by the influence of divine truth, and by the outgoing of the affections in response to the love of Christ. And so I have a measure of fellowship with the Roman Catholic hymn-writer, Bernard of Clairvaux, when I sing:

> Jesus the very thought of Thee,
> With sweetness fills my breast.

For fellowship is a spiritual exercise the measure of which is not prescribed by us arbitrarily, but is dependent on the measure of our mutual appreciation of the Lord and His truth. So that I may have, and must have, some fellowship with all who in any measure have a love for the Lord and His word.

Again, with some I have *full* fellowship. This is not merely a question of our belonging to the same assembly or circle of assemblies. Two people may belong to the same assembly or to a similar assembly, and have no fellowship at all! Unconverted people have been known to belong to assemblies, and of such the apostle John said, "They went out from us, but they were not of us". It is a good thing when spiritual conditions in an assembly make false professors feel that it is no place for them. Such were those of whom the apostle thus speaks. They were never really in fellowship.

But not merely unbelievers, but believers themselves may be in an assembly without being really in fellowship. They may be in a carnal condition – and the flesh cannot be in fellowship.

They may even be living in sin, like the man in 1 Corinthians 5, who had to be put away. What happens when a believer belonging to an assembly commits a scandalous sin? You say, "Well, we put him out of fellowship". You do not. What you do is to put him away from among you; he was out of fellowship before you put him away. He was out of fellowship both with God and with the people of God, when he committed that sin.

On the other hand, one can be put away wrongfully from an assembly by people of the Diotrephes-type, without being put out of fellowship. No one can truly put you out of fellowship but yourself. In the case of Diotrephes it was he rather who was out of fellowship when he acted in that high-handed way – not those who were cast out.

These extreme cases are used by way of illustration, but it should be evident to all that it is possible for true believers to be nominally or visibly identified with a Christian assembly and yet, for a variety of reasons – worldliness, carnality, unjudged sin, a critical attitude, a sectarian spirit, etc. – to be far from knowing and experiencing the reality of true Christian fellowship.

Fellowship is not Passive. When I read in Acts 2. 41, 42, that the 3,000 converts continued in the apostles' doctrine, and in the fellowship, I understand that it was no mere passive continuance in visible association with the church, but an active and practical continuance in the things that make for fellowship. And this is God's plan for all of us.

In 2 Corinthians, 6. 11–13 and 7. 2, 3, we see how Paul was conscious of a great lack in the fellowship of the believers. His mouth was opened and his heart was enlarged toward them, but they were straitened in their affections. He besought them to receive him, since he had wronged no man, defrauded no man, corrupted no man. What kind of reception was he asking for? Certainly he was not asking for permission to break bread with them. That is very often what we mean by reception. But Scripture never speaks that way. The reception Paul asked for was reception to the confidence and affections of the saints in a real and genuine way, just as they had a large place in his heart.

Travelling brethren sometimes have sad experiences. One has known what it is to arrive in a strange town with eager expectations of fellowship, only to be received in a cold official way, on presentation of a letter of commendation, "to the breaking of bread", without any manifestation of the love and cordiality (and hospitality) that belong to the fellowship of the saints. Such experiences serve to illustrate the difference between ecclesiastical recognition and true Christian fellowship.

In 1 John we learn that "if we walk in the light, as he is in the light, we have fellowship one with another". Fellowship with one another can only be maintained as we maintain fellowship with God. Walking in the light is not a static condition. It implies occupation with and progress in the things of God. As we continue in the doctrine (i.e. teaching), we continue in the fellowship. This is not merely a question of continuing in the doctrine of the gospel, but also of being enlightened as to the mystery of the Church, formerly hid in God, and of knowing our place in it. Much that is called fellowship today is no more than a mutual regard for those who belong to the same ecclesiastical clique, or party or circle. But Christian fellowship can never have a sectarian basis or find its inspiration in considerations of sectarian agreement. The understanding of the mystery would free us from every kind of sectarian spirit. Sectarianism is the masterpiece of Satan to destroy or restrict the true fellowship of saints, and we should be set against it. The very question of fellowship has become a bone of contention among brethren, and we should not be ignorant of these devices of the enemy. The discord is mainly created by the existence of divergent views on fellowship, and because of this I will now state a few Scriptural guiding principles.

Scriptural Pointers. 1. Ideally, our fellowship would be with all Christians everywhere, the only restrictions being those imposed by considerations of discipline or lack of spirituality in ourselves or others. The "mystery" would then be a precious practical reality.

2. Such a fellowship would find its expression in every local assembly gathered in a scriptural way and in subjection to the Holy Spirit. Since every local assembly should be a micro-cosm, or setting forth in miniature, of that which is true of the Church universal, there should be no man-made restrictions of the fellowship that saints are called to enjoy.

In the local assembly, as seen in Scripture, there are, of course, divine appointments which every Christian may be expected to recognize. A scripturally-gathered assembly exhibits certain essential features, as follows: It is composed of true believers only, and these believers, having been baptized in accordance with the Lord's ordinance in Matthew 28, have been gathered unto the name of Christ, acknowledg-ing Him as their true and only centre. They do not follow the pattern of the congregations of Christendom generally, but recognize the sufficiency of the name of Christ and of His Word. They are subject to Scripture in all things and meet in the simplicity that was characteristic of apostolic times. They have no clergyman to preside over them, but meet in the recognition of the common priesthood of believers. For ministry they depend on gifted men whom God has raised up, and they recognize the prerogative of the Holy Spirit to administer these gifts. They meet every Lord's Day, in accordance with apostolic example, for the purpose of breaking bread, and the worship which accompanies this ordinance is worship in spirit and in truth. It is the centre of the church's activity. The oversight of such an assembly is cared for by elders, men of experience and spirituality, men of good testi-mony and good example, whom the Holy Spirit has raised up for this purpose. Human appointments are not made for any such spiritual activities, nor are workers paid any salaries, but ministers of the Word look to God alone for their support. Such an assembly is recognized as the house of God and the pillar and ground of the truth. It is set to defend the truth of God, as revealed in His Word, and to maintain the highest standard of holy living, in accordance with that truth. It is also a centre of gospel activity and has fellowship in missionary work in distant regions.

Such an assembly is a divine institution. With such an assembly I may have fullest fellowship, for it is walking in the light and so has fellowship with God. But with sectarian bodies as such, I cannot have fellowship, for all sects are works of the flesh, according to Galatians 5. In all of them there is disobedience to the revealed will of God, and in most of them the essential features of a Christian assembly are entirely lacking.

3. If there is such a thing as the local assembly today, it is recognizable as the house of God, and because of its adherence to scriptural principles, my privilege and duty will be to have fellowship with it and fully support it, if I personally am walking in the light. The agreement will be there that makes fellowship possible. Such an assembly will not be found to be on sectarian ground. It will have no features that would be unacceptable to anyone seeking to walk in the light.

On the other hand, all congregations formed after a human pattern have many features that are unacceptable to the obedient Christian. The mind of God is replaced by the mind of man in the matters relating to God's own house; this is a very serious matter. My agreement or fellowship with the Lord in such matters makes it impossible for me to have fellowship with anything that is contrary to His mind. With Christians belonging to such bodies I may have fellowship in an individual way, but with the collective companies which take the place of churches while ignoring the revealed will of God, it is impossible for me to have fellowship without being unfaithful to the Lord.

4. Nor is interdenominationalism God's thought for His people. Whereas many Christians think that the desirable path for them is to remain in the denomination of their choice and to co-operate with other denominations as often as there may be opportunity, such an attitude assumes that sectarianism is a matter of indifference to God, or that it even meets with His approval. 1 Corinthians chs. 1 and 3 teach us otherwise. Instead of Christians stepping over their denominational

barriers occasionally to have fellowship with one another, the mind of God is that they should disown the barriers altogether and meet on the common ground of His Word.

5. Reception, as we have already seen, is a welcoming of a fellow-believer to all the privileges and responsibilities of assembly fellowship. There is no precedent for receiving a believer merely to the breaking of bread, or in any other restricted sense. God's assembly is the place where every believer belongs and if he recognizes it as such, he should be welcomed to its fellowship in the fullest sense. If, however, he does not recognize it as such, he cannot feel that his proper place is there, nor can he know true fellowship, or be in harmony with what is done, no matter how willing we may be to receive him. True fellowship is always reciprocal; it cannot be one-sided. And our reception of a believer, whether for a day, or a year, or an indefinite period, is always on the same ground: it implies our recognition of him as a suitable person to share in all assembly privileges and duties; it likewise implies his recognition of the assembly as a divine institution, functioning in accordance with God's will. If it were otherwise, the participation of such a believer would not be an act of obedience, and fellowship would be a formal thing. The use of the assembly as a convenient stopping-place on occasions for the breaking of bread only, while retaining allegiance to a sectarian body, is to ignore the true nature of the fellowship.

6. The mystery of the Church, properly understood, would lead us to the repudiation of all fellowships of a merely human order. It is sufficient that God has created a fellowship for us, and this fellowship finds its expression in the recognition of every true believer as one with whom I have a spiritual link, and of every true assembly as a divine institution that I am called to support and minister to. Other man-made fellowships are either too extensive or too restricted. The true path is the one which God Himself has traced for us in His Word.

7. The measure of my fellowship with individual believers or assemblies will depend upon the measure in which I and

they are walking in the light. No one can compose for me a list of assemblies and say: These you may have fellowship with! That would be the essence of sectarianism. Rather if I am in fellowship with the Lord, I will walk with Him in the midst of the golden candlesticks, taking account of conditions, thankful for all that can be approved of, and seeking also to remedy what may not be in order.

Let us never forget that suggestive picture in the letter to the church of Laodicea. The Lord is outside the door knocking and seeking fellowship. Let us see to it that our fellowship is made available to Him first of all. He appreciates it. And as regards the saints, rather than being over-fearful lest our fellowship be wasted on unworthy objects, let us fear lest our fellowship be below the standard that the elect of God have the right to expect in us.

On Fellowship – a Discussion

by E. L. LOVERING

All quotations are from the Revised Version

YOU MAY REMEMBER that in the last chapter* we listened in to a group of young people discussing the subject of "Baptism"; we join them again on this occasion to find them equally engrossed in considering the very important matter of "fellowship". One of them is reading Acts 2. 41–42, "They then that received his word were baptized: and there were added unto them in that day about three thousand souls. And they continued stedfastly in the apostles' teaching and fellowship, in the breaking of bread and the prayers".

They were all agreed that here was a clear indication that all believers in the Lord Jesus Christ should witness a good confession by baptism and that this should be followed by a life guided by the principles of the New Testament, and in association and partnership with other believers. There were no "isolationists" or free-lance Christians in God's plan for His people. Indeed as they continued reading in this passage

* See page 97.

they were in no doubt that in the first days of the early church, "all that believed were together and had all things common".

At this point there was much discussion on how far it was now possible or advisable to hold possessions in common and to say that "ought that any man had was his own". "Was this communism?" one dared to remark. An immediate reply came from several of the company, that this was an act of voluntary giving, and not a command of the State. It bore no resemblance to present day political communism.

It was obvious as the discussion continued that this matter of "fellowship" in the New Testament covered many aspects of truth and it was suggested that a summary of basic facts would be helpful. Four main themes appeared to emerge from the scriptures that were read and the thoughts that were expressed. These were, that, firstly,

Fellowship Implies a Condition. It was not essentially a matter of being joined to any *circle, brotherhood, union, church* or assembly, but that all believers "were called into the fellowship of his Son Jesus Christ our Lord", 1 Cor. 1. 9; there was a partnership with our Lord Jesus Christ Himself, which was vital and eternal. John tells us that "our fellowship is with the Father and with his Son Jesus Christ", 1 John 1. 3.

Reception into fellowship was an acknowledgment in the name of the Lord Jesus Christ of those who had already been received into the fellowship of His Son, for Paul wrote in Romans 15. 7, "Wherefore receive ye one another, even as Christ also received you, to the glory of God".

However, it was observed that it was possible to be outwardly "in fellowship" with a company of believers and yet to be spiritually "out of fellowship". In this connection John again wrote, "If we say that we have fellowship with him, and walk in the darkness, we lie, and do not the truth; but if we walk in the light, as he is in the light, we have fellowship one with another, and the blood of Jesus his Son cleanseth us from all sin", 1 John 1. 6–7. In 1 Corinthians 5 the man who had been living in sin was "out of fellowship" with God and his fellow-believers long before he was "put away" from their company. Are we constantly "in fellowship"?

Secondly, it was observed that

Fellowship Involves Communion. Union and communion are two distinct facts. Union with Christ is eternal and secure and is ours by faith, but communion can be broken by sin and restored by contrition and confession.

With regard to fellowship with unbelievers, the matter was plain and direct. Various scriptures were read, among them, 2 Corinthians 6. 14–15, "Be not unequally yoked with unbelievers; for what fellowship have righteousness and iniquity? or what communion hath light with darkness? And what concord hath Christ with Belial? or what portion hath a believer with an unbeliever?". Here there was some heart searching as to partnership in business, friendships, and obligations to the home and state; all these matters required much prayer and thought and must not be treated lightly without grave and often tragic results.

At this stage in the discussion, the question was raised as to how far one may have fellowship with other Christians whose persuasions differed from one's own. It was agreed that some things were a matter of personal conscience and must not be imposed upon another. God was our judge in these things, and before Him we stand or fall. However, even where one felt personally at liberty to do this or that there should always be a concern that all should be done to the glory of God and without giving offence either to unbelievers or believers, 1 Cor. 10. 31–33. (See especially Rom. 14. 1 to 15. 7; 1 Cor. 8. 1 to 11. 1).

It was decided that the present break-up of family life among certain Christians, under the guise of "no fellowship" was an utter travesty of truth. The Lord Himself had declared, "What therefore God hath joined together, let no man put asunder", Matt. 19. 6. Woe to the man who does!

In 1 Corinthians 10. 16 we read, "The cup of blessing which we bless, is it not a communion of the blood of Christ? The bread which we break, is it not a communion of the body of Christ?". It was noted here that the "*cup*" was mentioned before the "*loaf*" and one of the company remarked that this was the order in the experience of a believer, namely, the saving power of the death of Christ which makes him a fellow-member of the body of Christ, the church. It was pointed out that throughout the whole of our Christian experience, seven days of each week, God has richly furnished for us a table in the wilderness in the presence of our enemies. Enjoying what He has provided in Christ we have fellowship with Him and with all who share at the same table through His grace.

In worship at the Lord's supper, as in witness and in work, the principle and ground of fellowship was equally true. Here we remember the Lord Jesus Christ in company with other believers and proclaim His death until He comes, which is undoubtedly the highest privilege afforded any child of God, I Cor. II. 23–26.

"We seem to have been occupied very much with our privileges", said one of the company, "but surely there is another side to fellowship". Yes, indeed, there is, for with every Christian privilege there is a corresponding responsibility. This brought them to the third point, that

Fellowship Inspires Contribution. Previously we have thought of fellowship as "a sharing in", but it can also mean "to give a share to". So many scriptures were referred to at this point, that it is only possible to allude to a few representative ones. There is fellowship in giving.

Paul spoke of the churches of Macedonia, and commended them for their "fellowship in the ministering to the saints", they were liberal in their material gifts, 2 Cor. 8. 4. Again in Romans 15. 26 we read "for it hath been the good pleasure of Macedonia and Achaia to make a certain contribution for the poor among the saints that are at Jerusalem", and in 2 Corinthians 9. 13 "they glorify God for the obedience of your confession unto the gospel of Christ, and for the liberality of your contribution unto them and unto all". This was practical fellowship with believers in need.

Paul further exhorted the Galatians, "let him that is taught in the word communicate unto him that teacheth in all good things", Gal. 6. 6. This encourages practical acknowledgment of the spiritual help received from those who teach us the Word of God.

The writer to the Hebrews reminds us "to do good and to communicate forget not: for with such sacrifices God is well pleased", 13. 16. Remember then that fellowship means *give*, as well as *get*, and that it is more blessed to give than to receive.

Finally, it was observed that

Fellowship Invites Co-operation. When at the Saviour's command the disciples, after a night of toil and failure, put out into the deep and let down their nets for a draught, so great was the catch, that they beckoned unto their *partners* in the other boat, that they should come and help them. This was true fellowship, or partnership in bringing in the nets and sharing in the blessing. When the gospel net is cast are we partners in prayer and practice? Paul wrote of his mission to the Gentiles with the gospel, that "when they perceived the grace that was given unto me, James and Cephas and John, they who were reputed to be pillars, gave to me and Barnabas the right hands of fellowship, that we should go unto the Gentiles", Gal. 2. 9. The disciples were neither critical of, nor competitors with, their fellow fishermen, but partners and workers together.

Paul wrote of the women who "laboured with me in the gospel", Phil. 4. 3, for service in the gospel is far more than verbal ministry for an hour on the platform; this, after all, is but the climax to a work of preparation both in prayer and practice.

It was now time to draw the discussion to a close and it was suggested that they should read in turn a verse in which the word *fellow* occurred in combination with another noun. Here are some of the verses which they read:

fellow-disciples,	John 11. 16;
fellow-citizens,	Eph. 2. 19;
fellow-members,	Eph. 3. 6;
fellow-soldier,	Phil. 2. 25;
fellow-servant,	Col. 1. 7;
fellow-prisoners,	Rom. 16. 7;
fellow-heirs,	Eph. 3. 6;
fellow-partakers,	Eph. 3. 6;
fellow-worker,	Phil. 4. 3;
fellow-elder,	1 Pet. 5. 1.

It was generally agreed that the subject of fellowship was one which not only enriched the mind in its study, but ought to fill the life of every Christian with its joyful privilege and serious obligations. They left the group that evening asking their own hearts, "Am I *really* in fellowship?".

Letters of Commendation

by J. R. CHARLESWORTH

THE WAY IN WHICH such letters were used in New Testament times is shown by the following eight examples.

A Letter of Confirmation, 2 Cor. 3. 1–6; 13. 1–6. The *constraint* of Paul is seen as, with *courtesy,* he replies to the Corinthian believers' request for a letter confirming his status. These saints were themselves a living epistle – that is proof enough! Need a father be commended to his children? Paul's only concern is the defence of God's glory. How do we react when misjudged?

A Letter of Confidence, Acts 15. 23–27. What a contrast! Here the *competence* of Paul and his companions is proclaimed as they *contend* for the truth. Cf. 1 Cor. 16. 3.

A Letter of Consolation, Eph. 6. 21–22. The *comradeship* of Tychicus is mentioned as Paul sends his friends to Ephesus, knowing that personal *contact* and *communion* with this beloved brother will strengthen the Christians throughout the whole region. When "on holiday" do we consider the needs of those to whom we go?

A Letter of Concern, Col. 4. 7–9. The *consecration* of Tychicus is highlighted – he is a fellow-bondman. Paul wishes to *communicate* with the Colossians. Let us receive one another in a similar spirit of mutual welfare and comfort.

A Letter of Confession, Philemon 10–21. The *conversion* of Onesimus (a name meaning profitable) is described. Now, with *contrition,* the former unprofitable servant returns to be a true Onesimus. A letter of commendation is not intended merely as an introduction to the Lord's supper, but to happy fellowship in all the worship and work of the local assembly, which will thereby benefit, vv. 14–15.

A Letter of Conviction, Acts 18. 27. Aquila and Priscilla in Ephesus help Apollos whom they then commit to the disciples in Achaia, *convinced* that he will be useful there. Only that which is commendable can be commended; having been helped, Apollos then helps others. The "helps", 1 Cor. 12. 28, not the hinderers, Gal. 5. 7, are gifts of God.

A Letter of Consideration, Rom. 16. 1–2. The *compassion* of Phebe as she *cares* for the disciples is an example of the great yet silent ministry of sisters in the Lord. The Roman saints had to look after her as she had looked after others.

A Letter of Congratulation, 3 John 12. The *constancy* of Demetrius deserves this *compliment*; cf. Phil. 2. 25–30. In other words, give praise where praise is due. Every Christian shall "have praise of God", 1 Cor. 4. 5.

Additional Notes

by JOHN HEADING

Second Corinthians not only contains a direct reference to "epistles of commendation", 3. 1, but two of its major sections are in themselves examples of letters of commendation. Paul was journeying to Corinth from Ephesus by a roundabout route, through Troas, 2. 12, and Macedonia, 7. 5. In this last district, Titus brought to Paul the good news of the Corinthians' repentance after having read the first Epistle. Most of the Corinthians would now receive Paul again as an apostle, but a few in Corinth were still rebellious. To each group, the Holy Spirit pens a letter of commendation regarding Paul.

The *first* letter consists of chapters 3–6, and is written to the *majority* who would receive Paul. The plural form "we" is used throughout, and the apostolic *servant* is traced in detail. Far from being an automatically printed form, the letter traces the special type of ministry the apostle engaged in, ch. 3, the vessel through which this ministry was accomplished, ch. 4, the hope and evangelistic zeal of the minister, ch. 5, and the enlarged character of the minister though always separated from darkness and unbelief, ch. 6. In the light of such an example, how can brethren remain in doubt as to what to write when confronted with such a pleasant task for a brother or sister?

The *second* letter consists of chapters 10–13, and is written essentially to the *minority* who would still not receive Paul. The singular form "I" is used throughout, the Holy Spirit stressing the apostolic *service*. Here we find the motives and policy of the apostle, ch. 10, his sufferings and his future plans, chs. 11–12, while in chapter 13 the final approval of the apostle is shown by the very work already achieved in Corinth.

Letters of this kind are a pleasure to write for the Lord's glory, and a pleasure to read publicly in the receiving assembly.

WORSHIP AND PRAYER

⊂⊃⊂⊃⊂⊃⊂⊃

The Lord's Supper

by T. FITZGERALD

Introduction. We shall assume that we are approaching the subject of the Lord's supper for the first time, taking nothing for granted. We commence, therefore, with what is simple and elementary.

There are two ordinances only, authorized by our Lord, and described in the New Testament for the observance of believers in this present age, Matt. 28. 16–20; Luke 22. 14–20.

1. The first of the two ordinances, as described throughout the Acts, is the baptism of believers by immersion in water, and was observed on confession of faith in Christ as Saviour and Lord. This was done publicly and once only, and introduced the believer into the fellowship of the church or the assembly, Acts 2. 41, 42; 8. 36–39.

2. The second ordinance instituted for believers of this age, called the Lord's supper, was, unlike baptism, to be observed repeatedly. It is a continuous celebration of a past event, and let us ever remember that *celebrations* or *commemorations* of an event *are not repetitions* of that event.

We celebrate the Lord's death each first day of the week (as was the custom of the early church), but we do not crucify our Lord again, nor offer up again His flesh and blood to God. See Luke 24. 33; John 20. 19, 26; Acts 20. 7; 1 Cor. 16. 2.

The Titles Given in the New Testament to this Ordinance. 1. *Negative.* No names or titles as used by men or churches are found there, such as:

    i. The Sacrament;
    ii. Holy Communion;
    iii. The Eucharist;
    iv. The Sacrifice of the Roman Mass.

We therefore discard these names, while ever remembering that it is a holy and solemn occasion; a season of worship and of thanksgiving (Greek, *eucharisteo*, I give thanks) to God.

    2. *Positive.* We use the New Testament names such as:
      i. The breaking of bread, Acts 2. 42; 20. 7;
      ii. The Lord's supper, 1 Cor. 11. 20.

What do These Signify? 1. *The Lord's Supper* indicates a meal, the common food of which all present partake. The believers feed on the same "food luxurious (which) loads the board". Though simple elements, yet "the wine how rich, the bread how sweet, when Jesus deigns the guests to meet". The bread and cup are His own appointed elements, and no man has any right to alter them.

The supper is the last meal of the day. The night of the judgment of this world is to follow.

    2. *The Breaking of Bread* is a term which describes the act or manner of observing the feast. Each believer breaks the bread and drinks of the cup. We eat and drink personally and give thanks. The *supper* may be prepared, but unless we *eat* the broken bread and *drink* the outpoured wine, we do not keep the feast as instituted by the Lord. Referring to the bread, He said, "Take eat". Referring to the wine, He said, "Drink ye all (everyone) of it"; see Matt. 26. 26-27.

We Have the Highest Authority for This Ordinance.

    1. It was instituted by the Lord Himself on earth, just before His crucifixion; see Matt. 26. 26-28; Mark 14. 22-25; Luke 22. 19, 20. When men want to verify the validity of an institution or custom, they refer to the original documents. We, therefore, refer back to the New Testament. The institution of the Lord's supper is an historic fact recorded in the Gospels. Regarding the sufficiency of Holy Scriptures, even the

established Church of England states in Article 6, "that whatsoever is not read therein, nor may be proved thereby, is not to be required of any man, that it should be believed as an article of the Faith".

2. This ordinance was confirmed by our Risen Lord from heaven, in the special revelation given to the apostle Paul, with added instructions as to the doctrine and meaning of its observance, 1 Cor. 11. 23–32.

3. From the earliest times of Church History and throughout the centuries up to the present, the Lord's supper has been observed in all lands where the light of the Gospel has penetrated. Although it has been spoiled of its simplicity and spiritual profit by human inventions and traditions, the ordinance is an established fact recorded in history.

Some Things we Should Remember as to our behaviour and responsibility in observing this ordinance.

1. *Negatively*. No malice or wickedness should be allowed in the heart or conduct. *Positively*. Sincerity and truth should characterize the believer's manner of life, 1 Cor. 5. 6–13.

2. There should be unity and harmony among the saints. It is sadly possible to come together for the worse and not for the better, and to fail in rightly eating the Lord's supper, 1 Cor. 11. 17–22.

3. Self-examination, or judgment of ourselves should precede attendance at the Lord's supper, 1 Cor. 11. 28.

4. Spiritual discernment should be in exercise. To make much of the symbols and fail to enter into the true and deep meaning of the Lord's body given up and His blood shed in death, leads to cold formality and will bring the participant under the judgment of God, 1 Cor. 11. 27–34.

5. The period of its observance. There will come a time

when its observance shall come to an end. The symbols will no longer be needed. "For as often as ye eat this bread, and drink this cup, ye do shew the Lord's death till he come". Then in glory with Himself, the saints will see Him face to face, "as he is". The symbols will then give place to the privilege of beholding the once-crucified but ever living Lord.

> Too soon we rise, the symbols disappear;
>   The feast, though not the love, is past and gone;
> The bread and wine remove, but Thou art here—
>   Nearer than ever – still our shield and sun.

> Feast after feast thus comes and passes by.
>   Yet, passing, points to the glad feast above,
> Giving sweet foretaste of the festal joy,
>   The Lamb's great bridal feast of bliss and love.

The Lord's Supper

by A. G. CLARKE

"THE LORD'S SUPPER", I Cor. 11. 20, is termed also *"breaking of bread"*, Acts 2. 42, and is primarily a common expression for partaking of a meal, and is so used in Scripture, Acts 2. 46; 20. 11; 27. 35, 36; cf. Mark 6. 41, etc.; "bread", lit. loaf, for the dividing of which the Jews did not use knife. Later, the phrase "the breaking of the loaf" came to have special reference to the observance of the Lord's supper. *"Eucharist"* is a non-Scriptural term, but closely connects with one of the principal acts at the supper, namely "thanksgiving" (Greek *eucharistia*), and but for its ritualistic associations could not be considered objectionable. "*(Holy) Communion*", a term based upon 1 Corinthians 10. 16, expresses certain aspects of the supper. The wholly idolatrous conception of the "mass", as practised in the Roman Church, will be dealt with later.

Institution. In the New Testament we have four records of this, Matt. 26. 26–30 (dispensational order); Mark 14. 22–26 (chronological order); Luke 22. 14–23 (moral order); 1 Cor. 11. 17–34 (essential order). With three other passages relating thereto, Acts 2. 42; 20. 7; 1 Cor. 10. 16, 17, there are *seven* references in all. A *parting command*, "This do", Luke 22. 19; 1 Cor. 11. 24, 25, twice spoken; thrice recorded.

Exemplification. Practice of early disciples clearly indicated, Acts. 2. 42; 20. 7; 1 Cor. 10. 16. Writings from sub-apostolic times frequently refer to the importance of this ordinance and show the universality of its observance among Christians. The churches soon departed from the first simplicity of the scriptural pattern, however, and there gradually developed in certain circles a highly-elaborate ritual, often associated with definitely idolatrous practices. The breaking of bread is a collective exercise, and continued regularly, whereas baptism is a single initiatory rite for the individual believer.

Participation. It is most important to recognize that only true believers in our Lord Jesus Christ are entitled to partake of the Lord's supper. Participation by doubtful adherents and even known unbelievers as thereby receiving the very "means of grace" is wholly contrary to sound doctrine. See Acts 20. 7, "disciples"; 2. 41, 42, "they that received his word . . . baptized . . . continued stedfastly . . . in the breaking of bread". Here we may point out other terms designating the same class, namely "believers", Acts 5. 14; "Christians", 11. 26; "brethren", 11. 29; "saints", Rom. 1. 7. Moreover, only believers sound in the faith and godly in their walk should be welcomed, 1 Cor. 5. 11; 2 John 9–11; Titus 3. 10, 11; 2 Thess. 3. 6, 14, etc. If evidence is forthcoming of these requirements there is no warrant in the Word of God for imposing any further restrictions whatever. On the other hand, it is not consistent with godly order to issue a general invitation to the assembled company for anyone who wishes to participate. There should be real personal exercise of heart on the part of each believer concerned.

Signification. This may be exhibited in a seven-fold way. The Lord's supper is:

A Gathering of His Church, 1 Cor. 11. 17–21. The breaking of bread is not a subordinate gathering of the assembly – a mere appendage to other services. On the contrary, it is the normal gathering of Christians, the very central feature of the Christian order of worship. Acts 20. 7 strongly indicates this, and is supported by 1 Corinthians 11–14, in which chapters the term "come together" occurs just seven times and nowhere else in Scripture of the church meeting. In Troas the disciples gathered for the specific purpose of "breaking bread". They did not gather to hear the famous missionary-preacher Paul. Remembrance of the Lord in the manner He Himself had enjoined was the governing thought in the hearts and minds of the believers. In denominational "churches" the central point of a meeting for "divine worship" or "public worship" is the sermon, which is not worship in the scriptural sense at all. The supper beautifully expresses the oneness of the Body of Christ, the Church; the union of that Body in all its individual members (a) with the Risen Head in heaven and (b) with one another; also the communion flowing therefrom, 1 Cor. 10. 16, 17 R.V. marg. Note the double significance of the one loaf (a) as symbolizing His own precious body, 1 Cor. 11. 24, and (b) as symbolizing His mystic Body, the Church, 1 Cor. 10. 16, 17. The reversed order of cup and loaf here gives the order of the believer's experience, i.e. first, appropriation of the merits of the atoning blood ("cup") then the resulting membership of the "body" (loaf); 1 Corinthians 11 gives the order of observance.

A Memorial of His Person, 1 Cor. 11. 24, 25 R.V. Note "This do", i.e. it is not a matter of retrospection simply but an *act* of commemoration, and that not of His death but of His Person ("for a remembrance of me"). It should not therefore be compared to a memorial service for a long-dead national hero or a notable martyr in a great cause. We gather on the first day of the week, the Lord's resurrection-day, not on the day of His death, and ours is the joyful celebration of One who, having accomplished the atoning work of the cross, rose triumphant from the tomb and ascended to the right hand of God. Moreover, we commemorate Him not so much as a long-absent One but as One ever-living and graciously present according to His own promise, Matt. 18. 20.

A Token of His Love, I Cor. 11. 23 ("the night in which he was betrayed"), cf. John 13. 1. Love delights to *serve* and to *give,* Matt. 20. 28; Luke 22. 19; John 10. 11, and is measured by the extent of its sacrifice. As we partake of the supper, the Lord is afforded an opportunity to impart a further impulse to our devotion to Him in a fresh realization of His love.

A Pledge of His Covenant, I Cor. 11. 25; Luke 22. 20. Every divine covenant mentioned in Scripture has its distinctive sign, e.g. the sign of the Mosaic covenant given to Israel was the weekly sabbath, Exod. 31. 13, 17; Ezek. 20. 12, 20. The "sign" of the new covenant is the cup of which we partake at the supper, Luke 22. 20, for it symbolizes His blood shed in ratification of it; see Heb. 9. 15–22. For further teaching on the new (better) covenant, see Heb. 7. 22; 8. 6–13; 10. 16–18; 12. 24; 13. 20; 2 Cor. 3. 6–18.

A Partaking of His Feast, I Cor. 11. 26 ("eat . . . drink"). Some are averse from referring to the Lord's supper as a "feast". *Rightly* understood, however, there seems no valid objection to the term. It surely is a fitting occasion for believers to express the joy of their reconciliation to God, Luke 15. 22–24, made possible only on the ground of the death of His Son for us, Rom. 5. 10, 11; cf. the significance of the peace-offering, Lev. chs. 3 and 7. Personal participation is indicated by the four imperatives, "Take – eat – drink – do". The Lord's supper is the symbol of a broader concept – the Lord's table, I Cor. 10. 21. These are not interchangeable terms, though we often treat them as such. The "table" represents fellowship in all the gracious provision the Lord has made for His redeemed people. At this the believer is always "sitting", cf. Psa. 23. 5, but he sits at the supper but once weekly. 1 Corinthians 10 contrasts the "table of the Lord" with the "table of demons", which latter stands for all the worldly provision the devil prepares for his devotees, even in the moral and religious spheres. The Christian should have no fellowship whatever with such. He should do nothing to compromise his testimony for God before the world or to stumble a weaker brother (see context). Christ Himself is the unseen Host and Ruler of "the feast", John 2. 9. The table is spread by Him at great cost to Himself, but freely to us. "Table" also speaks of abundant grace and a generous sufficiency, 2 Sam. 9.

A Proclamation of His Death, I Cor. 11. 26 R.V. The A.V. word "show" has been misunderstood and is often cited as "show forth". The Greek however indicates not *representation* but *proclamation,* not showing to God but witnessing to men. It is the gospel in object-lesson, I Cor. 15. 3, 4. Same Greek word is used in 2. 1; 9. 14 and often elsewhere in sense of "to preach". Baptism also is a gospel testimony through eyegate, the emphasis being upon resurrection, whilst the supper stresses the death of our Lord. The combined witness of the two ordinances is very strong. It has been pointed out that the announcing is not in the "breaking" of the loaf but in the eating and drinking (text). We may perhaps see the death of our Lord already set forth in the separation of the loaf (body) and the cup (blood). Both the fact and the significance of His death are announced.

A Prophecy of His Coming, I Cor. 11. 26. "Till he come" is Paul's inspired comment. Here is the glorious consummation for which we look. It sets a limit upon the observance of the ordinance, so precious to all true believers. It is also a clear indication that obedience to the Lord's parting command must not be neglected in this waiting time.

> Backward look we, drawn to Calvary,
>   Musing while we sing;
> Forward haste we to Thy coming,
>   Lord and King!

Celebration. Keynote – *simplicity* according to the Scriptural pattern. Departure seen in Christendom, grievous errors and ritualistic practices having obscured original meaning. Loose observance also destroys its true character, I Cor. 11. 20 ff. At first observed by Christians in connection with a social meal, later called "love-feast" (Greek *agape*), Jude 12; 2 Pet. 2. 13 R.V.; I Cor. 11. 21, 22; and probably Acts 2. 46 as a necessary arrangement owing to numbers. For worship the Christians still gathered with the rest of the Jews in the temple. The practice shows also that the early communal order did not involve the break-up of family life. Appearance of abuses and other considerations eventually led to the separation of the Lord's supper from ordinary and social meals, 1 Cor. 11. 34. It is to be regretted that the social character of Christianity is largely lost sight of today. The Word of God avoids laying down laws of celebration. Scope is thereby given to Christian liberty, devotion and obedience.

Day and Time. Injunction is "as often", 1 Cor. 11. 25, 26, not "as seldom" or "as often as you may choose". This indicates frequency, not a yearly observance (as was the Jewish Passover), or thrice yearly or monthly. Acts 20. 7 denotes regular practice; disciples met on the first day of the week for this specific purpose. Paul had arrived at Troas the previous Monday but, though his journey was urgent, v. 16, he called no special meeting but patiently waited till the ensuing Lord's Day, after which he departed without further loss of time, vv. 11, 13. It is significant that our Lord first appeared to His own on His resurrection-day and on successive "first-of-the-week" days, symbolic of "new creation" day, whereas the Jewish Sabbath looked back to the old creation order. Greek "*kuriakos*" (only twice in the N.T.) links the Lord's supper and the Lord's Day, 1 Cor. 11. 20; Rev. 1. 10. 1 Corinthians 16. 1, 2 gives indirect support. The word "supper" need not determine *time* of day. It is fitting that worship and breaking of bread should have first place in all Christian exercises.

Elements. Controversy over their composition to be eschewed. It was at the Passover meal that our Lord instituted His supper, but the two must not be confounded. He took a loaf of bread and a cup of wine as simple elements ready to hand. The emphasis in the New Testament is never on "bread" and "wine" but always on "loaf" and "cup" as fitting symbols of the Lord's vicarious death. With us the elements are already set aside before we gather. In Scripture no lesson is drawn either from composition of the bread or contents of the cup. The wisdom of this arrangement is appreciated in lands where wheaten loaves and grape juice are unobtainable. The modern practice of cut wafers and individual cups, however, quite destroys the significance of the supper as a "communion", etc.

Distribution. In the Scripture regulating the order of this gathering, 1 Cor. chs. 11–14, it is important to notice that no president, whether leading elder or other "official" person, is seen. The claim to have special authority to administer the elements entirely alters the character of the supper, and is plainly contrary to the Word of God. Even apostles had no official status in this respect, but simply took their place with the rest of the saints. Acts 20. 11 is no exception as this refers to taking an ordinary meal (verbs all in singular, denoting individual acts) – Luke and others had probably already gone aboard the ship, v. 13. Clerisy today is strongly entrenched behind this unscriptural practice of allowing only "ordained" ministers or other appointed persons to "officiate".

Regulation. In 1 Corinthians 11. 17 to 14. 40, Paul deals with disorders in the gathering of the church and gives divine regulations for (a) observance of the Lord's supper, 11. 17–34; (b) use of spiritual gifts, chs. 12–14 (their endowment, 12, energy, 13, exercise, 14).

That one gathering is contemplated after the pattern of Acts 20. 7 is here shown by the use of *characteristic words* – (a) "come-together" (Greek *sunerchomai*) seven times in section, not elsewhere in New Testament of the church; (b) "give-thanks" (Greek *eucharisteo*) 14. 16, 17 with 11. 24; (c) "whole assembly", 14. 23. Most significant is it that the Spirit of God is not mentioned after 12. 13. He retires from view, so to speak, in favour of the Lord Jesus, who is recognized in the midst as Head of His Church and Host at His supper, John 16. 14. On the other hand, the *personal responsibility* of those taking part is emphasized (21 imperatives used in ch. 14). Common expression (often heard) "leading of the Spirit" occurs only twice in the New Testament, Rom. 8. 14; Gal. 5. 18, and is connected with the believer's walk, not with worship. However, if not walking by the Spirit during the week, we cannot expect to be "led of the Spirit" at the supper. The Spirit's prompting is not by some supernatural impulse, not by unintelligent zeal and certainly not by a fleshly desire to display gift (all errors seen in the church at Corinth), nor by purely emotional exercise, but through the spiritual understanding and spiritual discernment of spiritual persons, 1 Cor. 14. 14, 15, 19, 20. While regulation of order is seen primarily in connection with "tongues" and "prophecy" (gifts which have passed) seven *underlying principles* are discernible; (i) not everyone to take part, v. 26 (ironical); (ii) Messages limited to two or three and in turn, vv. 20–31; (iii) Speech to be in language heard and understood, vv. 6–11; (iv) Consideration to be given to other gifted persons present, vv. 30, 31; (v) Gift to be under self-control, vv. 32, 33 – the appropriateness or otherwise of what is said is to be judged by others, not by the speaker concerned, v. 29; (vi) Constant aim to be edification, vv. 12, 26 – "building up" not "pulling down" ministry – five words fitly spoken may encourage the spirit of worship, v. 19 – not vain talking, 1 Tim. 1. 3–7; Titus 1. 9; (vii) Everything to be seemly (in outward deportment) and harmonious (appropriate to the occasion). See 2 Cor. 3. 17 – liberty is neither licence nor legality, which are both manifestations of fleshly activity. If merely a question of unintelligent zeal, elders should correct and instruct in a spirit of patient grace.

Procedure. Breaking the loaf has no ceremonial significance, but is for convenience of the company, especially if loaf is large and crusty, otherwise *need* not be broken. All "break" it in the sense of partaking, 1 Cor. 10. 16, 17; our Lord's body was not "broken", John 19. 36; 1 Cor. 11. 24 R.V. So with pouring of the wine, where such is done, no special meaning attaches to the act. In the already separated loaf (body) and cup (blood) we may see death set forth. All ritual order and use of formulae must be avoided. Insistence on details is of no importance, and only genders strifes, 2 Tim. 2. 23; Titus 3. 9. As with the gospel meeting and all other gatherings of the church, there is nothing secret about the Lord's supper, in marked contrast to Masonic and other Lodges, which originate in the ancient mystery-cults of pagan-

ism (note incidental reference to "many lights", Acts 20. 8;
cf. 1 Cor. 14. 23–25).

Preparation. 1 Corinthians 11. 27–32 is of solemn importance. Corinthian excesses may not occur today, but
irreverent behaviour and meaningless formality are far too
common. Distinguish between *unworthy persons* partaking and
unworthy manner, which is in view here. A divided fellowship,
a discordant spirit, distracting thoughts, disturbing movements, are all unworthy of the presence of the Lord. A
defiled conscience hinders remembrance and worship. Prior
self-examination is therefore necessary and sin should be
judged, confessed and cleansed, 1 John 1. 9, otherwise the
chastening of the Lord is invited. Such judgment, v. 29, is
temporal not eternal. Verse 28 removes all excuse for absence.
Another's faultiness does not alter the obligation "this do".
If personally involved, one should follow the procedure given
in James 5. 16; Matt. 18. 15ff and the principle of Matthew
5. 23, 24. Note that our Lord prepared His disciples for the
supper by the feet-washing, an action of deep symbolic
importance as the context shows, John 13. 1–10.

Superstition. As pointed out already, many erroneous
doctrines and practices have gathered round this originally
simple ordinance. Perhaps the most serious are:

Transubstantiation. This doctrine of the Roman Church,
introduced A.D. 831, teaches that "at the instant of consecration the elements are changed into that body which was
born of the virgin; the outward appearance only remains as
before". The commemorative aspect is thus changed into a
celebration of the idolatrous mass, during which, at the
elevation of the host, communicants adore Christ as being
actually present. To quote further, "there is offered to God a
true, proper and propitiatory sacrifice for the living and the
dead". A most ornate ritual, so attractive to the flesh, accompanies the performance. Contrast Heb. 7. 27; 9. 14; 10. 10–14.

Consubstantiation. Lutheran doctrine dating from the
Reformation in sixteenth century. This movement, though it

accomplished much, did not break completely free from established clerical order. Certain errors of doctrine and practice remain in the "Reformation Churches". Consubstantiation teaches that Christ is bodily present with the elements at the moment of partaking.

Misconception. Certain Scriptures are often misapplied to the Lord's supper. John 6. 48-58 has no direct reference thereto, for the supper had not then been instituted. It has to do with appropriation of Christ by faith for eternal life, v. 54. 1 Corinthians 5. 7, 8 does not point to the Lord's supper; see R.V. marg. Passover typifies the once-for-all sacrifice of Christ as the Lamb of God. The seven days' festival that immediately followed ("unleavened bread") typifies the whole round of the Christian life, which is to be "kept" free from spiritual leaven – "malice" (in motives), "wickedness" (in conduct). One name, either "Passover" or "unleavened bread", often covered both feasts; Luke 22. 1; Mark 14. 12 with Lev. 23. 5, 6. As to breaking bread where there is no established assembly: 1 Corinthians 11 gives the assembly order, but this does not rule out the exercise of the privilege by believers in circumstances of a temporary nature, e.g., those travelling aboard ship, etc. Our Lord instituted the ordinance for "disciples" before the church was in actual existence. It is significant that the breaking of bread is predicated of "disciples", not of the assembly, in Acts 2. 42; 20. 7; cf. Luke 24. 30, 35 in keeping with Matt. 18. 20.

Summary. The believer's relation to the Lord's supper is
  an Act of Submission – One's *will* exercised – Response to *His authority* – Result, the Joy of *Obedience*.
  an Act of Devotion – One's *heart* exercised – Response to *His love* – Result, the Joy of *Mutual Attachment*.
  an Act of Appropriation – One's *faith* exercised – Response of *His grace* – Result, the Joy of *Satisfaction*.
  an Act of Adoration – One's *spirit* exercised – Response to *His deity* – Result, the Joy of *Worship*.
  an Act of Communion – One's *brotherly love* exercised – Response to *His kinship* – Result, the Joy of *Fellowship*.

an Act of Expectation – One's *hope* exercised – Response to *His promise* – Result, Joy of *Anticipation*.
an Act of Self-examination - One's *conscience* exercised – Reponse to *His holiness* – Result, the Joy of *Restoration*.

Readers who are fortunate enough to have been left undisturbed, to enjoy the remembrance of the Lord in simplicity, will hardly credit the determined attempts which are being made in some quarters to hedge around the Lord's Supper with all kinds of rules and regulations. If they question the usefulness of going so fully into the question, we ask them to believe that this examination of the subject will be welcomed by many Christians, who are sorely perplexed by efforts to restrict their liberty and regiment their worship, under the plea of closer conformity to the Scriptures. Even those who are happily unfamiliar with such efforts, would do well, by careful consideration of what is here discussed, to fortify themselves against possible infiltrations of these devitalizing ideas.

Legality and the Lord's Supper

by HARRY LACEY

(The accounts of the institution of the Lord's supper should be read, preferably in the Revised Version: Matt. 26. 26–28; Mark 14. 22–24; Luke 22. 19–20; 1 Cor. 11. 23–25.)

CONSIDERABLE PERPLEXITY is created in the minds of Christians by the differing attitudes to the Lord's supper which exist not only in Christendom but even amongst assemblies of the Lord's people. Apart from the wider extremes of refusal to celebrate it at all on the one hand and of making it a dramatic ritual and a sacrifice on the other, one aspect of truth emphasized at the expense of another produces distortion. The wisdom of the law of Deuteronomy 31. 9–13, which calls for periodical restatements, is evident. Uniformity is undesirable, but fresh examination of the circumstances and associations of the institution of the Lord's supper are profitable from time to time.

The Passover and The Lord's Supper. There is a tendency to confuse the Passover with the Lord's supper. It was at the Passover meal that the Lord instituted the Lord's supper, and that altogether unexpectedly. He took the ordinary bread and the ordinary cup of that meal and adapted them to a new use. Yet, careful distinction between the two is established in our records.

Matthew and Mark distinguish between the use of the loaf for the Lord's supper and its use for the Passover by *eulogeo*, an element in the meaning of which implies *consecration*. At the same time the idea of consecration must not be exaggerated, because Luke and Paul in parallel accounts say simply that the Lord gave thanks, as He did whenever food was taken, Mark 8. 6; Matt. 15. 36; John 6. 11, 23, or as any devout person would, Acts 27. 35. What is implied occurs when an ordinary loaf is taken for use at the Lord's supper. Luke distinguishes by showing that it was *after* the Passover supper and *after* the Lord said He would not drink of the fruit of the vine, that the Lord's supper was instituted. No less than five chapters fall between reference to the Passover and the Lord's supper in 1 Corinthians; see 5. 7–8 and 11. 23. The feast in chapter 5 is the Jewish Feast of unleavened bread and its spiritual counterpart now in a life unleavened with evil.

This distinction emphasizes the replacement of the Passover supper by the Lord's supper, rather than any perpetuation of it in a modified form. The Passover was prospective, and was superseded by that which is retrospective and distinct in both form and object.

The Lord's Supper and the New Covenant. The association between the Lord's supper and the new covenant is one which, though patent in Scripture, is largely missed. Indeed, some go so far as to deny that present-day believers are in covenant relation with God.

Christ's words "this is my blood of the covenant", Matt. 26. 28 R.V., recalled for the eleven men who sat at the last Passover (Judas probably left before the meal ended, John 13. 31), and who knew the Old Testament Scriptures, the words of Moses at the institution of the Sinai covenant; see

Exod. 24. 8 and Heb. 9. 20. Consequently, the Lord's supper indicates primarily a new legal bond which binds Christians to the Lord and Him to them. Such a bond was originally made in the body and blood of a sacrifice; see Gen. 15. 8–10 and 17–18. Hence the Hebrew idiom "to cut a covenant". The Lord's supper symbolizes the fact that it was in the very body and blood of Christ that this covenant was cut.

Paul's statement that he and his fellow-servants were ministers of a new covenant is final in evidence that believers now are in covenant relationship with God; see 2 Cor. 3, especially vv. 5–6). It is this covenant which, as to its better character, 7. 22, its surety, 7. 22, its mediator, 9. 15, its newness, 9. 15, its terms, 8. 10–12 and its everlastingness 13. 20, is treated of in Hebrews.

This association with this covenant is especially precious and not without its moral effect. Those who celebrate the Lord's supper simply and regularly find that it serves to develop a consciousness of the assurance of salvation. On the other hand, it is noteworthy that where it is not observed, or is corrupted, the "falling away" and other hurtful doctrines obtain. That all four accounts of the institution of the Lord's supper connect it with the new covenant demonstrates that it is pre-eminently "the supper of the covenant".

The Significance of the Blood of the Covenant.
A tendency to limit the range of contemplation at the Lord's supper exists and manifests itself in different ways. Some forbid anything but contemplation of Christ in His devotedness to God (the burnt offering aspect of His Person and work). Others forbid anything but contemplation of Christ's perfect character evidenced in His life of purity and grace (the meal offering aspect of His Person and work). But the many contrasts between the blood of the old covenant and that of the new show that these restrictions are unwarranted.

The Sinai covenant was instituted in the blood of burnt offerings and peace offerings, Exod. 24. 5, but Christ stated that His blood of this covenant was shed for many for the remission of sins, Matt. 26. 28. It was trespass offering blood; see Lev. 5. 14 to 6. 7, and note that this sacrifice was devoted to the removal of sins. And the shortened account

of Christ's words in Mark with the omission of "unto remission of sins" and the consequent reading "for many"
Mark 14. 24, which heightens the idea of persons, shows
that the blood of the covenant is sin offering blood, see Lev.
4. 1–35, and observe that this sacrifice was that by which
forgiveness of persons was secured.

The blood of this new covenant therefore is not only that
of Christ in contrast to that of beasts, but it is trespass offering
and sin offering blood in contrast to the blood of the old
covenant. To prohibit contemplation of Christ's sufferings
for sins during the celebration of the Lord's supper is opposed
to the very words of Christ.

Profound contemplation of Christ's suffering for sins
will produce not only thankfulness for their removal and
forgiveness, but will surely develop that love for righteousness
and hatred of iniquity which is characteristic of Him Himself,
Psa. 45. 7.

Students of the offerings will observe that priests were
to eat sin and trespass offerings in the holy place, Lev. 7. 6;
6. 29. It is noteworthy that failure to do so was one of the
first recorded errors of priests, Lev. 10. 16–20.

Progress of Doctrine in the Accounts of the Supper.
That it would be as wrong to limit thoughts at the celebration
of the Lord's supper to the trespass and sin offering aspects of
Christ's Person and work, on the one hand, as to the burnt and
meal offering aspects on the other, will be seen from the
progress of doctrine which is evident in the four accounts of
the institution of the Lord's supper.

The accounts in Matthew and Mark stress the establish-
ment of a covenant and emphasize the foundation thereof in
atonement. That in Luke stresses the character and the benefi-
cents of that covenant. He transposes the words blood and
covenant, putting the covenant first and adding the adjective
"new". Thus he heightens the idea of the covenant itself and
the newness of its character. By omitting mention of sins and
bringing in the word "you", with its more personal touch
than the word "many" of the former accounts, acceptance is
suggested. The distinctive feature of the Pauline account
is *remembrance*. This is not mentioned in Matthew or Mark;

in Luke of the cup only, but in the Pauline passage of both loaf and cup. The development of ideas appears to be:

Matthew	—	the covenant and the trespass offering;
Mark	—	the covenant and the sin offering;
Luke	—	the newness of the covenant and its blessings;
Corinthians	—	the new covenant and the Lord Himself.

Early Celebrations of the Lord's Supper. There is profit in reviewing the early celebrations of the Lord's supper. These were less formal and less ecclesiastical than latterly. It was celebrated in Jerusalem in a household way, Acts 2. 46. When partaking of an ordinary household meal, in the same way as the Lord Himself did, they took an ordinary loaf and ordinary cup to remember their Lord in the sweetness of their first love and under the unction of the Holy Spirit freshly imparted by the Exalted Christ.

As the new era developed, the celebration seems to pass from the household to the churches. It appears (as Acts 20. 6-12 describes) that a weekly gathering took place, and, whilst this served primarily for the breaking of bread, vv. 7, 11, it did so also for preaching and for conversation; *dialegomai*, v. 7, and *homileo*, v. 11. Evidence that there were meetings for the breaking of bread exclusively, others for prayer exclusively, and yet others for preaching exclusively, hardly seems apparent in our records. The impression that a fresh unbiased reading of 1 Corinthians 11 to 14 creates is that the same meeting is in mind throughout. It must not be supposed, therefore, that Spirit-led attention to the Scriptures on subjects appropriate to the Lord's supper is out of place.

The meal at which the supper was celebrated seems to have been transferred to the churches also; see 1 Cor. 11. 21, 22; Jude 12. Undisciplined behaviour thereat violated the sanctity of the Lord's supper. Restraint as to eating, drinking, 1 Cor. 11. 21, speaking in tongues, 14. 23, teaching, prophesying, singing, 14. 26, and the proper conduct of women, 14. 34-35, was cast off at Corinth. This section of the Epistle, 1 Cor. 11-14, was written to regulate these matters, and the regulation of them seems to amount to a prohibition of the meal, 1 Cor. 11. 22, thus making the Lord's supper a sacred and central feature of church gathering.

The emphasis upon the Lordship of Christ in this passage is very considerable and should be allowed its solemnizing effect.

Subsequent Ideas of Celebration. From the coarse encroachments upon the Lord's supper, the pendulum swung over to ecclesiasticism. The mingled formality and meticulousness of Ephesus indicates a tendency, Rev. 2. 2–4, which developed into prescriptions of form and order in the second century. Soon the spirit of sacerdotalism resulted in the theory of transubstantiation, which claims that the bread and wine when consecrated become the actual body and blood of Christ. It also claims that in the act of dissolving the bread in the mouth of the communicant death takes place. Thus the supper is changed to a sacrifice and, instead of proclaiming the Lord's death, 1 Cor. 11. 26 R.V., parodies its once-for-all character by professing to repeat it interminably.

The Priesthood of Believers and The Lord's Supper. It is sometimes said that it is distinctively as priests, or as a priesthood, that believers celebrate the Lord's supper. This statement should be off-set by the fact that the Epistles which deal with priesthood, 1 Peter and Hebrews, do not deal with church order, and the Epistles which deal with church order especially, 1 Corinthians and 1 Timothy, do not directly mention priesthood. It should also be remembered that Gospel service, Rom. 15. 16 R.V.; the aggregate activities of a Christian community, Phil. 2. 17; the sharing of goods, Heb. 13. 16; Phil. 4. 18, and the offering of praise, Heb. 13. 16, are all shown to be spiritual sacrifices acceptable to God by Jesus Christ. It is therefore hardly with propriety that the priesthood of believers is limited to celebration of the Lord's supper. Rather is it that because Christian priesthood embraces all else of genuine Christian life, it also embraces the Lord's supper.

Though it appears from 1 Peter 5. 1–6 that organized church life was contemplated by Peter when he wrote, it was not to churches as such that he addressed himself. It was to believers scattered throughout an area at least as large as Great Britain. The one priesthood that he contemplates as functioning must therefore have been, as he says, a *spiritual* house.

Sometimes the word *coming* is given an ecclesiastical sense, but its use in Hebrews indicates a wider idea and hardly countenances this narrowed sense; see Heb. 7. 25; 10. 1; 11. 6.

A very real difficulty exists in attempting to envisage the functioning of the royal priesthood, 1 Pet. 2. 9 (which is the same priesthood in another aspect), in a way in which its members are associated with one another tangibly. The same difficulty appears when attempt is made to envisage believers throughout five Roman provinces meeting together tangibly as a holy priesthood. But when the conception is allowed to be an abstract idea rather than a concrete one the difficulty melts, as it does when it is seen that members of a nation (one of Peter's co-extensive figures of Christians) can exercise the privileges of citizenship though as far apart as Land's End and John o' Groats.

Of the priesthood of believers it has rightly been written

Tho' sundered far, by faith they meet,
Around one common mercy-seat.

Although believers in each locality should meet in tangible fashion to break bread and enjoy the privileges of Christian fellowship and priesthood, yet it is not by so meeting that they become a priesthood nor that then only are they a priesthood. They are a priesthood then simply because they are always a priesthood.

It follows therefore also that neither is it only those who so meet that form part of this holy and royal priesthood. To exclude genuine believers from the spiritual house and holy priesthood involves denial that they are the people of God.

Modes of Address at The Lord's Supper. As a development of the association of priesthood with the celebration of the Lord's supper, it is sometimes maintained that priesthood has to do with God as God, and that it is therefore wrong to address Him as the Father. It must be remembered that priesthood could not in the Old Testament be associated with the Father, because He is not revealed therein as such. Nor could it, in the very nature of the case, be in the Epistle to the Hebrews, because those to whom it was written had not yet realized that this present era is distinctively the era of the revelation of the Father. However, the book of the Revelation shows unmistakably that all those loosed from their sins are made priests to His God and *Father*; see 1. 6 R.V. and J.N.D. Indeed, since the advent of the Son, worship is characteristically worship of the Father. It is as such that He seeks worshippers. Consequently, address to God as Father may not be forbidden without direct collision with the words of Christ, John 4. 21–24.

Another development of this conception of priesthood is that address to the Lord Jesus Himself is discountenanced. Although it must be remembered that one aspect of truth is that our approach to God is by the mediatorial offices of Christ, it must also be remembered that, at the close of the three greatest writings of John, the Lord Jesus Himself is given significant prominence. When believers were together in a meeting with the Lord in their midst, He was worshipped personally. The record of this fact is intended to be instructive, John 20. 26–28. Almost the last words of the Bible are addressed to Him, Rev. 22. 20. The close of the first Epistle of John speaks of the Son as the "true God and eternal life". Moreover, the oneness of the Father and the Son excludes setting aside the Father when the Son is addressed. To see the Son is to see the Father, John 14. 9. And it seems implied also that to honour the Son is to honour the Father, John 5. 20–23. Furthermore, it is clear that believers will be priests of Christ in the future, Rev. 20. 6. The approach of the saints to the Lord is so sacred that legal prohibitions and regulations of address seem profane. Piety and acquaintance with the Scriptures will cultivate spiritual taste and lead to becoming modes of address as occasion requires.

Many readers when they discover that the following message is based upon the Old Testament Offerings will be tempted to pass it over. If they do so it will be to their own loss and perhaps the loss of others. A former generation found great delight and profit in the study; perhaps it was over-done but it is a thousand pities that so many should now go to the opposite extreme and neglect the subject. We regard this message as important and we believe that careful attention to it could result in the enrichment of assembly worship.

Worship and Prayer in Relation to the Assembly

by S. ALEXANDER

(READ PHIL. 3. 3; JOHN 4. 23; NUM. 28. 2; I TIM. 2. 1-4)

UNTIL DEEPLY WROUGHT UPON by the Spirit of God, the believer is incurably self-centred and individualistic. This becomes manifest even in assembly life and worship, in which the emphasis is only too frequently placed on blessings which have reached us through the grace of God, and even thanksgiving is largely limited in scope to the work of Christ which has rid us of the guilt and consequences of our sins. In assembly government and order the individualistic and self-centred tendency is also seen in the desire to dominate one's brethren and impose upon them one's own thoughts, preferences, conceptions and plans, thus reducing the Headship of Christ and the sovereignty of the Spirit to empty doctrines having no issue in living experience.

Corporate Life. We, as the Lord's people, greatly need to have our thoughts as to the worship of the church lifted to a higher level and also to know what the ministry of intercession truly is. It is here that the failure to realize the corporate nature of the church's life is so frequently manifested. In worship the member whose voice is heard is not so much speaking as an individual believer, as for the moment representing, and becoming the voice of, the assembly. As the praises of God are thus uttered and the worthiness of Christ expressed, the hearts of all kindle, join in warm assent, and the fervent Amen is heard. It is as truly the worship of the assembly as when all voices join in a hymn of praise. Anything that is purely individual in character is an indication of spiritual weakness: the glory fades, the life seems checked, the fire dies down. The highest level of worship is reached when all hearts kindle in fervent response and the voice is truly the voice of the church. The recognition of this will greatly help us to offer that which is well-pleasing to God and worthy of His acceptance. The church is a company worshipping in the heavenlies and is therefore occupied with the heavenly Lord, not with earthly things, however beautiful. That which properly belongs to our private life should not intrude into assembly worship. Thanksgiving for the mercies of the week, for deliverance from peril, for the beauties of nature, the singing of the birds, the blossoming of the trees, etc., all can find true expression in our private or family devotions. There it is fitting and precious. The corporate worship of the church, gathered around the Person of the Lord, is other than this and belongs to a different realm. There, the one supreme, exclusive and inclusive occupation is Christ. It is our glorious privilege to speak the praises of the Son in worship of the Father.

Worship in the Assembly. It is a fact never to be forgotten, that we are sinners saved by God's sovereign grace, but when we come before the Lord in the assembly and particularly when gathered around the Lord to remember Him, we are there not as sinners but as saints or "holy brethren", a priestly company in union with Christ, and rejoicing in our acceptance in the Beloved. It is our privilege thus to serve Him in the sanctuary. We should therefore have done entirely with self-occupation in any shape or form, and be exulting in the perfections of God's beloved Son, in whom He always finds His delight. As we are led out in worship by the Spirit of God we shall be shown increasingly what the Son is to the Father. This will occupy our hearts, and find fitting expression. The burnt-offering aspect of Calvary will be more in our thoughts than the sin offering. We shall speak of Christ offering Himself to God "for an odour of a sweet smell", Eph. 5. 2, rather than as dying "for our sins", 1 Cor. 15. 3. We can learn much in this connection by a careful consideration of the worship of God's ancient people as set out in the Pentateuch. The offerings prescribed for the individual worshipper and for the nation are full of instruction. The difference between the individual and the collective is clearly marked. The offerings of the individual worshipper are voluntary, those for the whole people are commanded. The individual could bring a peace offering, a meal offering or a burnt offering, according to his own desire, Lev. chs. 1–3. The Lord would smell a sweet savour, whichever was brought. But when it was a question of the corporate worship of the nation, when the people gathered together to hold a feast unto Jehovah, then everything was prescribed in the most minute detail. Nothing was left to human judgment or discretion. The explicit instructions given in Numbers 28–29 are most impressive. The amazing thing is that we so little recognize the significance of these instructions.

The Burnt Offering. It is a striking fact that both in the voluntary sweet-savour offerings of the individual worshipper, and those enjoined upon the whole congregation, the emphasis is upon the burnt offering. God begins with that when He speaks to Moses in grace out of the tent of meeting, Lev. 1. 1. That which differentiated the burnt offering from the other sweet-savour offerings was the fact that the whole animal was burnt upon the altar and went up to God as fragrant incense, Lev. 1. 9, 13, 17. It mattered not whether the offering was a bullock, a sheep or goat, or two turtle doves or young pigeons, all ascended to the Lord as an odour of a sweet smell. Only the ashes were left as a testimony to a completed sacrifice. Neither the worshipper nor the priest had any share in the burnt offering. It was wholly for God. This speaks loudly and blessedly of that aspect of the atoning sacrifice of Calvary which was for the heart of God alone.

Individual Worship. The individual worshipper need not go to this length; there were other and lesser offerings which could be presented and which would come up to God as a savour of Christ. There was the meal offering, Lev. 2. Only a portion of this was burnt upon the altar. The remainder was for the priest. There was the peace offering, Lev. 3, of which again only a portion was burnt, the rest being shared between priest and worshipper. These were precious as expressing different aspects of the person and work of the Lord Jesus. But the burnt offering, most impressively, comes first. It is a searching question which we should do well to ask our own hearts: how much do we know in our personal intercourse with God of this, upon which the chief emphasis is laid? The burnt offering, with which the worshipper becomes identified by the laying on of his hands, Lev. 1. 4, represents the highest form of worship and the deepest appreciation of what Christ is to God. Is not the worship of the assembly often on such a low level because the individual members know little of this in their private communion? If our personal appreciation of Christ does not rise to the level of the burnt offering, we can hardly expect the Holy Spirit to make us the church's voice as it seeks to offer that which God desires to receive.

Corporate Worship. The importance which God places upon the burnt offering in the corporate worship of His people is plain for all to see in Numbers 28 and 29. Here we pass from that which was voluntary to that which was enjoined. The various periods are enumerated. (i) The daily sacrifice. (ii) The Sabbath. (iii) The new moon. (iv) The Passover and feast of unleavened bread. (v) The feast of weeks. (vi) The feast of trumpets. (vii) The day of atonement. (viii) The feast of tabernacles. The introduction to them all is in these impressive words. "Command the children of Israel, and say unto them, my oblation, my food for my offerings made by fire, of a sweet savour unto me, shall ye observe to offer unto me in their due season". Four offerings are named, (i) The burnt offering, associated with which, in every case, were the (ii) meal offering and (iii) drink offering. Then there came (iv) the sin offering. Let it be remembered that the sin offering, whilst making worship possible, is not, in itself, a worship offering. Though the fat of the sin offering was burnt on the brasen altar, representing the preciousness of Christ to God even when making propitiation for sin, it is not one of the sweet-savour offerings. It speaks of Christ in His atoning sacrifice as meeting the deep need of man, while the burnt offering brings before our hearts what He is to God the Father. Now note where the divine emphasis lies and how strong it is. The aspect of Calvary with which we are most easily impressed is that the Saviour was on the cross dealing with our sin. "Behold the Lamb of God, which taketh away the *sin* of the world". This, together with the trespass offering, by which our *sins* are dealt with, is that which calls forth our praise. It is natural and fitting that in our spiritual infancy the sacrifice of Christ, in its manward aspect, is most appreciated. The newly-born soul rejoices in its deliverance and sings:

> My chains are snapt,
>   The bonds of sin are broken,
> And I am free.
>   Oh let the triumph of His grace be spoken,
> Who died for me.

But when we come to the assembly of God, when it is a matter of the corporate worship of the Lord's people, we must rise to higher levels. That which is made possible by the sin offering should occupy us. If these chapters in Numbers are carefully read it will be observed that, during the year no less than 1,243 animals were sacrificed as burnt offerings while only 32 were slain as sin offerings. Thus there were 39 burnt offerings for every sin offering. This loudly proclaims that, however blessed it is that man's need has been fully met, the divine side is of vast importance. We must seek to bring to God that which He so impressively calls His food: that is, we must pass on to that pure worship represented by the sweet-savour offerings.

The more the details are studied the more is this driven home. The principle is found to apply not alone to the more joyous occasions such as the feast of tabernacles, the crown and fulness of the whole year of worship, but was also true of the Passover and the day of atonement. The Passover, with the feast of unleavened bread, was instituted to keep in remembrance the deliverance of the people from Egypt's bondage. Yet there were 70 burnt offerings prescribed as against 7 sin offerings. On the day of atonement when the people were called upon to afflict their souls in remembrance of their many sins, there were 9 burnt offerings as compared with 3 sin offerings. It is surely impossible to miss the spiritual significance of this. The assembly, in its worship, should be far more occupied with what Christ is to God than with the man-ward blessings. However much we may rejoice in sins for-given, and sin put away, we must learn to rejoice more abundantly in the satisfaction brought to the Father, and enter into fellowship with God, in those aspects of Calvary, which declare the devotedness of Christ to the Father's will, and His preciousness to the Father's heart.

The Meal Offering and the Drink Offering. Then again it must be remembered that the burnt offering was to be accompanied with its appropriate meal and drink offerings. It is not alone the death of Christ, but His life of spotless purity and devotion to the Father, represented by the meal offering, which was to be had in constant remembrance. And what of the drink offering? If the burnt offering was wholly consumed upon the altar, the drink offering was a fitting accompaniment. It graphically portrays the lavish devotion of the worshipper, his intense joy in the appreciation of God's portion in His Son. It is scarcely possible to conceive of anything more expressive of intense devotion in worship than the pouring out of strong drink before the Lord. There is something unspeakably precious suggested here. David would not drink of the water of the well of Bethlehem; his mighty men had secured it at the jeopardy of their lives, and he poured it out before the Lord. Only God is worthy of such devotion. So the worshippers, seeing the various sacrifices ascending as whole burnt offerings to God, were filled with holy joy, and that was expressed by the pouring out of wine in His presence. Carnal minds might esteem this to be stupid waste. But nothing is waste which is acceptable to God, however extravagant it may seem. The heart of the infinite God is gladdened by that which is a sweet savour of Christ unto Him. The burnt offering, with its accompanying meal and drink offerings, was continuous. No day in Israel's history might pass without the morning and evening sacrifice: no Sabbath but must have its additional burnt offering: no new month could be entered upon but it must be marked in the same way: and so through all the year. It was a constant presentation to God, in type, of a whole Christ, in His infinite perfections, and of the Godward aspects of both His life and death.

What Christ is to God. This tests our spiritual life. If it be on a low level our worship will be concerned with our blessings. We shall be self-centred, even in our approach to God. The higher the level, the more we shall be occupied with, and seek to express, the preciousness of Christ to God, and the greater will be our joy. On the day of atonement there were 3 burnt offerings for each sin offering; in the feast of tabernacles, expressive of overflowing joy, the proportion was 24 to 1. May we have grace to learn the deep and blessed lesson, and so when we are gathered around the Person of our Lord, bring to our God and Father that which He seeks from His people. It is the Father who seeketh worshippers, and worship "in spirit and in truth" will be evermore a telling forth of what He is as revealed in the Person of His Son.

God and Father, we adore Thee,
　　Now revealed in Christ the Son,
Joying in Thy holy presence
　　Through the work that He has done.

In Thy presence we behold Him
　　Object of Thy heart's deep love;
Boundless theme of adoration
　　In that scene of joy above.

In Thy grace Thou now hast called us
　　Sharers of Thy joy to be,
And to know the blessed secret
　　Of His preciousness to Thee.

Corporate Prayer. If the emphasis in the worship of the assembly is thus on the divine side, the same is true of the ministry of intercession. Fellowship with God in His revealed purposes is of far greater importance than the meeting of human need. Not that the latter is to be neglected. By no means; it is a question of proportion and balance. The Lord will ever meet need as it is laid before Him in believing prayer by the church. But divine, age long and universal purposes have been revealed in the Word, and God desires to have a people in true fellowship with Himself in relation to these matters of vast import. If He does not find this fellowship in the church assembled for prayer, where shall He look for it? If the accomplishment of divine purpose depends in any degree on the co-operation of His people – and it surely does – how important that we should rise to the height of our privilege. The Holy Spirit is in, and with, the church to bring divine purpose to pass. Every need of man will be dealt with "according to his purpose". That is, as we are concerned with the bringing to pass of divine ends, all related matters will be brought in by the Spirit of God. As the church learns to pray in the Holy Spirit, Jude 20, the divine passion will find expression through the lips of God's people, and the divine compassion will fill the hearts of the saints as the sorrows and sufferings, the perplexities and pains of the Lord's people are brought before them. The love of God for a lost world will throb and thrill in the heart, and intercession on behalf of "all men" will be intensified.

The End in View. The Lord is seeking to move through the church, not only to accomplish His present purposes in the earth, but also by its worship and prayer to make it the vessel of divine fulness, as it is found in union with its Head, the appointed Heir of all things. The final summing up of all things in Christ, that is, the full realization of the kingdom of God, is the end in view. The kingdom is to be administered by the Lamb and His wife, from the heavens, when the marriage has taken place. It is therefore of great moment that the church should learn to rise to the full thought of God as to worship, and fulfil its ministry of intercession on a similar level. The local assembly is the workshop in which God, by

His Spirit, will bring this to pass. The Lord discipline our hearts in these matters and so prepare the way for the revelation of His glory! "Unto him be the glory in the church and in Christ Jesus unto all generations for ever and ever. Amen", Eph. 3. 21 R.V.

Prayer to the Lord Jesus

by E. W. ROGERS

INCREDIBLE AS IT MAY SEEM to some, yet it is unfortunately true that many believers have been seriously unsettled by teaching which insists that it is wrong to address the Lord Jesus in prayer and praise. This view is being propagated with a zeal worthy of a better cause. Even hymns which saintly and well-taught men have written, and which for generations have proved such wonderful channels for the expression of the praise and worship of devoted hearts, are drastically amended if any words in them are addressed to the Lord Jesus.

If any brethren are fully persuaded in their own minds that it is wrong to address the Son, surely no one would wish to override their consciences or coerce them into acting contrary to their convictions. We would rather pray that God would "reveal even this unto them". This is not the difficulty. The unfortunate part is that too often these brethren are not content to let the matter rest there, but they impose a burden on the consciences of others and require their fellow-believers to follow them, when, as we contend, they have no Scriptural warrant for so doing. In this way serious injury has sometimes been done to the affections of the saints and this is a grave matter. Furthermore, spontaneity of worship has been hindered and in many cases a legalistic spirit has tended to put supposed correctness of form in the place of reality of heart. Nor does the tendency stop there – gradually the meeting for the remembrance of the Lord has been hedged about with increasing restrictions of one kind and another. The whole thing has been made an unhappy bone of contention and a cause of deplorable division. Believing that the phase will pass and that things will eventually fall back into their proper perspective, we would fain leave it there, but so much harm is being done meanwhile, that whilst we have not the slightest desire to augment the controversy we feel that the question must be faced.

We believe that such teaching is unscriptural and liable in the end to obscure the true glory of Christ. At the same time we realize that the proper balance must be preserved, and we must be on our guard lest we allow one extreme view to drive us to the opposite extreme. Admittedly prayer and praise is more generally addressed to the Father, through the Son, by the Spirit as the following Scriptures show: Eph. 5. 20; Col. 3. 16, 17; Heb. 13. 15; John 4. 23; Jude 24, 25. All three Persons of the Godhead are involved and these Scriptures recognize their respective activities towards the saints and their interrelations with each other. But this is not the question. The question is: "Is it wrong to address the Son?".

What becomes of the Lord's saying, "That all men should honour the Son, even as they honour the Father", if we are to honour the Father in praise and worship and yet decline to honour the Son in the same way? If in Revelation 1. 6, "to him be glory and dominion for ever and ever. Amen", Christ's worthiness to receive praise is clearly stated, how can it be wrong to render it?

Although it is sometimes contended that the Lord was personally addressed only in the days of His flesh, our readers will have no difficulty in remembering many instances where the Lord was addressed not only after His resurrection, but actually after His ascension. We mention a few striking cases which will repay careful consideration.

(1) Stephen, a man "full of faith and of the Holy Ghost", "full of faith and power", prayed to the Lord Jesus to receive his spirit and forgive his murderers, Acts 7. 59, 60.

(2) On the Damascus road Saul sought and received directions from the Lord Jesus, Acts 22. 10.

(3) Three times Paul besought the Lord with regard to a thorn in the flesh, 2 Cor. 12. 7-10.

(4) Paul gave thanks to Christ for putting him into His service, 1 Tim. 1. 12.

In face of the above no one can question the believer's right to address the Lord Jesus in prayer and praise. This much is generally conceded *to the individual* by those who support the theory we are now discussing, but they dispose of such Scriptures by contending that what is permissible in the individual is not permissible in the assembly. It is difficult to see on what logical grounds such a contention can be maintained. If it is right for individuals in their private devotions to address prayer and praise to the Lord Jesus, how does it become wrong to do so, when those self-same individuals meet together with the express purpose of re-membering Him?

As is only to be expected when a theory has to be main-tained, various arguments are advanced, but we do not find them convincing. Some of these arguments are complex and depend on inferences and deductions which may sound impressive, but we advise our readers not to allow any involved arguments to becloud a simple issue. For example – we are told that the children of Israel, when gathered for worship, did not address their high priest, and seeing that Christ is our Great High Priest it must therefore be wrong for us to address Him. This is a very precarious piece of reasoning which overlooks several considerations. We can certainly learn many precious lessons from the ordinances of the tabernacle, but we must be careful. The Epistle to the Hebrews shows that Christian worship is on a much higher plane and our privileges far greater. In any case, it would have been so manifestly improper for the children of Israel to offer praise or prayer to a sinful man like themselves that we cannot rest the aforesaid deduction on the mere fact that they did not address him. Dare we argue that, because it was improper for them to address their failing high priest, it is improper for us to address our beloved Lord, whose Person is infinitely more glorious than Aaron, and whose Great High Priesthood, whilst wonderfully illustrated in the Aaronic priesthood, is nevertheless of an altogether different and superior order? In any case, even if it could be proved that it is incongruous for us to address Him as our Great High Priest (and we cannot

see that it is), it does not settle the question at issue for the
very simple reason that He sustains towards His people many
other precious relationships.

It seems to us that such arguments would never have been
advanced but for the determination to support a cherished
theory. We do not propose to go further into these arguments
because we feel that space will be better employed in setting
out some plain facts to show that the Scriptures supply
several instances of prayer and praise being addressed to
Christ in gatherings of the Lord's people. This is a sufficient
answer. If Thomas, in a gathering of disciples on the first
day of the week, exclaimed in wondering worship. "My Lord
and my God", John 20. 28, and received no rebuke from the
Lord for doing so, but only for his failure to realize it earlier,
on what grounds are we to be prevented from pouring out
our hearts to the One to whom we owe so much, when we
meet with His promised presence and for the express purpose
of remembering Him? This could only result in an unnatural
restraint on our truest instincts and would surely limit the
liberty of the Spirit. If the disciples as a company "worshipped" (same word as John 4. 23, "worship the Father")
Christ just before He was received up into heaven, Matt.
28. 17, is there less reason to worship Him now that He is at the
right hand of the Majesty on high, far above all principality
and power? Was it not a large assembly in Acts 1. 24 which
prayed, "Lord . . . show whether of these two thou hast
chosen"? Seeing that Peter had just referred to the Lord
Jesus and seeing that the choice of apostles is attributed to
Christ, 1. 2; 9. 15, no unprejudiced reader will have difficulty
in believing that the simple title "Lord" as generally used in
the book of Acts and elsewhere in the New Testament here
means the Lord Jesus.

Furthermore, we have several instances where it is clearly
indicated that believers were in the habit of calling upon
Christ. When the Lord Jesus instructed Ananias to go to Saul,
Ananias pointed out that Saul had authority from the chief
priests to "bind all that call on thy name", Acts 9. 14, suggesting that it was the accepted and well known practice of the
saints. That this practice was general in the churches is clear
from 1 Corinthians 1. 2, "all that in every place call upon the

name of Jesus Christ our Lord, both theirs and ours", on which passage Dean Alford writes, "It is a direct testimony to the divine worship of Jesus Christ as universal in the church". Without question, Ephesians 5. 19 contemplates assembly gatherings, "Speaking to yourselves in psalms and hymns and spiritual songs, singing and making melody in your heart to the Lord". In view of this we cannot help feeling that the ruthless deletion from hymns of any words addressed to the Lord Jesus is a proceeding most grievous to the heart of the Father, and most dishonouring to His Son. When Timothy was instructed to cultivate fellowship with like-minded believers, they were referred to as "them that call on the Lord out of a pure heart", 2 Tim. 2. 22. It is straining things to say that those whose fellowship was to be sought because they called on the Lord would not call upon the Lord when they met. Or again, if the Spirit and the bride are found united in Revelation 22. 17 in saying, "Come", to the needy, can we say that the prayer of verse 20, "Even so, come, Lord Jesus", is not fitted to the bride's lips, but must be confined to the private devotions of the individual believer?

Who that reads that grand passage in Revelation 5 will not feel that if such rapturous ascriptions of praise are to be rendered to Christ first by the company of the four living creatures and four and twenty elders, all prostrate before the Lamb, offering the prayers of the saints, and singing praise to Christ, then by the assembled hosts of angels, and at last by the whole creation praising God and the Lamb together, it must be a serious thing to hinder those who would worship Christ in the humbler assemblies of earth?

Much more is involved in this matter than may at first appear and we appeal to any of our readers who may meet this theory not to allow any specious argument to move them away from the plain statements of Scripture. Whilst it is true that praise and worship is more generally to be addressed to the Father, through the Lord Jesus Christ, let us cherish the liberty given us by the Scriptures to offer to our Lord and Saviour the homage of our hearts.

"Worthy is the Lamb that was slain to receive power, and riches, and wisdom, and strength, and honour, and glory, and blessing", Rev. 5. 12.

The Prayer Meeting

by DENIS CLAPHAM*

PRAYER HAS ALWAYS BEEN made to God by the churches, and it is certain that where there is spiritual life and faithfulness to the Lord it will be maintained by them until the end of their existence. In view of this, we do well to ask how best we can take part in the prayers of the church to which we belong. Some Christians, maybe, think that prayer in the church is only for the few, or, it may be, that there are some churches where prayer is only irregularly made. If our study helps to enlighten or revive such, our aim will be achieved, and God will be glorified by an increase of intelligent and believing prayer.

In any matter affecting church life there is no need to be confused by complex regulations and elaborate ritual. We have only to be willing to do what the Scriptures say, and in regard to prayer, as all else, we shall know the truth and be freed from the traditions of men by which so much that is corrupt has been introduced. Our aim ought to be to discover what the Lord requires, and what the Scriptures say.

If we are to appreciate why the early church met to pray, we must remember that the original church at Jerusalem was made up of disciples, most of whom had known the Lord Jesus before His ascension. Many of them had seen His example, and heard His teaching about prayer, Matt. 5. 44; 6. 5–11; Luke 18. 1–8, and some of them could recall His encouraging words to them on the night He was betrayed, John 14. 13–14; 15. 7, 16; 16. 23–27. They were, therefore, in a unique position and readily responded as one to His influence. Thus their corporate prayers were an acknowledgment of the grace that had brought Christ the Saviour to them, an expression of their common allegiance to Him as their Lord, and a proof of their belief in the fulfilment of the promises which He had made to them while still with them. Through belonging to Him they recognized that they belonged to one another, and in making their supplications and prayers with one accord they were also expressing their love for, and the confidence

* This article has been specially written for this book.

and interest which they had in, each other. As devout Jews, they had been in the habit of going together to the temple to pray at the appointed hour, but as a company of disciples of the Lord Jesus they had so much more in common that they increasingly met in their own homes. Against this background it is written of them that, "they continued steadfastly in the apostles' doctrine and fellowship, and in breaking of bread, and in prayers", Acts 2. 42.

In the beginning there was a clear line separating the church from the rest of men. The earliest believers publicly identified themselves with the Lord Jesus by baptism, accepted His reproach and openly dissociated themselves from the generation of unbelievers which had refused the Just One, and crucified the Lord of glory. This made the church an object of hatred to be persecuted, and drove the believers together to pray for boldness to witness without fear of man. So urgent were their needs at times, and so great the peril to which their leaders were exposed, that they frequently gathered together in secret and prayed until the answer came – sometimes in an unexpected way, Acts 12. 5–17. When their sphere of witness became enlarged, and men were called by the Holy Spirit to the work of preaching the Gospel throughout the world, the churches supported them by prayer, 2 Thess. 3. 1; Col. 4. 3.

These are some of the reasons that prompted the earliest prayer meetings. Unitedly and spontaneously, sharing common interests, needs and blessings, they made their requests, gave thanks and called upon the name of the Lord; and they did this because it was His will that they should, 1 Thess. 5. 17–18.

If we ask how the earliest prayer meetings were conducted, we must search the Scriptures for the true answer. Many believers, in failing to do so, have become severely restricted by set forms of prayer, while others, tolerating loose and unscriptural practices, have exposed themselves to ridicule. "Let all things be done decently and in order", 1 Cor. 14. 40, holds good for the prayer meeting as much as for every other kind of church meeting. Who would presume to say that one meeting is more important than another, or that on the Lord's Day a different standard of conduct is required from that which is permissible at other meetings of the church on any other day? Every gathering of the church is in the same Name; at all meetings the same Lord is over all, and in all; and the holy requirements of God are to be met by all who present themselves before Him at all times.

When coming to the Father in prayer, believers come into the presence of a holy God who is a consuming fire. Prayer meetings should therefore be conducted reverently and in godly fear with the grace which is available for this. The internal, moral and spiritual condition of all who meet to pray is of the greatest importance. Having regard to time, place, procedure and all other external conditions, is insufficient to please God if the saints are in a carnal condition. An unforgiving spirit, a proud mind, an unthankful heart, debt, falsehood, or any other form of unrighteousness, not to mention indulgence in wickedness permitted by society today, are all things which prevent prayer being effectual. It is written, "And if we know that he hear us, whatsoever we ask, we know that we have the petitions that we desired of him", 1 John 5. 15. But it is also written, "If I regard iniquity in my heart, the Lord will not hear me", Psa. 66. 18.

The Scriptural way of conducting a church prayer meeting is ascertained mainly from 1 Timothy, although there are other indications of the New Testament pattern scattered throughout the rest of the apostle Paul's letters. From these we learn that the prayer meetings of the early churches were supported by all their members. It was required of them that they had a steadfast will, and a mind to persevere in praying. Casualness, or halfheartedness, would betray a lack of appreciation of the great importance attaching to prayer to God, Rom. 12. 12.

In praying, the men were to pray with their heads uncovered, while the women were to have theirs covered. The reason given for this is that, as the head of the woman, the man has authority over the woman. In the man's presence, therefore, it is necessary for the woman to wear on her head a token of her subjection. A spiritually minded person will find peace and joy in practising this divine injunction, 1 Cor. 11. 2–16.

Prayers were to be made so as to be understood by all,

and so that all could add their Amen. It is not necessary to make long prayers. Five intelligent words will always be more to the point than five minutes of unreasoned, or unseasoned talk, 1 Cor. 14. 15.

Prayer "in the name of our Lord Jesus Christ", "unto God and the Father", indicated a church's appreciation of the authority, character, rank, majesty, power, excellence, and other attributes of Christ, through whose death all believers have been reconciled to God, Eph. 5. 20. But, in order that God might take account of prayer, it is essential that it be "in the Spirit", which means that it must be both prompted and composed by Him. The Holy Spirit teaches believers what is according to the will of God through His Word, and then enables them to express themselves accordingly, Eph. 6. 18.

Prayer meetings have been held throughout the dark night of this present age, an age in which all who belong to it are spiritually asleep. There is need therefore at all times, and especially when praying, for believers to be spiritually alert. It is possible for them to succumb to the world's influence, because of the weakness of the flesh, and to fail to keep awake. Effective prayer then ceases, Col. 4. 2.

In 1 Timothy there is a section dealing with the kind of behaviour required by God of Christians in their church life. It gives reasons why rulers should be prayed for, and the order for united prayer, ch. 2; and the qualifications of overseers and deacons, ch. 3. What was written to help Timothy at Ephesus until the apostle Paul could join him, has been given to the churches to guide them until the Lord Himself returns. From chapter 2, we learn that a church's prayers form a vital part in the divine strategy for the blessing of mankind. In the interests of men generally, and of believers in particular, the churches are given the opportunity to pray for the world's rulers and leaders. Social unrest, industrial strikes, revolutions of all kinds, and even wars may be averted through the supplications, prayers and intercession of those who know what it means to be in touch with the throne of grace in heaven.

Wherever the church meets to pray, it is always to be the men – the word is the specific word indicating the male sex – who take the lead publicly and audibly. They are to be men who only practice what is consistent with the nature of God. When they lead in prayer it is to be without wrath towards others, or unbelief towards God. Women in the church pray silently from the heart, in modest dress, displaying the marks of godly women. These things are related to the divine pattern in the creation of male and female. From the book of Genesis there is much to be discerned of the mind of God relating to the sexes. In the New Testament the truth as to their respective responsibilities in the Lord is developed.

We have now briefly looked at the spiritual marks of the prayer meeting. These will never be effaced, for they are seen in the imperishable Word of Truth. They will always challenge every church that yearns to prevail with God. The application of these Scriptural principles can revitalize churches. True overseers well know this, and under their leadership we may yet expect a measure of revival of spiritual life and power in our times. If in these days of lukewarmness there are but few believers who humbly recognize the last state of the church, let not the few be discouraged or dismayed. "The effectual, fervent prayer of a righteous man availeth much", James 5. 16. "If two of you shall agree on earth as touching any thing that they shall ask, it shall be done for them of my Father which is in heaven", Matt. 18. 19.

SPIRITUAL GIFTS AND SERVICE

⬤⬤⬤⬤⬤⬤

The Holy Spirit's Guidance in the Life and Activities of the Assembly

by W. W. CAMPBELL

As BELIEVERS, both individually and collectively, we are completely dependent on the Holy Spirit in our life and activity. As individuals we are born again of the Spirit, we are sealed by the Spirit, the Holy Spirit is the earnest of our inheritance, He is the power whereby we understand and know the things which are freely given to us of God, taking of Christ's things and showing them unto us. Individually our bodies are temples of the Holy Spirit, a token that they will share in the final quickening of resurrection, Rom. 8. 11.

The Holy Spirit is equally the beginning and end of the life and service of the assembly. It is by the baptism of the Holy Spirit that believers have been brought into the body of Christ. The local church is a temple of God by the indwelling Spirit. He is the power of the church in worship, in prayer and in testimony. It is quite impossible for believers to separate their lives into two compartments, one individual and the other collective, for the very simple reason that the local church is composed of individuals, and it is what we are as individuals that makes or mars the power and effectiveness of the church. Many of the activities of the church should also be the activities of the individual. For instance, the church has its life of worship, of prayer and testimony, but if the individuals who compose the church never engage in these exercises at any time other than when gathered in assembly, how can the life of the church be other than impoverished, and its witness ineffective?

When we come together as churches to engage in worship

and the remembrance of the Lord in the breaking of bread, or for prayer, or edification, we profess to recognize the Holy Spirit's sovereignty and guidance in the ordering of our activities, but if as individuals we know nothing of the leading of the Spirit, is it likely that we shall be qualified to discern His movements in the gathering of the saints? It has become all too common to regard the leading of the Spirit as having to do with a crisis in the life of some servant of God of unusual spiritual stature, but not for the majority of the people of God.

We are but stating a commonplace fact when we say that in the practice of our lives, both as individuals and as churches, we do not give the Holy Spirit the place which the Scriptures do. When Paul was combating the Galatian defection, the teaching that only in law-keeping could believers attain to spiritual manhood, he comes right to the source of all that was unique and original in Christianity, and in a trenchant question asks, "This only would I learn of you, Received ye the Spirit by the works of the law, or by the hearing of faith?", Gal. 3. 2. This was undoubtedly the outstanding experience of the Christian, for the Holy Spirit was the creative force in the Christian church. It is from this realization that we have been removed by the passage of time, and it is back to it that we need to return with all our hearts.

The Holy Spirit and the Individual Believer. In Galatians 4. 4, we read that "when the fulness of the time was come, God sent forth his Son". The word *exapostello* is used signifying, to be sent forth out of the presence of one who is to be represented by the one sent, so that the Lord Jesus came forth from the presence of God to be His representative. In Galatians 4. 6, we read "and because ye are sons, God hath sent forth the Spirit of his Son into your hearts". Again the word *exapostello* is used, so that the Holy Spirit has come forth from the presence of God to be His representative. The Holy Spirit is for God, in our hearts, what the Lord Jesus was in the world. He is the power for all truly Christian living. "If we live by the Spirit", says Paul, "by the Spirit let us also walk", Gal. 5. 25 R.V. The believer has to choose the type of life he is going to live, either after the flesh or after the Spirit. The life that is by the Spirit is the life that is Spirit-led, and it is the antithesis of the life that is lived under the law. In the life that is Spirit-led, there is freedom, fruitfulness, variety, and originality; whereas in the life that is lived under the law, there is bondage and the constant repetition of man's failure and disappointment.

In Romans 8. 14, the placing of believers as sons in the family of God is connected with the leading of the Spirit. Sonship of believers in Galatians 4 is shown to be the result of Christianity being the mature dispensation, in contrast to the period under the law, which was the time of tutelage. In Galatians 5, we learn that there is the mature life which is in accord with the mature dispensation, and that is the life that is Spirit-led, not necessarily filled with recurring crises in which the intervention of God is manifest, but rather filled with the fruit of the Spirit in increasing measure. It is in the life which is Spirit-led day by day, producing likeness to Christ and conformity to the will of God, that God does intervene to give guidance in the crises of life. The general character of Paul's life was a willing submission to the Lordship of Christ, and again and again the Lord intervened to direct the course of His servant, sometimes causing him to know the way wherein he should go, and at other times giving him this knowledge from the way things developed, that the path he had taken was of God.

The Holy Spirit and the Assembly. If the leading of the Spirit is a thing unknown in our daily lives, it is really idle to talk about it in the assembly; it just will not happen. It is to 1 Corinthians that we have to turn in thinking of this subject in the assembly, and chapters 12 and 14 are the passages that must be considered. Many of the Corinthians had been idolaters, and the pagan temple-worship was marked by all kinds of excess, and the devotees abandoned self-control and came under the power of evil spirits. "Ye know that when ye were Gentiles ye were led away unto those dumb idols, howsoever ye might be led", 1 Cor. 12. 2 R.V. The Christian assembly is also directed by an unseen power, the Holy Spirit of God; but whereas the pagan temples were filled with all kinds of excess, the worship and service of the church is to be free from it, and, in order that it shall be so, the apostle lays down some guiding principles:

1. The man who speaks in the Holy Spirit magnifies the Lordship of Jesus, not only in what he says, but also in what he is, 1 Cor. 12. 3.

2. Spiritual profiting is the purpose of spiritual manifestation, 1 Cor. 12. 7. Such is the wide range of need and the variety of purposes to be served in the will of God when the assembly gathers, that they can only be met by the unhindered operation of the Holy Spirit in all His bountiful variety.

3. To edify the church is to be the humble and sincere desire of spiritual men, and by this rule all exercise is to be judged, whether to approve or to keep silence. This is the burden of a large part of chapter 14.

4. The activities of the understanding and of the Spirit in those who lead the assembly are not to be divorced. Paul says "I will pray with the spirit, and I will pray with the understanding also", 1 Cor. 14. 15. There is therefore a great need to heed the exhortation, "Brethren, be not children in mind; howbeit, in malice be ye babes, but in mind be men", v. 20 R.V. We are not to act on impulse. We are to apply to the task of leading the church in prayer or worship minds that have been disciplined and matured in the school of God, while seeking humbly that our contribution may be in the Spirit.

5. Spiritual men, in the exercise of their gifts, will bow to the commandments of God as revealed in His Word. They will own the teachings of Christ's apostles, as found in the New Testament Scriptures.

6. The leading of the Spirit does not mean the end of self-control, for the spirits of the prophets are subject to the prophets.

These then are some of the principles by which those who seek to voice the needs of the assembly in prayer, its praises in worship, or its edification in ministry, are to be guided; and by these same principles the others are to judge as to whether or not any contribution is a manifestation of the Spirit.

The Leading of The Holy Spirit in the Assembly

by HENRY STEEDMAN

THE WORSHIP of God must be in spirit and truth. Such only are true worshippers and these are sought by the Father to be His worshippers. True worship presupposes a suitable spiritual condition in the saints. Apart from this there can be no acceptable movement or expression Godward. Such a condition is essential to the leading of the Spirit, John 4. 20–24. These are the circumcision (circumcised with the circumcision made without hands), who worship by the Spirit of God, and glory in Christ Jesus, and have no confidence in the flesh, Phil. 3. 3; Col. 2. 11, 12.

One must be in the Spirit to be led of the Spirit, and that before any audible or leading part can be taken in worship, song, prayer or ministry. The leading of the Spirit is known when saints are in communion with the Father and the Son, and no wilful inconsistencies exist among them. There must needs be spirituality and accord with the will and Word of God. Provision has been made for infirmities, varied apprehensions, measures of spiritual growth and capacity. But, as for carnal ways, worldliness or known sin in life, or evil associations, these grieve the Spirit and hinder His ways in and among the believers. Quench not the Spirit, 1 Thess. 5. 19.

It is futile to legislate for the leading of the Spirit in assemblies where and when the state or conditions are not agreeable to Him.

Surely there is need among us for purgation of every form of evil. The old leaven must be put away from every quarter that we may be a fresh lump. How intrusive is the flesh. How prone we are to take mere natural impulses and sanctimonious feelings for the leading of the Spirit. Let us search our own heart as to these things.

The marks of being Spirit-led are clearly set before us in 1 Corinthians 14. Such an one will speak within the *understanding* of those who hear, whether the speaking is Godward or manward. The Spirit-led speaks to *edification and profit, distinctly and instructively.*

The same applies to singing, praying and giving of thanks. One might give thanks well and yet fall short of edifying others. Verbosity is irreverent and profitless to all. Our spirits should be subject to us. The lack of spiritual discrimination as to the line of things the Spirit is bringing forward accounts for interruption, when inappropriate hymns or even irrelevant Scriptures are read, when one or more digress into long prayers, or when unseasonable so-called ministry is imposed on the saints.

These things ought not so to be. License and monopoly are also foreign to the Spirit's leading. The body is not one member but many. Let there be that waiting on and for God. Let us consider one another, in honour preferring one another, esteeming others better than ourselves in all lowliness of mind. When saints are kindly affectioned one to another in brotherly love, it opens the way for definite guidance of the Spirit in the gatherings.

"Keep thy foot when thou goest to the house of God, and be more ready to hear, than to give the sacrifice of fools: for they consider not that they do evil. Be not rash with thy mouth, and let not thine heart be hasty to utter anything before God: for God is in heaven, and thou upon earth: therefore let thy words be few", Eccles. 5. 1, 2.

One must be led by the Spirit of God before he can lead others according to God. Self-led ones can only lead others astray.

It is only when the Spirit leads that God is worshipped and glorified, Christ magnified and saints edified. Let each one examine himself in the light of the Word of God, and desist from everything that would hinder the Spirit.

"Where the Spirit of the Lord is there is liberty." How pleasing to God when saints are truly in the Spirit in subjection to the Headship and Lordship of Christ. It is an evidence of low spiritual conditions when things are merely kept going in meetings.

The silence of communion is sometimes broken by intrusive pretentious performance on the part of poverty-stricken minds assuming to be led of the Spirit, and instead thereof simply imposing their vain ideas on the saints. Rather, let us worship in the Spirit, walk and serve in the Spirit, pray in the Spirit, remembering neither to grieve nor to quench the Spirit at any time. "But ye, beloved, building up yourselves on your most holy faith, praying in the Holy Ghost, keep yourselves in the love of God, looking for the mercy of our Lord Jesus Christ unto eternal life", Jude 20, 21.

A Scriptural List of Assembly Meetings

by E. TIPSON

IN MATTHEW 18. 20 we read the words of our Lord when He said, "For where two or three are gathered together in my name, there am I in the midst". The words *"gathered together"* represent one word in the Greek (*sunagō*) and that word when used in connection with the church in the New Testament gives us a complete list of seven different kinds of meetings that every assembly ought to have. The word is also used of other gatherings, such as Herod gathering together the chief priests and scribes in Matthew 2. 4, etc., but the word as used only in connection with the church gives the following list:

The Prayer Meeting, Acts 4. 31, "And when they had prayed, the place was shaken where they were *assembled together*". Here the word is translated "assembled together". It is surely very significant that the first meeting of the church where this word is used is a prayer-meeting, especially as nowadays, if attendances signify anything, the prayer-meeting is generally looked upon as the *least important in the* church. We should remember that Matthew 18. 20 was spoken in connection with prayer.

Two things should be noted of this meeting: First, that the word used for prayer (and there are several) is the word used of the Lord praying in Gethsemane, which in Hebrews 5. 7 is described as "when he had offered up prayers and supplications with strong crying and tears". That is, the kind of praying meant – Gethsemane praying. Second, it was prayer that shook the building and was accompanied by the filling of the Holy Spirit. Do we know anything of such prayer-meetings today? Only when the church realizes again the important place of the prayer-meeting amongst the other church meetings, will there be a reviving amongst us.

The Teaching Meeting or Bible Address, Acts 11. 26, "they *assembled* themselves *with* the church, and taught much people". This is also a very important meeting. Often, alas, it is badly attended and thus the people lack instruction in the things of God, not because there is no provision for such instruction, or a lack of teachers, but because they do not assemble at that meeting, not realizing perhaps the importance of being instructed in the things of God.

What was the teaching in New Testament days?

Jesus and the resurrection, Acts 4. 2. ⎫
The Word of the Lord, Acts 15. 35; ⎬ DOCTRINE
   18. 11. ⎭

To do whatsoever Christ commanded ⎫ PRACTICE
   them, Matt. 28. 20. ⎭

It is very needful to teach doctrine to believers. Someone said to Dr. Dale of Birmingham when he commenced to give his famous addresses on the deep subject of the atonement, "Your congregation won't stand for it". "They will have to stand for it", said the doctor, and stand for it they did.

Elders who watch for souls and have the care of the ministry should see that regular and consistent ministry on the doctrines of Scripture is supplied to the believers.

But doctrine is not all. There should be a balance in

teaching as the Lord commanded His disciples before He left them, "Teaching them to observe (i.e. to *do*), whatsoever I have commanded you". Practice as well as precept.

The Missionary Meeting, Acts 14. 27, "And when they were come, and had *gathered* the church *together*, they rehearsed all that God had done with them". Note that missionary meetings are not a modern innovation. They were amongst the first of the church's gatherings. Note also the purpose of the meetings – not to tell of what the missionary had done and thus glorify him, but what the Lord had done. See how much the first missionaries needed to learn this lesson.

In Luke 9. 10, we are told that the apostles returned and they told Him all that *they* had done. See also Luke 10. 17: "the seventy returned again with joy, saying Lord, even the devils are subject unto *us*". They did add, "through thy name", but there was the exaltation of what they were and had done; and so the Lord had to rebuke them with the picture of Satan falling – surely a hint that they were also in for a fall, if they persisted in rejoicing in that kind of thing. To these He immediately gave, by illustration, the right attitude to take, as we see in verse 21. "In that hour Jesus rejoiced in spirit, and said, I thank *Thee*, O Father". What a difference!

See Mark's version of Luke 9. 10. The apostles gathered themselves to Jesus and told him all things, both what *they* had done and what *they* had taught, and He said unto them, "Come ye yourselves apart into a desert place, and rest a while", Mark 6. 31. That was the best place for those filled with what *they* had done and what *they* had taught!

In Acts 15. 3, 4, 12, we get further light as to what made up their missionary addresses: (i) the conversion of the Gentiles, (ii) all things that God had done with them, and (iii) what miracles and wonders God had wrought. This is the kind of work God wants His people to be interested in. A father is always pleased if his boy asks what he is doing, and our Father loves to see His children taking an interest in what He is doing.

The Elders' Meeting, Acts 15. 6, "and the apostles and elders *came together* for to consider of this matter". This was a matter which had caused "no small dissension and disputation", and the elders had a meeting to consider it, at which there was also much discussion. It was a question of wrong doctrine being taught to the believers, and had all the elements of a serious division in the church. Yet see how wisely it was handled. Firstly, on the way down to the meeting the brethren did not spread the disaffection, but rather held missionary meetings, vv. 3, 4, 12, to fasten the people's minds on what God was doing in the spread of the gospel, rather than the disputed things. Secondly, see where they turn for their final authority on questions – the Word of God. It was what God had done, what the Lord Jesus had done, and what the Holy Spirit had done, that was the final word with them.

We may note, of course, that this was not a meeting of local elders strictly; nor indeed of elders only. It was the apostles as well as the elders that came together, and these not from one particular locality. It nevertheless establishes as a precedent the fact that it was regarded as wise for elders to come together in their care and concern for the teaching and spiritual welfare of the saints. And further, an apostle, because he was an apostle, did not cease to be an elder; see 1 Pet. 5. 1.

Elders' meetings are very necessary to the welfare of the church. Remember elders watch for your souls. And happy is the assembly that has wise and godly elders. The state of a meeting can usually be determined by the kind of elders found there. But they need your prayers, and probably most when you disagree with them. Let the elders realize their tremendous responsibility and the others their responsibility to pray for them, instead of criticizing them.

The Bible Reading Meeting, Acts 15. 30. "when they had *gathered* the multitude *together*, they delivered the epistle; which when they had read, they rejoiced for the consolation (or exhortation, see margin)". The same word for reading is used in Acts 8, where the Ethiopian and Philip had a Bible Reading together on the 53rd chapter of Isaiah. How profitable that was!

Why is it that so many Bible Readings are unprofitable?

That is the only word that adequately describes some. And why is it that they have fallen so much into disfavour and decay? Is it not that often brethren come together to consider a portion of the Word of God without ever having spent five minutes beforehand studying that portion; and so, when they come together no one has a single profitable thought to give to the rest of the assembly? If you get several godly brethren, who have prayerfully and carefully studied the same portion of the Word before coming to the meeting, you may rest assured that you will get a really profitable Bible Reading, and the saints will go home, as the saints in The Acts went home, rejoicing.

The Breaking of Bread Meeting, Acts 20. 7, "when the disciples *came together* to break bread". When? On the first day of the week. This is proof positive that the Christians did not keep the Jewish Sabbath; for these travellers were there (Troas) for seven days, v. 6, and thus were there on the Jewish Sabbath, the day before; but they did not break bread on that day, but the first day of the week.

What a precious meeting this is, acknowledged and enjoyed more than any other meeting by the majority of believers (if the attendance is any guide!). And yet, here a word of caution is needed. If it is considered by some that this meeting is so important that it is all that is necessary for one's soul, and they become what are called "once a week" believers, then let them consider that God, by His Holy Spirit, did not put this meeting *first* on the list He gave us, and let it be remembered that He gave all the others as equally necessary. Thus, if the others are neglected, however precious this one may be, it is not sufficient for the growth of the soul, nor for the up-building of the church.

The Discipline Meeting, 1 Cor. 5. 4, "In the name of our Lord Jesus Christ, when ye are *gathered together,* and my spirit, with the power of our Lord Jesus Christ, to deliver such an one unto Satan . . .". Here is the saddest meeting of all. Is there not the suggestion here that this should be a *special* meeting for the purpose? I think the practice of just "reading out" a person at the end of a morning meeting, and then forgetting the person, is quite wrong. If a special meeting were convened for the occasion where the one is read out, and then the assembly got down to earnest and tearful prayer for the dear one, who has fallen by the way, that he or she may be restored, how often would it result in the erring one being brought back into happy fellowship with the assembly again. As J. N. Darby once expressed it, "We should think of the dear fallen one as if she were our own daughter". What a difference that would make in our attitude to the one "put away".

Remember that the church at Ephesus was known for its exact correctness as to doctrine, and how *they could not bear them which were evil*, yet they themselves were in a loveless condition and ready to be set aside by God as far as their testimony was concerned.

May God help each one of us to make use of all these meetings that God has ordained for the blessing and welfare and growth of His people, and it is certain there will be a more healthy state amongst us.

The Gifts of the Holy Spirit in Service

by R. FORREST-HALL

Our Service. God's purpose is that every one of us shall be like Christ and this process begins down here. Our progress depends on our devotion to, and service for, our Risen Lord, Rom. 8. 29; Phil. 3. 8–10; John 15. 14.

Acceptable service should, therefore, be the ambition of every Christian; his Lord expects it of him and indeed makes it the test of his worth and the basis of the rewards, much or little, which he will receive. "I know thy works" is stated of every one of the seven churches in Revelation chapters 2 and 3. The only other points common to the addresses to the seven churches are that it is the Spirit Himself who is speaking and that in all cases one can be an overcomer.

At the judgment seat of Christ, we are told in 1 Corinthians 3 that judgment will be based on the works done, not on the *quantity* but on the *quality* – "of what sort it is". The test will be extremely thorough and the figure used is of a fire burning up the wood, hay and stubble. The materials which stand up to the test, gold, silver and precious stones, are only refined by fire, which takes away the dross that they may shine or sparkle brighter.

The Holy Spirit. The believer today is not likely to be in the position of those in Acts 19 who had not heard whether the Holy Ghost was given, Acts 19. 2 R.V. He will know that the Holy Spirit is equal with the Father and the Son and is one with them in the Trinity.

He is mentioned in Genesis 1 as taking part in creation, in Matthew 1 in the incarnation, in Hebrews 9. 14 in the death of Christ and in Acts 2 as descending from heaven after the ascension, and dwelling in believers. Since that day the Holy Spirit has been in direct touch with believers on the earth continuously.

Apostles and Prophets. Ephesians 4. 1–16 gives us the gifts of the Holy Spirit for service down here in a practical setting, the gifts being given for the express purpose of building up and binding together God's people.

In verse 11 they are enumerated, apostles, prophets, evangelists, pastors, teachers.

Apostles and prophets are stated first as they were the foundation gifts of the church, Eph. 2. 20.

At Pentecost (the position of Judas having been filled) there were the twelve apostles. Paul came later (last of all as he says). They were given special authority as leaders and teachers in the early church. In the case of Peter he was given the keys of the kingdom of heaven, Matt. 16. 19, which he used, one to open the door to the Jews, Acts 2, and the other to open the door to the Gentiles, Acts 10. After that, the doors having been opened, the keys were no longer necessary. Peter had been given the honour of first preaching the Gospel to Jews and Gentiles. The Lord Jesus Christ Himself has the keys of death and of hell, Rev. 1. 18.

The apostle Paul was chosen to record the unique mystery

of the New Testament, the Church (consisting of all believers in this present dispensation) which is the Body and the Bride of Christ (so much nearer to God than Israel His servant, Psa. 136. 22). Further, he became the great apostle of the Gentiles who speedily became the majority in the Church and greatly benefited from his pioneering and teaching labours and authority received direct from the Lord.

It was mainly the apostles who wrote the New Testament.

In answer to the Lord's prayer in John 17, there was complete unity among the apostles (apart from two difficulties later resolved).

The prophets spoke with authority and were empowered to foretell future events as Agabus in Acts 11. 28. They worked with the apostles and sought to maintain the purity of the faith, as Judas and Silas, Acts 15. 32. Luke and Mark were especially used of God.

There are now no apostles and prophets since:

1. The foundations of the Church have been laid.

2. The canon of Scripture is complete and they could not therefore add to its authority or tell us anything new. That which is perfect is come (the Scriptures) and therefore that which is in part is done away (prophecies, etc.); see 1 Cor. 13. 8–10.

Evangelists, Pastors and Teachers. The next gift mentioned in our verse is that of evangelist. It is the great gift for the extension of the Church. Philip in Acts 8 was a model evangelist. He preached Christ the Saviour of the world to the crowds in Samaria; Jesus the personal sin-bearer to the seeking soul. He was subject to Scripture, obeyed instantly the Spirit's promptings and used initiative and judgment at the right time.

It is a work to be done as Paul told Timothy, 2 Tim. 4. 5, not a striving for a place of prominence.

Young people are especially suitable for such exacting work and can find a joyous outlet in such service for enthusiasm and zeal. Paul, the great evangelist, lost no time after conversion and baptism "but straightway he preached

Christ in the synagogues, that he is the Son of God", Acts 9. 20. He told the people what he knew.

A passion for souls is the motive to make disciples (not merely converts), who will go on themselves to serve and live for God, Matt. 28. 19 marg.

To be a true pastor is a definite gift. Many have no gift for speaking and are not of a studious disposition, they may be even quiet and retiring, but a gracious, sympathetic, understanding personality can help enormously in the building up of God's work. Visiting sick ones, shielding the weak, encouraging the backward or youthful, restraining the forward, such work is necessary to build together the assembly and consolidate the work of the evangelist. It is not necessary to be counted a member of an oversight to do such work. The God who calls His servant to this work will enable and sustain him in it.

An example of a pastor in Scripture is Barnabas, a good man who exhorted the converts to cleave to the Lord, Acts 11. 23.

Appropriately, the last gift mentioned is that of teacher, for he follows the evangelist and pastor in seeking to build up converts so that they may be established in the faith and abound in it, Col. 2. 7. The teacher can expound Scripture, giving sound doctrine, holding fast the faithful word, Titus 1. 9. He should be able rightly to divide scriptural teaching, dispensationally, in types, for daily living, for church truth and prophetic truth. He gives babes milk, for temptations the bread of life, strong meat for adult believers, honey for the mature saint, 1 Pet. 2. 2; Matt. 4. 4; Heb. 5. 14; Psa. 119. 103.

Ezra "prepared his heart to seek the law of the Lord, and to do it, and to teach in Israel", Ezra 7. 10. Note the order. Learning from God's Word heart knowledge, and practising it himself, the true teacher is fitted to teach God's people today.

Objectives. Ephesians 4 tells us the object of the gifts to the Church. They are given (a) that we may walk worthily, (b) for humility and patience, (c) to promote unity and peace, vv. 1–3, so that we are effective workers and there is healthy growth of the body of Christ, v. 16.

Gifts Given for Profit. God has chosen to work through men and women (often quite obscure ones at that!) and He has done this in preference to carrying out His purposes independently. We who are God's servants are therefore called with the high honour of entering into partnership with Him. The whole Trinity is vitally interested. The Father's work is carried on as the Lord Jesus uses the gifts given to His servants and these gifts come from the Holy Spirit, 1 Cor. 12. 4–6.

The gifts of the Spirit are many-sided. They are given for the profit of God's people. He is a free and munificent Giver: He expects us to use His gifts in the most practical manner possible. This is illustrated in the stories of the talents, Matt. 25. 14–30, and of the pounds, Luke 19. 12–26. In each case one servant made no use of his gift at all and he who received one pound buried it (instead of making it work) in a napkin or, as the word really is, a sweatcloth! Does this speak to us today? In the stories, the use of the gifts meant more gifts, more blessings. So it is with us. In business, a firm turns over its stocks to make profits and the greater the turnover, the greater should be the profit. We should turn over our gifts to the same end of profit, bringing glory to God and blessing to men, Rom. 12. 11.

Wisdom. The first of the individual gifts stated in 1 Corinthians 12 is wisdom. It is significant that this gift is stated first because in this same chapter some gifts (not specified) are declared to be greater than others, v. 31. What does Scripture tell us about wisdom? Proverbs 3. 19 states that by wisdom God founded the earth; Psalm 104. 24 that by wisdom He does all His works. Turning to the New Testament, we read of the Lord Himself that He grew not only physically, as is natural, but in wisdom, and this is put first, Luke 2. 52. The Lord is described as the wisdom of God, 1 Cor. 1. 24 and in Him "are hid all the treasures of wisdom", Col. 2. 3. The Scriptures are called the wisdom of God, 1 Cor. 2. 7, 13. The most outstanding characters in the Scriptures are specially stated to have been men of wisdom: Joseph, Gen. 41. 39; Moses and Joshua, Deut. 34. 9; David, 1 Sam. 18. 14; Solomon, 1 Kings 4. 29–34; Daniel, Dan. 2. 23, and Paul,

1 Cor. 3. 10. That wisdom is difficult to define and is hidden from natural man is clear and is emphasized in the book of Proverbs, as well as its transcendent value to those who have it in any measure. Proverbs 4. 7 tells us it is the principal thing, to be obtained at all cost. Young people should seek it early, Prov. 8. 17. Good manners are not acquired overnight and neither is wisdom. The development of all worthwhile gifts takes time – a lifetime. Seeking for it, it is found by faith and a real desire, in the measure of God's will for each one of us, James 1. 5-7; Matt. 7. 7-11. The service of God is the highest calling a man can have. It should be worked out with the maximum of wisdom. This is necessary for ministry in the spiritual things, 1 Cor. 3. 10, and the material things of the assembly, Acts 6. 3.

Knowledge. Knowledge is the next gift mentioned. Learning comes very much easier to some than to others. It is not merely a matter of opportunity to learn being given to some and not to others. Aptitude to learn is a real gift. Scripture truth is by no means easy to understand, once one has passed the first and easy truths of salvation by faith in Christ's finished work on the cross. By familiar usage it may seem easy to some, but as soon as a great doctrinal matter is discussed seriously, the knowledge which is merely super- ficial is shown up. Rightly to divide God's Word requires real knowledge, and the multiplicity of sects and schisms shows how far from a real knowledge of the truths regarding the Church and essential doctrines are a vast number of people, including many sincere believers. A balanced grip of truth concerning the Gospel, the Christian Church, God's purposes for Israel, prophecy, the types, the Trinity, the work of Christ, Christian morality, etc., is required and those with the necessary knowledge have the responsibility under God to impart it. It should be passed on as simply and helpfully as possible, care being taken not to be proud of what is known, or puffed up, 1 Cor. 8. 1, 2, and to avoid unnecessary controversy and pseudo-scientific so-called difficulties, 1 Tim. 6. 20. A great deal of the ministry enjoyed in assemblies comes to us from brethren who have had to spend much time in patient study, preparing for the service of tomorrow or possibly ten years hence. It is right that others should recognize this and seek to encourage God's servants in every way possible, by attention, meeting all expenses and something adequate in addition if there is any dependence. This latter is especially important in these days of rising costs of living and any lack of attention to it is a grave dishonour to God's servant and the gift given for the edification of the church. We cannot judge people with a whole-time ministry if we are not prepared to finance adequately the ministry we have. There is a great need for those with the gift of knowledge in assemblies today.

Faith. Faith is a special gift of God. The faith referred to in this chapter is not that exercised in becoming a Christian, but the faith given specially to some believers as their gift to be exercised in special ways. The name of George Muller springs instantly to mind. Few could have done the work he was called to do. God raised him up with a remarkable gift which was faithfully used and resulted in untold blessing. So careful was Mr. Muller that God alone should be glorified, that he regularly took extreme precautions to see that nothing but simple faith in God was exercised to carry on the tremendous work which developed. Undoubtedly faith was the mainspring in the lives of men like the Wesleys, William Booth, A. N. Groves, Dr. Chalmers, Livingstone and a great host of God's saints chiefly unknown. Faith, in the adverse scene in which their lot was cast, was a first essential, and God gave them it in the measure needed, and they on their part obtained a good report like many before, Heb. 11. 39. May we, whose lot is cast in different circumstances, have the gift of faith according to God's sovereign will and glorify Him in using it aright. It is, perhaps, a more universal and basic gift than the others mentioned so far. It has enabled many to rise above illness or trying circumstances in a victorious manner.

Sign Gifts. The other gifts are sign gifts to the early church showing God's power with the believer. Unbelievers were healed, Acts chs. 3, 19, Timothy was not, 1 Tim. 5. 23. The prayer of faith can still be effective, but the large-scale apostolic blessing has ceased, both in healing and other miracles. Nobody can now raise a person from the dead as Peter raised Dorcas, Acts 9.

Prophecy was very important and took precedence over teaching, 1 Cor. 14. 30, but now Scripture is completed the gift has ceased, 1 Cor. 13. 8. Peter and Paul used the gift of discernment in order to make clear the gospel truths, Acts chs. 8, 16, and in the latter case a miraculous cure was effected showing the link between discernment and miracles.

Tongues were given for edification and, if in public, required interpretation. The gospel, through tongues, was preached to all nations on the first day, Acts 2. 5, 6. Now-a-days, foreign languages have to be painstakingly acquired, although, no doubt, divine help is granted. Carey learnt Sanskit and other languages as he cobbled shoes in Northamptonshire, equipping himself to serve God magnificently in far off India.

Now Concerning Spiritual Gifts

by J. H. HUGHES

SPIRITUAL GIFTS are for spiritual saints. Chapter 12 of the first Epistle to the church at Corinth opens with the significant word "*now*". The beloved apostle is about to describe the working out of the gifts of the Spirit in the assemblies of God's people, and looking back through the Epistle to chapter 2. 15, we find his allusion to the man who is "spiritual", but at once he adds, that he could not speak unto them as spiritual, but as unto carnal, as unto babes in Christ. Following that, there are no less than nine chapters occupied with questions arising out of the carnality of these believers, chapters containing precious truths indeed, but nevertheless branding this rich assembly as being "carnal" rather than "spiritual". And there are grievous sins enumerated – lust, idolatry, jealousy, strife and others. Who does not know the Spirit-quenching effect of any of these if allowed to continue in assembly life. We may therefore with profit ask ourselves if we are in the spiritual state where Paul could address us in the terms of this opening expression.

"I would not have you ignorant". Yet very many believers are ignorant in these matters, and few manifestly possess spiritual gifts. To possess is to enjoy; not a talent hid in the earth, but in full use and blessing. The hall-mark of the Spirit is expression, yet many saints exhibit no particular manifestation of Christ. May these few notes encourage all of us to seek spiritual gifts, for "to each one is given the manifestation of the Spirit to profit withal", v. 7 R.V., so if there is no manifestation we may well ask "Where is the Spirit?".

We note first the contrast between the Spirit of God and the idols of the Gentiles, the latter being dumb. "They have mouths, but they speak not", Psa. 115. 5, and like Baal's prophets of old their devotees may be as active as they like, but "there was neither voice, nor any to answer, nor any that regarded", 1 Kings 18. 29. Let us beware of being dumb in the church, for "He hath put a new song in my mouth", Psa. 40. 3, and "Let the redeemed of the Lord say so", Psa. 107. 2. "The shout of a king is among them", Num. 23. 21. He is coming back with a shout, so we had better be vocal now, or we shall be in poor condition to meet Him when He comes. Let dumbness be to the unregenerate who have no tongue to praise with, but we will remember that "in his temple doth every one speak of his glory", Psa. 29. 9.

Next we observe the happy harmony in diversity, 1 Cor. 12. 4. Spiritual gifts are diverse, but are always harmonious. An English wood on a morning in spring is a delightful place, where many birds blend their songs. Each brings his individual glory, marked and distinct, but the paeon is one, and the harmony perfect. So here it is revealed that the churches are in unison with the divine Trinity with a view to God's glory in the world. We may put it in this way – the Father works; the Son ministers; the Spirit enables. As in the miracle of the loaves, the Father provided the repast; the Son ministered it, and the Spirit, through the disciples, distributed to the multitudes. The writer was recently in an "all electric home". Around were all the modern appliances to make life comfortable and pleasant. The ultimate source of it all was a generating station providing the power. Secondly, many factories had combined to produce the articles around me, and lastly a switch here and there put all these things to their proper use.

So there again was variety in harmony, a trinity of operation, all working for the blessing of the household. Similarly we all have our proper place and part, all working for the profit of the whole assembly. And so it is when all the saints fill their proper God-given place, but alas, how often discontent, jealousy, and spiritual indolence mar the harmony of a gathering, and the Spirit is quenched.

One cannot emphasize too earnestly the purpose of all gifts. It is "to profit withal", that is, for the profit of all. They are for the common good. We are indebted to each other to minister the gifts in the assembly. None of us would rob another, but many saints are running up a long account of spiritual debt which they apparently feel no urge to discharge. The fact is that many Christians are too selfish to want to help others. This is a great sin. They return from a meeting saying, "I didn't get anything", but it has not occurred to them to take anything, unless it were a coin for the offering. Yet Paul distinctly says, 14. 26, "when ye come together, everyone of you hath" – what? We are intended to be channels of blessing, but it is sadly possible for all we receive to be drained away and lost. It is true to say that the life of many assemblies would be revolutionized if all went to the meeting with Paul's five golden words in heart and mind – "What shall I profit you", v. 6. We all have something to give for the common good, and "God loveth a cheerful giver". "Freely ye have received, freely give", Matt. 10. 8, said the Lord Jesus, so let us meet in that spirit, that all may go away the richer for having come together.

Finally, there is the great but oft-neglected truth of the sovereignty of the Holy Spirit in the churches. Who can measure the blessing that the recognition of this truth has meant during the past 150 years? He has sent forth a host of messengers with the gospel into the four corners of the earth. Happy is the assembly where His authority is supreme. Nor must we take too much for granted because our form of gathering is correct. It is sadly possible to have no authority at all, or on the other hand, the authority of some forceful personality, and in either case the Spirit is robbed of His rightful place, which is spiritual dishonesty. Only by prayer and the most humble and constant obedience to the written

Word can the assemblies of God's children continue in the path of testimony, exhibiting in their conduct that lofty and exalted conception of truth by which the world will know that "God is in you of a truth", 1 Cor. 14. 25. This is the most difficult of all things to maintain, and most sects take the easy path of a stated ministry, to the ruin of their corporate testimony. A stated ministry hinders the Spirit in His working, and an appointed minister may easily displace Him. But we may well remember that "a" minister is better than "no" minister, and the saints fail in their testimony if they forget that we come together in the spirit of 1 Peter 4. 10 – "As every man hath received the gift, even so minister the same one to another, as good stewards of the manifold grace of God". Where this is so we may rely on the Spirit to produce the love and loveliness of Christ in the churches; we may look to the Lord and expect to be endued with power from on high; and we may expect to be able to express ourselves to His glory. To this end we should ever seek to serve one another, and encourage God's people everywhere to seek the fellowship which gives full scope for the operation of the Spirit in the assemblies of the saints.

Prominence or Profitableness in the Assembly

by E. H. Betts

WHEN THE APOSTLE Paul said, "covet earnestly the best gifts; and yet shew I unto you a more excellent way", 1 Cor. 12. 31, he had in mind the life and activities of the assembly. There is no doubt about this, for the passage in which these words occur, 1 Cor. 12. 31 to 13. 13, is set as a jewel in the very heart of a group of chapters dealing with assembly life and activity. We have in fact these subjects amongst others: coming together for the Lord's supper, ch. 11, diversity of gifts and functions within the unity of the body, ch. 12, the mainspring of all assembly activity, namely love, ch. 13, and lastly, control of gift with a view to comely order when the whole assembly is come together, ch. 14.

Love of Prominence. Paul was painfully aware of the tendency in Corinth to indulge a carnal fancy for the ostentatious – a fondness for the exercise and display of those gifts which may bring the possessor into prominence. Knowledge was in high esteem, to the detriment of love and tender care for the weak conscience. But knowledge puffs up, said the apostle, whereas love builds up, 8. 1. Tongues – the gift lending itself to display – stood at a premium in Corinth. And of it Paul said, surely not without a keen-edged play on the sense of the word "edify", "He that speaketh in an unknown tongue edifieth himself; but he that prophesieth edifieth the church", 14. 4.

Here, then, in our verse, 12. 31, the apostle is about to bring to light an important secret, the secret of profitableness in assembly life and fellowship – the means and the guarantee of edification. And we have at once "Though I speak . . . and have not *love* I am *nothing*".

The Secret of Profitableness. We may well give heed to his burning words. For a like fondness to that of the Corinthians for display may be ours too. What value, we must admit, we set, all of us, on eloquence! What primacy of place is readily yielded amongst us to the facile ministry of speech! What powers of entertainment it may hold for us! But dwell for a moment on the tremendous import of this concessive clause: "Though I speak with the tongues of men and of *angels* . . ." Could we but hear one thus richly gifted, should we not hang on his lips? Should we not treasure up the very sounds themselves and as long as possible enjoy their mere reverberations in our memories? Indeed. And yet there is a condition. "Though I speak . . . and have not love, *I am nothing*". Here is the secret itself. Love is the spring of vitality, of living force, of effectiveness in all we do. If love is not my urge, my impelling force and my compelling motive, no matter what my clarity, my fluency or my use of stored-up truth, *I am nothing*.

We must not allow ourselves to think that in using these words "I am nothing", the apostle has inadvertently fallen into an extravagant form of speech. He means what he says. He means it, literally. For love, divine love, inworking in the hearts and lives of the members of the assembly, is the very "stuff" of assembly life. Without it, whatever notable gift may be exercised, whatever talent may be laid under contribution or stores of Biblical knowledge brought into play – without love, we repeat, there is no real contribution to assembly life or assembly growth, no heightening of the beat or throb of the life of its real being.

The Hallmark of Life. For love, divine love, has been implanted in every saint of God. We have been made partakers of the divine nature, 2 Pet. 1. 4. And God *is* love. That is His nature, 1 John 4. 8, 16. The Spirit says by the apostle John, "We know that we have passed from death unto life, because we love the brethren. He that loveth not his brother abideth in death", 1 John 3. 14. Here is a challenge which may well halt every one of us in his steps; for love, we see, is the very hallmark of life. When, accordingly Paul says, "Though I speak . . . and have not love, I am nothing", he refers not to human sentiment or to mere emotionalism; nor is he thinking of the milk of human kindness, desirable though this be. Much less does he mean the sweetness and amiability of the natural man. For though this is an excellent thing in its right sphere, yet under the figure of honey it was prohibited as an ingredient of offerings made by fire to God. What the apostle did intend us to understand by love is the operation, the movement towards our brethren, the controlling activity, of this new implanted nature and the complementary rejection and merciless judgment and refusal of the old nature. If we wish to know whether it is by the one or by the other that we are being moved and motivated, let us make ourselves intimately acquainted with the marks, the lineaments – in short, the character – of divine love as set forth in that great classic chapter, 1 Cor. 13. Let us bear in mind, as we study it, that its great and only perfect exemplification is seen in Christ, and especially in that which moved Him to go to and to endure the cross, with its death of public shame and mental anguish and physical agony.

The Marks of Love. Here are the features of love as found in 1 Corinthians 13.

It bears long and patiently, and so has no outbreaks of ill-temper or petulance.

It is kind, for it is intrinsically unselfish.

It does not covet the possessions or the gifts of others, for again, being essentially unselfish, it rejoices in the well-being of its brethren.

It does not show off. Never once could our blessed Lord be detected in, or suspected of, so doing.

It is not self-complacent: it is, contrariwise, self-sacrificing and esteems others better than itself.

It does not seek its own advantage, prominence or way.

It is not provoked to paroxysms of anger. (The word "easily" in 1 Cor. 13. 5 A.V., has been interpolated in translation.)

It does not think up evil of people, especially of its brethren.

It does not hail the fall of another, though that fall may seem to open up avenues of advance for itself or its friends.

It does rejoice in the truth and its prominence, whatever the cost.

It bears (and so covers) all things for the good of its brethren.

It bears up in hope above all untoward circumstances.

It believes good of the brethren, in spite of appearances.

It endures when prophecies, tongues and knowledge pass away; and it will endure for ever and ever.

The Quality of Love. *That* is Calvary love – "love divine, all loves excelling". That is the love of which the seed or germ has been planted in every saint of God. That is the pulse of life which if cultivated will produce times of refreshing, fruitfulness for God, revival.

But we see that love is made of sterner stuff than natural amiability. Love is prepared to suffer. Love would go to the wall. Further, let us remember those words of deepest divine truth, "As many as I love, I rebuke and chasten", Rev. 3. 19, for they convey to the mind an oft-forgotten quality of the love of God, of which we speak. Love does not always set out to gratify. It may hurt. For true love would see its object free of evil. This is a truly divine property of love. "Whom the Lord loveth he chasteneth, and scourgeth every son whom he receiveth", Heb. 12. 6. Divine love is that which if necessary "seeketh me through pain".

The Cultivation of Love. Let us cultivate this precious life, this love, within ourselves, and encourage it in others. Let us, in the light of the cross, where we, in all that we are by nature, were judicially terminated in the sight of God – let us be merciless to self. We cannot live in a vacuum. Either the old self or the new nature is in control. The new nature is love. It has the vitalizing, refreshing characteristics and qualities we have set down above. But only as we are kept near to the cross can it be in active operation. "I am crucified with Christ: nevertheless I live; yet not I, but Christ liveth in me", Gal. 2. 20. "Not I, but Christ." Let us keep this up. Let us translate into practical everyday living and assembly life that which is true of us in our standing before God. Let us walk in Him, rooted and built up in Him. If we live in the Spirit, let us walk in the Spirit. And then we shall see the lovely array of spiritual fruit which will be forthcoming, Gal. 5. 22, 23, love, joy, peace, longsuffering, gentleness, goodness, faith, meekness, temperance (i.e. self-mastery, self-contol). Perhaps, from the practical standpoint, the last of these is the greatest, and in assembly life and fellowship the most needed.

Certain it is that if only six in an assembly of average size walked according to this rule, it would bring to that assembly a stirring and a refreshing heavenly breath. If the majority so walked in consistency, there would be revival. "In Christ Jesus, neither circumcision availeth any thing, nor uncircumcision, but *new creation*. And as many as walk according to this rule, peace be upon them, and mercy, and upon the Israel of God", Gal. 6. 15, 16. A.V., J.N.D.

Ministry – Deaconship

by A. G. Clarke

(1 TIM. 3; 1 PET. 4. 10, 11; 1 COR. 14)

Definition. As used in the Word of God, "ministry" denotes any form of service rendered to the Lord or to others. Examination of passages where the Greek word ("diakonia" and its cognates) occurs, immediately confirms this. "Deacon" is a transliteration not a translation, and simply means "servant". The service performed may be a regular occupation or only a temporary commission. Derivation points to an earlier Greek word signifying "to hasten after", "to run an errand", etc. "Diakonos" expresses the servant's relation to his work; "doulos" (bond-servant) expresses the servant's relation to his master. In the New Testament the former refers to a domestic servant, John 2. 5–9, and to a civil ruler, as servant of the State, Rom. 13. 4, 6. It is used of Christ Himself as Servant of Jehovah, Rom. 15. 8; and of Paul, Apollos and Timothy as servants of the Lord, 2 Cor. 3. 6; 6. 4; 1 Cor. 3. 5; 1 Thess. 3. 2 R.V. There were younger men who served the apostle Paul and other leaders, Acts 19. 22; Col. 4. 7; Philemon 13. There were servants of the churches, Acts 6. 2; 11. 29 with 12. 25 – including a woman, Rom. 16. 1. Even Satan has his ministers (lit. "deacons"), 2 Cor. 11. 14, 15. A related verb is used of angels, Mark 1. 13; of women, Mark 1. 31; 15. 41 with Luke 8. 3; 10. 40; and of Christ, Mark 10. 45; Luke 22. 27. The commonly-held view of a Christian "minister" is of one who holds clerical office in a church, usually at a stated salary, following theological training and subsequent "ordination" at the hands of superior clerics or "elders". This is a grave misconception. The idea of one "minister" or "pastor" over a local church is wholly foreign to the Scriptures. In 1 Timothy 3. 10–13 both the A.V. and R.V. show glaring examples of a mistranslation in the interests of ecclesiastical practice. "Office of a deacon" represents a form of the one Greek word meaning "to serve". Cf. verse 1 where "office of bishop" represents simply "overseership". Philippians 1. 1 shows that the "deacons" were a well-recognized group in the assembly. The expression "ministering brethren" gives the true idea.

Commission. The current ecclesiastical practice of "ordination" to service is a clear usurpation of the prerogative of God Himself, the authority of the Church's Risen Head and the functions of the Holy Spirit, 1 Cor. 12. 28; Eph. 4. 11; 1 Cor. 12. 7–11. Note that the seven stars, Rev. 1. 20, are seen in the hand of the Lord. As to apostolic practice, Paul gives directions to Titus regarding the choice of elders, Titus 1. 5, but nowhere do we find directions for the appointment of ministers.

Servants are appointed directly by their own Master, 1 Pet. 4. 11. It is obvious that natural gifts cannot be bestowed by ordination of men, much less so spiritual gifts. Lack of education, however, is no commendation. Natural ability may be turned into spiritual channels but this is not to be confounded with education *for* the ministry. Peter and John were not illiterate men but they had not been trained in the recognized theological schools, Acts 4. 13. Saul of Tarsus had exceptional ability, theological training and high attainments, Acts 22. 3; Phil. 3. 4–6, but under the mistaken idea that he was serving God he was working, in fact, in violent opposition to Him, Acts 23. 1; 26. 9; 1 Tim. 1. 13. How like many misguided persons in Christendom today!

The source of all spiritual gifts is the Risen Christ, who endows. The power for its exercise in ministry is the Holy Spirit, who endues, 1 Cor. 12. 4–11; 1 Pet. 4. 11; Eph. 4. 30; 5. 18; Luke 24. 49; Acts 1. 8. All fleshly activity in the things of God is wholly unacceptable to Him.

Function. Among God's people two forms of ministry (i.e. service) appear; (i) Service according to grace-gifts bestowed by Christ as Head of His Church, and (ii) Service of a temporal and special nature. These are differentiated in Acts 6. 2–4 – in spiritual things (ministry of the Word); in temporal things (ministry of "tables").

(i) *Service according to the grace-gifts* ("*charisma*") *of the Risen Christ.* Four main passages should be studied – Eph. 4. 7–16, for the universal church aspect; 1 Cor. 12. 4–31, for the local church aspect; Rom. 12. 3–13 and 1 Pet. 4. 7–11, for the personal aspect. In Ephesians, our Lord is seen as an illustrious Conqueror returning from a successful campaign against His foes and proclaiming His great victory at Calvary by the distribution of bounty. His "gifts" are men for the welfare and enriching of His Church. Five major grace-gifts are mentioned. Two were passing, as belonging to the foundation period of Church-building, Matt. 16. 18; Eph. 2. 20, and three permanent. *Apostles and prophets* both possessed unique authority and miraculous gifts as those through whom the Lord revealed New Testament truth, the former by personal teaching, John 14. 26; 16. 13, 14; Gal. 1. 11, 12, the latter by inspirational means, 1 Cor. 14. 30. The apostles had seen the Lord, 1 Cor. 9. 1; Acts 1. 21, 22, and were specially chosen to be witnesses to His resurrection, Acts 3. 15; 5. 32; 10. 41; prophets communicated the mind of God by a direct word from heaven. With the completion of the New Testament Scriptures fully revealing the will of the Lord for His people, the need for this great gift passed. The permanent gifts are *evangelists,* whose proper sphere is the outside world, and *pastors and teachers,* whose sphere is in the assembly. The evangelist concentrates on preaching the gospel, planting new assemblies or bringing converts into existing ones; he is concerned with the church's expansion. The pastor (lit. shepherd) and teacher concentrate on caring for the saints; "shepherding" pointing to occupation with souls, "teaching" to occupation with the Scriptures. The shepherd's work is mostly in private; the teacher's work is in public; they are concerned with the church's consolidation. The teacher has largely replaced the prophet, 2 Pet. 2. 1, as one who communicates the mind of God (but now from the Scriptures instead of by revelation) and speaks to edify, vivify and mollify. Edification builds up, exhortation stirs up, comfort binds up, 1 Cor. 14. 3. Note that his ministry is constructive, not destructive, a point sometimes forgotten by platform speakers.

1 Corinthians 12 enumerates grace-gifts in a local assembly, and it is significant that "evangelist" is omitted, for his work lies outside the immediate circle, though in full fellowship with it, v. 28. Here, too, passing and permanent gifts must be distinguished. Prophecies, tongues and even "knowledge" (cf. "word of knowledge", v. 8; i.e. of divine truth apart from written revelation), were of this temporary character,

13. 8–10. Note that in Ephesians, a later Epistle, the "sign" gifts are entirely omitted. A most important truth emphasized in 1 Corinthians 12 is that every individual believer shares the Christian ministry as a member of the Body of Christ. Not one member of our physical bodies is useless or merely decorative, and no believer is without some gift to be exercised for the welfare of the whole assembly, vv. 12–27 with 4 R.V.; 1 Thess. 5. 11; Rom. 15. 14. Women also have their proper sphere in ministry. Some individuals may possess more than one grace-gift. It should be remembered that even the major grace-gifts are not in sole possession of those who are in what is termed "full-time service". Brethren who follow a secular calling are often well equipped for ministry of the Word. The call to "full-time" ministry comes with distinct guidance from the Lord and must not be taken up lightly, 1 Cor. 7. 20; Mark. 13. 34.

All divinely-appointed ministry is primarily for the glory of God through Jesus Christ, 1 Pet. 4. 10, 11. The main purpose of the greater gifts is to prepare and to fit all members of the body of Christ for the exercise of their proper individual function with a view to the balanced and harmonious development of the whole unto full growth and maturity, Eph. 4. 11–16 R.V. Ministry also is a stewardship, 1 Pet. 4. 10; cf. 1 Cor. 4. 1, 2; 9. 7, which looks to the day of accounting at the *Bema* of Christ. Diligence, love, patience and prayerfulness are some of the many qualities enjoined among exhortations which all servants of Christ need to lay to heart, Rom. 12. 3 ff; 1 Pet. 4. 7–11. "Gift" is not to be neglected or laid up, 1 Tim. 4. 14, and needs at times to be stirred up (rekindled as a fire), 2 Tim. 1. 6. The true servant seeks not popularity but to please God, Gal. 1. 10; 1 Cor. 7. 23; Matt. 6. 1 ff; the approval of the Lord is better than the applause of men.

(ii) *Service of a Temporal and Special Nature.* An assembly may choose anyone to perform a service that he or she may be willing and competent to undertake. See e.g. Acts 6. 1–6, where almoners were chosen in connection with the distribution of daily rations to needy widows. They were already well-approved servants of God, so they are not termed "deacons" although their service is called (lit.) "deaconing" ("ministration", v. 1, *diakonia*; "service", v. 3, *diakoneo*). Some of the seven, if not all, were able to minister in higher capacity. Philip is known to have been an evangelist, Acts 21. 8. Compare his activities, 8. 5–8, 26–40. Note what is said of Stephen, 6. 6, 8, 10. Another example of "deaconing" is found in 2 Corinthians 8. 18–24, and Phoebe, a sister in the Lord, is called a servant (lit. deaconess) of the church at Cenchreæ, Rom. 16. 1. It is evidently a divinely-established rule that if an assembly contributes funds, etc., it should have a voice in the selection of those who administer or distribute them.

Qualifications. The divine requirements are set forth in 1 Timothy 3. 8–13. There are seven; four positive, three negative. Note the high standard set, as with the "overseers"; cf. Acts 6. 3 where only temporalities are in view. Note also the four important essentials in the case of women who serve, v. 11. There must be consistency between preaching and practice. Service and spirituality should go hand-in-hand, 2 Cor. 6. 3–10; 1 Thess. 2. 1–12.

Regulation. Sometimes a brother may have gift suited to a small local company consisting mostly of immature believers, but not gift that would profit a united ministry-meeting consisting of Christians drawn from a wide area and of all stages of spiritual growth. Much distress is often caused by some who have no proper gift for public ministry yet persist in taking the platform and wearying the saints with profitless talking. It wastes both time and money expended in the arrangement of such gatherings. In flagrant cases of offence the principle of Titus 1. 10, 11 should be applied.

Recognition. Those who claim the call of God to ministry are to be proved (tested) as to soundness in the faith, consistency in life and capability in service and, if approved, "being found blameless" (i.e. no ground for complaint), they are to be permitted the liberty of serving among the saints according to their proper grace-gift, 1 Tim. 3. 10; Matt. 7. 15–20. The assembly is responsible thus to recognize and to provide room for those whom God has set in the midst, 1 Cor. 16. 15–18. It is important to remember that the assembly cannot appoint or control any grace-gift, and certainly should not hire or retain solely for its own benefit any servant of Christ. Even an apostle had no authority to direct a fellow-servant of the Lord, 1 Cor. 16. 12. Moreover the servant of Christ is not to be judged as to service, sphere and motive, for he serves in view of the *Bema* of Christ, Rom. 14. 4, 10; 1 Cor. 3. 5–15; 4. 1–5. Elders, as responsible leaders in an assembly, should ever be on the watch for signs of gift in younger men and encourage such, affording opportunity for exercise and development towards maturity, 2 Tim. 2. 2. In these days there appears to be need to stress the importance of Paul's injunction, which will ensure a true "apostolic succession" in the church of God, 2 Tim. 2. 2.

The Master supplies the needs of His servants, Luke 22. 35. His promises are all-sufficient to assure the one who has been charged with ministry. Nevertheless, where necessary, and particularly with regard to the greater grace-gifts, practical recognition by rendering financial support is enjoined upon the saints, 1 Cor. 9. 7, 13, 14 (evangelists); Gal. 6. 6 (teachers); 1 Tim. 5. 17–18 (elders who labour in the Word), "honour" here meaning "honorarium"; 3 John 5–8. Paul's example in special circumstances and for certain reasons should not be overlooked by servants of the Lord, Acts 20. 33–35; 1 Cor. 9. 18.

Compensation. For faithful service, recompense is promised, 1 Tim. 3. 13 cf. R.V.; also Matt. 25. 21, 23, 34ff. It will not be according to the measure of success but of faithfulness, 1 Cor. 3. 8; Rev. 22. 12.

Conclusion. It is sometimes asked, "How can I recognize gift in myself?". The following questions have been put forward in one way or another:

a. Is there *due ardour* for a particular line of service? – FERVOUR.
b. Is there *definite ability* for a particular line of service? – FACULTY.
c. Is there *divine approval* upon a particular line of service? – FRUIT.

Has the blessing of God been seen in service already rendered? Godly desire for the "greater gifts" is not discountenanced but encouraged, I Cor. 12. 31; 14. 1, 39. "Greater" means greater usefulness, not necessarily of greater prominence. None should seek a position that he has no ability to fill, but if he uses gift already possessed, the Lord may add further gift.

Ministry of the Word

by J. R. CHARLESWORTH

WE SHALL CONSIDER (i) the gift of public ministry; (ii) the brethren who minister; and (iii) the ministry which they present.

The Gift of Ministry is:

Appointed by God, Eph. 4. 7–16. This truth, which applies to all gifts among the Lord's people, cannot be over emphasized. Organized Christendom overlooks the exercise of divinely appointed talents; we must beware lest we should copy ecclesiastical systems about us. The Risen Saviour's triumph was celebrated by His giving gifts to His body, the Church. His purpose in doing this was that we "may grow up into him in all things, which is the head, even Christ", Eph. 4. 15. Any resort to carnal endeavour, Acts 8. 18–22, or human organization is to be deplored.

Some gifts have been of a temporary nature. The work of the apostles established the early stages in the building of the Church upon its one Foundation; and prophets, forth-telling the revelations of God, were necessary prior to the completion of the Holy Scriptures, Eph. 2. 20. But as essential today as at the inception of the Church are the *studying* evangelists like Timothy, 2 Tim. 2. 15, who rightly divide the word of truth as they seek the *salvation* of sinners; the *suffering* teachers like Paul, 2 Tim. 1. 11–12, who in truth and verity seek the *sanctification* of the sheep within their pastoral care; and the *sincere* elders like John, 3 John 4, who are able to teach as they seek the *spiritual welfare* of the saints.

Administered by God, Col. 1. 25–29. Our Lord not only bestows gifts, sometimes by transforming inert ability by the power of the Holy Spirit, but He administers the use of these gifts. We are to use, not abuse, this privilege. Individually and collectively we need to wait upon God, earnestly desirous of the best gifts.

The New Testament does not countenance one-man-ministry. But it equally condemns any-man-ministry! James exhorts: "Be not many teachers, my brethren, knowing that we shall receive heavier judgement", James 3. 1 R.V. Not all are preachers or teachers, gifts requiring much discipline and involving great responsibility. Let us not envy another's talent. For every one has a gift and every gift is valuable. How vital to Paul were the beloved physician Luke, Phoebe, Epaphras who laboured fervently in prayer, Priscilla and Aquila. "The eye cannot say unto the hand, I have no need of thee", 1 Cor. 12. 21. In any case, "platform" ministry cannot provide all the instruction needed by the various sections of the church community. Sisters, though exempt from public teaching, 1 Tim. 2. 12, act as guides to the young women, Titus 2. 3–4, and each saint can manifest "a pattern of good works". Thus it is that the Holy Spirit, knowing the circumstances and necessities of every assembly, is always willing to supply that which is required. In this way, as the Lord walks in the midst of the lampstands, administering to them, He will be silhouetted in their light.

Ministering Brethren are:

Accountable to Christ, 1 Pet. 4. 11. Teachers expounding error by life or lip, satisfying men with "itching ears", must be restrained from Bible teaching and constrained to understand the way of God more perfectly. Nevertheless every servant is accountable only to his Master. Realisation of this would prevent idle criticism and promote instructive counsel. Galatians 6. 6. refers to the support God-given teachers deserve.

> When your preacher is doing the best that he can,
> Pray for him, help him – He's only a man!

To judge my brother cruelly is to grieve the Spirit and gratify self. "Who art thou that judgest another man's servant?"

Teaching God's Word is a sacred occupation. The true Bible teacher is an influential instrument of the Holy Spirit, and he will appreciate the solemnity of his work. Within his ministry there can be no place for iniquitous words or foolish novelties. His task is to edify, not to entertain, and this he will do "as of the ability which God giveth". He will be above petty quarrels and factions, 1 Cor. 1. 11, contending earnestly for the faith which was once for all delivered unto the saints.

"It is required in stewards that a man be found faithful", 1 Cor. 4. 2, and he who honestly expounds the written Word will realize to whom he has to give account.

Acknowledged by the Church, 2 Cor. 4. 2. One of the duties of an assembly is to provide nutritious ministry for its members, Acts 2. 42, utilizing the godly teachers available. Paul pleaded with the Corinthians: "Receive us; we have wronged no man, we have corrupted no man, we have defrauded no man", 2 Cor. 7. 2. John was plainly not wanted at the church where the malicious Diotrephes was pre-eminent. These facts imply that every preaching brother who neither corrupts nor defrauds should be received. But Scripture warns against any speaker who has an eye to monetary gain, 1 Pet. 5. 2; cf. Acts 20. 33, or who rests upon a measure of popular esteem, 3 John 9, or who relies mainly upon persuasive eloquence, 1 Cor. 2. 1–4, or intellectual wisdom, 1 Cor. 2. 13. Jude 16 mentions that there are some with "men's persons in admiration because of advantage". Christians recognize the true teacher, for God speaks to them through him. Such recognition is commendation indeed.

Ministry must be:

Accurate in Content, 1 Cor. 4. 1. Ministry is not the propagation of what a man thinks; it is the proclamation of what God has declared, "that we may present every man perfect in Christ Jesus". A good example of teaching ministry is found in Neh. 8. 8. We can pass on profitably only that which has already profited our own souls. Consequently the more one studies the Holy Scriptures and responds to the Lord's leading in one's own life, the greater will be one's ability to speak as with the oracles of God. One's ministry will become increasingly authentic and authoritative, 2 Tim. 4. 1–4, educating the listeners in the doctrines of Christ.

Approached with Care, Col. 1. 25–29. Many scriptures advise us to avoid false leaders, e.g., Eph. 4. 14; 1 Tim. 4. 1; Heb. 13. 9; 1 John 4. 1. The Ephesian elders in Acts 20. 30 were warned that some of their own number would arise "speaking perverse things, to draw away disciples after them". At Corinth certain teachers had apparently formed cliques around themselves. Those competent to proclaim God's Word are bound to be the object of Satan's wily attacks. The minister of the grace of God must be careful to make sure that he directs his congregation away from himself and towards his Saviour. Nothing has more power to bring saints together within the unity of the Spirit than the exaltation of Christ.

Congregations and their needs differ, so that every occasion for ministry is unique. Seven churches are addressed in Revelation 2 and 3 but no two received the same message. There are times when similar circumstances prompt similar teaching (see Col. 4. 16), but it is obvious that the Bible teacher must seek the Spirit's leading concerning every address. A mother considers her child more than her cooking. So also will the teacher think more of the believers' needs than of his preaching niceties; more of his Saviour than of his sermon.

Again teaching shepherds must be careful to minister to, that is "*to serve*", the Lord's people. If a church is to be built up in its most holy faith then the work must be undertaken "with all humility of mind, and many tears". Paul writes: "we were gentle among you, even as a nurse cherisheth her children", 1 Thess. 2. 7. The present condition of the saints should be considered before delivering an address, e.g., a milk menu will not satisfy a congregation anxious for meat, while dry profundities could be burdensome to believers weary at the end of a hard week's work.

God has raised up His spokesmen in every age. One thinks of Enoch who prophesied, Noah who preached, Jeremiah chosen before his birth, Amos called from the fields, Isaiah challenged by a vision. Still today God is choosing, calling and challenging men to teach His Word. Such brethren will fearlessly denounce sin and faithfully encourage sanctification wherever their Master sends them.

The Place of Women

by FRANK HOLMES

"BLESSED ART THOU, O Lord, our God! king of the universe, who hath not made me a woman." So runs the Jewish office book, "Daily Prayers". This is an evil saying which feeds the worm of pride in the male heart and is opposed to the spirit of both the Old and New Testaments. It should find no echo in the hearts of Christian men.

Our Lord was supported in His ministry by women who travelled with His party and gave material assistance. Paul refers to "those women which laboured with me in the gospel". In his time women prayed and prophesied and he did not rebuke them, 1 Cor. 11. 4-5. At the same time Scripture commands women to be silent in the churches, and does not permit a woman "to teach, nor to usurp authority over the man, but to be in silence". There is no confusion or error in logic here. A little clear, unbiased thinking reveals that the Scripture takes a balanced view of the place of women in church life. If only we were all as balanced!

To be frank, some men who take an extreme view of the matter and treat women with contempt, would be the first to fight for women's rights if they themselves belonged to the opposite sex. Equally, some women who forget their modesty in these things would be the first to try to "keep women in their place" if they belonged to the opposite sex.

There is no doubt whatsoever that the Bible forbids women to speak during the gatherings of the church. There is in fact a surprising agreement on this point between scholars of very different persuasions. Where a writer has no barrow to drive he generally accepts the fact that the ministry of women in the church is forbidden in Scripture. To illustrate this point we quote, without stopping to express here our general reaction to the publication, from the *New English Bible*.

"As in all congregations of God's people, women should not address the meeting. They have no licence to speak, but should keep their place as the law directs. If there is something they want to know they can ask their husbands at home. It is a shocking thing that a woman should address the congregation."

"It is my desire, therefore, that everywhere prayers be said by the men of the congregation . . . A woman must be a learner, listening quietly and with due submission."

Now it may be that some turned to this new translation expecting to find some softening down of apostolic teaching on this question. Instead, the facts are stated rather bluntly.

If a person claims to believe the Bible, and yet is unwilling to accept its plain teaching on such a point as this, he will readily swallow a cheap, unscholarly interpretation, which involves the wresting of the Scriptures. The modernist is at least honest, for he says, "Obviously Paul wrote that, but it was just his prejudice against women". Of course in this matter some believers are modernists.

It is an historical fact that these things were almost universally accepted in Christendom up to Queen Victoria's reign. The few exceptions were largely enthusiastic movements marked by various excesses.

During Queen Victoria's reign the spread of education and the employment of women in offices and factories promoted a new conception of womanhood. Some of the changes were good and simply an outworking of Christian principles. Others had no appeal to godly women. But, as so often happens, the church was expected to bring its practice into line with that of the world, regardless of Scripture. And weak Christians, in their usual hurry to be fashionable, brought forward various reasons why women should teach and govern in the church.

The Bible does not exclude women from public ministry in the gatherings of the church without giving a reason. It is better to accept the reasons of Scripture than to invent your own. Thus the Bible does not say that women are not to teach because there have been more false teachers among women than among men. Facts do not support that. What the Word of God says is: "For Adam was first formed then Eve. And Adam was not deceived, but the woman being deceived was in the transgression".

It is not for us to question the decisions of God. He has decided that when the local church comes together women must not lead the worship or speak, because man had priority in creation and women led the way in the Fall. We must accept this as we accept the fact of everyone's involvement in Adam's disobedience.

But Christian women must not be required to accept a heavier restraint than God had laid upon them. It is hard enough for a godly and gifted sister to sit silent whilst an ungifted and fleshly brother holds forth to no profit. She must not be prevented from doing the work which God has given her. Outside the gatherings of the assembly she has a large field. Who so well fitted to work among women as women? Who so likely to understand children?

Women who have no gift for public speaking often do a valuable work in private visitation and in providing hospitality in their own homes. Who can doubt that a great reward will be given for such unostentatious service?

Women's Sphere and Service

by A. G. CLARKE

TO GATHER THE MIND of God on this subject it is necessary first to consider woman's origin.

Creation Order, Gen. 1. 27, 28; 2. 18–25. In His eternal counsels, God ever had before Him the glory of His beloved Son. This included the provision of a consort wholly suited by grace to be for ever in joyful fellowship with Him as the Christ, a suited vehicle for the display of divine wisdom in time, Eph. 3. 10, 11, and divine grace in eternity, Eph. 2. 7. God's order in creation must be viewed in light of this planned union of Christ and the Church, Eph. 3. 3–11; Col. 1. 26, 27. In relation to God, the woman was "created", Gen. 1. 27; in relation to man she was "made" (lit. builded) from his side,

Gen. 2. 22. Verse 20 has profound significance when considered in its context. God took evident delight in His creature-man's exercise of divinely-bestowed wisdom in naming beast and bird, but there was a deeper purpose in the act. It was demonstrated to Adam that his being was of an entirely different order and that among all the other creatures there was no true counterpart "answering" to him. The words "was not found" imply an unsuccessful quest. It seems clear that the Creator in consultation with Adam showed him that a suited consort could come only from his own body. The man's willing response as a free agent was to offer himself for the operation necessary to produce his bride. This not only adds force to verses 23, 24, but answers more closely to the wonderful antitype of Christ and the Church, Eph. 5. 25–32. It is evident that the Creator never intended woman to be in the place of independence. Her position, however, is not one of inferiority but of a unique dignity as representing the Church's relationship to Christ, a position to be worthily sustained according to divine arrangement, Prov. 31. 10–31. Without the woman man is incomplete and the divine purposes for him frustrated, 1 Cor. 11. 3; study context to verse 12.

The Fall did not alter the relative position between the man and the woman, but the effects upon the latter are stated in Genesis 3. 16; (a) suffering in childbirth, and (b) subjection to husband. Headship had been vested in the man before, but now the subjection of the woman was a matter of command rather than of her spontaneous attitude. Modern teaching and practice have largely overturned God's order resulting in much of the confusion seen in present-day society, 1 Cor. 11. 3.

Matrimony is according to divine arrangement, Gen. 2. 24, endorsed by our Lord, Matt. 19. 3–6; John 2. 1, 2; cf. Heb. 13. 4; cf. the implied rebuke against forbidding it, 1 Tim. 4. 3. Divorce was never intended by God, and modern practice in regard to this is another cause of the sad state into which society has drifted in these last days. Scripture teaching on the subject will be found in Matt. 5. 31, 32; 19. 7–12; Mark 10. 2–12; Luke 16. 18; Rom. 7. 1–3; 1 Cor. 7, etc. In periods of special distress, such as open persecution of the

Church, it may be expedient to refrain from, or postpone, marriage for a time in order to lessen the dangers and difficulties, 1 Cor. 7. 26–31. Then there are cases where servants of the Lord will suffer less distraction by remaining free from family ties (e.g. pioneer missionary work in unexplored territory), 1 Cor. 7. 32–35 with Matt. 19. 12. Paul himself was probably such an one, 1 Cor. 9. 5 with 7. 8. Marriage has definite commitments, and the New Testament by precept and example instructs in the respective duties of husband and wife, 1 Cor. 7; Eph. 5. 22–33; Col. 3. 18, 19; 1 Pet. 3. 1–7. In proper subjection to her husband, the Christian woman should be an example to the world, not an imitator of the world.

The Home is woman's own special sphere. 1 Timothy 5. 14 speaks of her as being the "house-ruler" (not husband-ruler). Her aim is to make the house into a home, and this can only be done where love is. She is to be "husband-lover" and "children-lover" (lit. Greek), discreet, chaste, good (i.e. beautiful in character) and a *home worker*, Titus 2. 4, 5. Income is mostly the husband's earning but much of the responsibility for expenditure is the wife's, who has to decide between necessities and luxuries, with conveniences in the middle place! The training of the children, especially in earlier years, lies chiefly with the mother. This is a privilege of the highest order and a solemn duty not to be neglected. Lack of well-ordered homes is one of the factors responsible for the incidence of juvenile delinquency today.

Adornment. The fall brought a change from the primeval condition, Gen. 2. 25. The attempt of the guilty pair to cover their shame proved a failure, Gen. 3. 7, 8. God in grace provided for their recognized need by the blood-shedding of a substitutionary victim, 3. 21, a foreshadowing of the redemptive work of Christ. Clothing is striking evidence of sin in the human race. Animals have no such self-consciousness. The Mosaic law enjoined a distinction between the attire of men and of women, Deut. 22. 5, and the words in the latter part of the verse imply that it is an abiding principle. Christian women are instructed to wear apparel that is seemly (lit. orderly) with modesty and discretion. Neither immodest dress nor slovenly attire commends the gospel. There is to be no ostentation or extravagance – she is to be approved by good deeds not by gay dress, by consistent works not by costly wrappings, 1 Tim. 2. 9, 10. God looks upon the heart not on the outward appearance, 1 Sam. 16. 7. This should encourage sisters who do not possess beauty of features and form. A meek and quiet spirit is precious in God's sight and therefore should be highly esteemed by Christians. Men of the world may be attracted by the artificial styles of fashion, but these are "corruptible" and soon to pass away, 1 Pet. 3. 3, 4; 1 John 2. 15-17; Rom. 12. 2. This does not rule out certain adjustments necessary for health and comfort in various climates, but conspicuousness is to be avoided whether in new fashions or old. As to "beauty aids" the only woman in Scripture mentioned as using them is Jezebel, an unenviable character surely for Christian sisters to follow, 2 Kings 9. 30; cf. the prophets' scathing denunciation, Jer. 4. 30; Ezek. 23. 40. As to the hair, this was designed by God, to mark the distinction between the sexes, 1 Cor. 11. 14, 15. Long hair is woman's glory, therefore such practices as bobbing, shingling and cropping in concession to passing fashion is not well-pleasing to the Lord, 1 Cor. 10. 31. Trimming for health reasons may be advisable on occasion, provided this is done with a clear conscience before God and is not offered in excuse. Woman is to be truly feminine, not masculine. Both nature and revelation reprehend a woman with shorn head, 1 Cor. 11. 6, 15. Many modern fashions and practices are really in revolt against the Creator's prescribed arrangement.

Redemption Order. In this there is no distinction of sex, Gal. 3. 28. All believers are alike in Christ Jesus – in Christ a new creation, 2 Cor. 5. 17. All are partakers of the heavenly calling, Heb. 3. 1, and all equally share the privileges of the Christian priesthood, 1 Pet. 2. 5, 9. This standing before God, however, must not be confounded with the present church order.

Church Order is to maintain a testimony before angels, 1 Cor. 11. 10; Eph. 3. 10, 11, and before men, 1 Cor. 14. 23-25. In the assembly the creation order still holds, 1 Cor. 14. 34, 35; 1 Tim. 2. 11, 12, the reasons being stated, (a) man's priority in his creation by God, cf. 1 Cor. 11. 2, 8, 9; (b) woman's frailty in her deception by Satan, 1 Tim. 2. 14, 15. Leadership is vested in the brethren in all assembly gatherings and among mixed audiences. This refers to both teaching and audible praying, 1 Tim. 2. 8, 12; "the men (lit. males) . . . everywhere". A gracious promise follows in verse 15. There would appear to be no restriction placed upon sisters speaking and praying in gatherings for women or children, provided only that the injunction as to head-covering be observed in accordance with 1 Corinthians 11. 2–16. Many women have natural ability for speaking, but neither this nor modern practice in certain "churches" warrants disobedience to the Word of God, however plausible the arguments. Apparent blessing upon such efforts is no safe guide, Matt. 7. 21–23; 2 Cor. 5. 9. We need ever to be on guard against the spirit of the age, Eph. 2. 2. Satan is always working to subvert the divine order, but his defeat is assured and his doom imminent.

Ministry. Christian women have a wide sphere of ministry in activities for which they are particularly suited. As a member of the Body of Christ, the Church, each has her function to perform for the edification of the whole, 1 Cor. 12. 7, 12 ff. Most wives and mothers will find their time chiefly occupied with home-duties. A well-ordered Christian household is a most powerful testimony for God in any neighbourhood. Experienced missionaries in pagan lands can testify to this fact. Elderly women, widows and unmarried sisters may have more opportunity to engage in outside work such as a Sunday School class, visitation of the sick and sorrowing, tract distribution, helping the singing in open-air testimony, women's gatherings and personal work among neighbours. Elderly sisters are enjoined to teach the younger, Titus 2. 3, 4; and we have an example of a sister in the home sharing in the enlightenment of a brother not so well instructed, Acts 18. 26. Especially if they are wives of elders, they may be able to render valuable assistance in undertaking investigations among womenfolk on behalf of the assembly, and perform other service, provided always they possess the necessary qualifications, which are, "grave, not slanderers (lit. *diaboloi*, i.e. not allowing themselves to become the tool of the devil – the slanderer – *diabolos*), sober (abstinent and circumspect),

faithful in all things (i.e. in carrying out any assigned duties)",
1 Tim. 3. 11. In the showing of hospitality to servants of God,
to other visiting saints and to lonely Christians, especially
young believers from ungodly homes, the wife obviously has
the greater share, 1 Tim. 3. 2; 5. 10; Titus 1. 8; Rom. 12. 13;
Heb. 13. 2; 1 Pet. 4. 9; example, Acts 16. 15, 40. Christian
doctors, nurses and school-teachers have an exceptional field
to witness and to work for the Lord. Examples of other forms
of service are found, Matt. 27. 55; Mark 12. 41-44; 15. 41;
Luke 8. 3; Rom. 16. 1; Acts 9. 36-39. In practice Christian
women have often proved most generous givers. The Scriptures afford many examples of women who displayed strong
faith and tendered devoted service to God. Among God's list
of "honourable mentions" in Hebrews 11 we find named and
unnamed women. Many a dear sister in Christ, little noticed
in the world, will surely meet in a coming day the approving
word of the Lord, "She hath done what she could", Mark
14. 8.

Misunderstood Passages of Scripture. It would appear
well to consider some of the passages advanced in support of
the public ministry of Christian women by those who wish
to introduce this unscriptural practice.

(1) 1 Corinthians 14. 34, 35. The prohibition here is said
to refer to "chattering" in the assembly gatherings. The
Greek verb used occurs frequently in the New Testament
but never in the sense of "to chatter". In this very chapter it
appears 24 times, 22 times clearly relating to ministry. Let the
student attempt to substitute the word "chatter" in any of
these and he will immediately perceive the resulting absurdity, verse 29, for instance! Besides, would not the chattering
of men be equally reprehensible? Why the restriction upon
sisters only?

(2) Acts 21. 9, 10 incidentally mentions that the four
daughters of Philip the evangelist had the prophetic gift.
There are no prophets now, so that in any case this affords no
example for the present. The only women claiming the prophetic gift in modern times have been mostly connected with
error cults. Note that Philip's daughters are not said to have
exercised their gifts in public. Then observe that when a

prophetic message is to be delivered concerning Paul, the Lord sends His servant Agabus all the way from Judæa instead of using Philip's daughters, who were already on the spot. Surely this is significant enough!

(3) Philippians 4. 3. Euodia and Syntyche laboured with Paul in the gospel, but it is unwarrantable assumption to suggest that they preached publicly. As we have seen, there are many ways in which sisters can co-operate in the Lord's work, apart altogether from speaking.

(4) John 4. 28–30, 42. Three things must be noted here; (a) the Samaritan woman's audience was "the men", i.e. those with whom she was acquainted and possibly had had unholy relations, hence must have been of a private nature; (b) hers was a simple testimony, not a public proclamation, 39; (c) she issued an invitation, "come", a suggestive form of service for Christian sisters today.

(5) Acts 1. 14. It is not to be inferred that the women prayed audibly. The order of the words indicates simply that they were present. Had the statement been, "These all, with the women, continued steadfastly in prayer", there would be some measure of ambiguity. As it is, the meaning is clear.

(6) Judges 4. 4–9. Advocates of women's public ministry must be hard put to it when they turn to such an Old Testament passage! There is no inconsistency even here, but rather a warning example. Rulers had ceased in Israel, 5. 7, showing that all was in confusion in the nation instead of divine order. Deborah took over the civil rule for lack of a man willing and able to do it. Barak was the military leader, but so weak and fearful that when an emergency arose he called upon Deborah to share the post of danger with him despite her warning, v.9. The incident shows utter weakness and failure among God's people. It was not an accession of new power and spirituality. Brethren who would introduce the public ministry of sisters thereby expose Barak-like qualities and augment sad failure in the church. Hebrews 11. 32 mentions Barak not Deborah, thus upholding the divine principle that where men and women are in association, even in weakness, leadership belongs to the man.

PASTORAL RESPONSIBILITIES

The Little Flock

by WILLIAM TREW

THE WORD TRANSLATED "flock" in Acts 20. 28 and in 1 Peter
5. 2–3 is probably the diminutive form of the word so translated in John 10. 16 R.V. Though the word is used by the
Lord Jesus to designate the aggregate of His own it seems
clear that the apostles, in the passages referred to above, use
the term as descriptive of the local assembly. Taking farewell
of the elders of the Ephesian assembly, Paul says, "Take heed
therefore unto yourselves, and to all the flock, over the which
the Holy Ghost hath made you overseers", Acts 20. 28, while
Peter exhorts the elders to "Feed the flock of God which is
among you, taking the oversight thereof, not by constraint,
but willingly; not for filthy lucre, but of a ready mind; neither
as being lords over God's heritage, but being ensamples to
the flock", 1 Pet. 5. 2–3.

The expression is a very beautiful one, and suggests a
number of ideas. It would speak to us of:

(1) Weakness in the presence of the enemy;
(2) Dependence upon the care of the shepherd;
(3) Surrender to the guidance of the shepherd;
(4) Unity thus secured and maintained.

It will be observed that the shepherd is charged with full
responsibility for the flock. It is expected that he will be
provider, protector, and *pattern,* and as such, characterized by
love and devotion, wisdom and skill, and patience and persistence. These qualities are seen in perfection in Him who is
"the great shepherd of the sheep". But He is the "chief
shepherd" also, and as such He has, in the exercise of His

care of the flock, appointed under-shepherds. It is required that these under-shepherds be like the Chief Shepherd

(1) In their love of, and devotion to, the flock;
(2) In their wisdom to feed, and skill to care;
(3) In their courage to guard against the attack of every enemy;
(4) In their leadership as ensamples to the flock.

This designation of office is descriptive of their work in relation to the assembly.

They Serve the Flock as having been Appointed by the Chief Shepherd and in Direct Responsibility to Him. Let the under-shepherds constantly bear this in mind. The Chief Shepherd, to whom the flock belongs, holds them accountable for the condition of that flock. Peter emphasizes this in a most striking way when he says, "not as lording it over your possessions", 1 Pet. 5. 3 J.N.D. The character of the elders' conduct in relation to the flock is what is in question, and the force of the exhortation is, "Do not be as persons who lord it over your own possessions, viewing the saints as something belonging to you". Overseers in the assembly are not a body of control, nor do they constitute a board of management. They are the gifts of the ascended Lord to the assembly. Fitted for their work by the sovereign Spirit, it is their ministry to the saints to maintain the authority of the Lord in a practical way, in order to develop the spiritual and moral condition of the assembly for His glory who dwells in the midst.

Let the members of the flock also bear in mind the fact that those who have been appointed over them by the Lord must render an account of their service "in that day". The exhortation is, "Obey your leaders, and be submissive; for they watch over your souls as those that shall give account, that they may do this with joy, and not groaning, for this would be unprofitable for you", Heb. 13. 17 J.N.D.

Their Work is to Lead as Ensamples to the Flock. It is the privilege of the under-shepherds to be in fellowship with the mind of the Chief Shepherd, so that they may guide the footsteps of the flock into ways that will meet with His approval, by the power and influence of their example, even more than their words of ministry. How solemn, if, by word or act, one who professes to be a leader influences any of the flock into ways that do not answer to His thoughts to whom the flock belongs.

David was a true leader of the flock of God's pasture, Psa. 78. 70–72, spoken of as "a man after mine own heart, which shall fulfil all my will", Acts 13. 22. His deep exercise on behalf of the people to whom he had been appointed guide was to restore the ark of God – the throne of God – to its rightful place in their midst, and unify the tribes under the authority of that throne, in glad submission to God's rule. This remains the work of the true leader. It is intended that the saints take character from their guides. Thus the true leader is one who can stand before the saints and say Gideon-like, "Look on me, and do likewise".

Their Work is to Guard against every Attack. Thus Peter, writing in view of days of fiery persecution, wrote to warn the shepherds of the flock of the coming of "the roaring lion", 1 Pet. 5. 8–9, and Paul, taking farewell of the elders of the assembly in Ephesus, raised his voice in warning also, Acts 20. 29, 31. He recognized two sources of danger: from outside there would be attacks upon the life of the assembly testimony, and from within, attacks upon the unity of the saints. It is evident that principles are developing today that threaten assembly testimony. The true leader, devoted to the interests of the Chief Shepherd in His flock, with eyes open to the dangers, and recognizing the source from which the attacks come, will lift his voice in faithful warning, though some, even of the flock, be found impatient of warning voices.

Their Work is to Feed. Peter's word to the elders of his day is addressed to all the under-shepherds: "Feed the flock of God". Though the word is wide enough in its significance to include all the work of a shepherd, it lays emphasis upon his responsibility to search out green pastures for the feeding of the flock. Psalm 23 describes the flock as cared for by the perfect Shepherd. According to that pattern, the under-shepherds model their service. How important it is that the flock be well nourished! In the church epistles of Revelation 2 and 3, the Spirit speaks very much of ministry that wrought havoc and ruin; while, in the Pastoral Epistles, He lays emphasis upon the importance of sound (healthful) teaching. The health of the flock depends upon its food; poisoned food will undermine the health of the saints, while the faithful ministry of every phase of divine truth alone can build them up, and secure the prosperity of the assembly. To that end the ascended Lord has given gifts to men. "He gave some . . . pastors and teachers . . . for the perfecting (the full development) of the saints", Eph. 4. 11, 12.

The great concern of the Chief Shepherd is His flock. Therefore, to the under-shepherds whom He has appointed, His word is, "Feed my lambs", "Feed my sheep".

Shepherd Care

by D. PARRACK

APART FROM JOSEPH AND MARY, the shepherds were the first in the scriptural record to see the Lord Jesus, Luke 2. 16. Their environment and occupation immediately prior to this revelation suggest lessons for those who seek to shepherd the flock of God today.

Firstly, they were *abiding in* the field. They had not slipped from warm beds for a few short hours to make a cursory check on the flock, nor had they brought the sheep down to a place where they could be watched over from the comparative comfort of their own homes. The place where nourishment could be obtained was up in the green hills, and for the sake of their charges the shepherds stayed up there with them. Certainly this implied inconvenience, probably hardship, possibly danger, but the prime concern was the wellbeing of the flock, and the comfort of the shepherds must be subordinated to the requirements of the sheep. It was not of course left to the sheep to make the choice; this was willingly made by the shepherds themselves.

"Feed the flock of God which is among you", 1 Pet. 5. 2, exhorts Peter upon writing to fellow-elders, the sense implying shepherding in its fulness rather than the mere provision of food. "Feed the church of God", Acts 20. 28, urges Paul in his farewell message to the Ephesian elders. But the provision of food convenient entails knowing where such food may be found. Fresh pastures are often necessary, but are discovered only after much searching. To be able to feed God's people involves first having fed deeply on God's Word oneself, 2 Tim. 2. 15. This may mean, as in the case of the shepherds in Luke 2, the denial of otherwise legitimate occupation of time.

Such ministry will involve both labouring in the Word and doctrine, 1 Tim. 5. 17, and the careful and illuminating public reading of the Scriptures. "Give attendance to reading", 1 Tim. 4. 13, was one of Paul's instructions to Timothy, a man of whom the apostle wrote to the Philippians, "I have no man likeminded, who will naturally care for your state", Phil. 2. 20.

To know the immediate needs of the flock means being close to them at all times. To safeguard the flock necessitates an awareness and recognition of what may be dangerous to them, together with the ability either to drive away the danger or to guide and shepherd the flock away from the dangerous locality. Wolves who seek to steal the sheep must be kept out; unwholesome pastures which would cause sickness and weakness must be avoided. Spiritual discernment, essential for both these activities, is cultivated only in the Lord's presence, where we learn to see things in their true perspective and from His viewpoint.

Secondly, these shepherds in Luke 2 were *keeping watch over* their sheep. They were not merely watching them in a cold dispassionate manner, ready to drag them back at the first or slightest hint of deviation. "Not by constraint . . . not for filthy lucre . . . Neither as being lords over God's heritage, but being ensamples to the flock", 1 Pet. 5. 2, 3, is the attitude that Peter encourages elders to cultivate. The writer to the Hebrews, enjoining obedience amongst believers towards their leaders, reminds them that "they watch for (over) your souls, as they that must give account", Heb. 13. 17. Shepherding cannot be undertaken in a spirit of superiority, or as an imposed task which is accepted as being necessary but undesired.

It can be undertaken only with deep assurance and conviction of appointment by the Holy Spirit, balanced by an equally deep affection for Christ's people and a consequent desire to serve Him by serving them. Watching over the flock will be motivated, not by a desire to ensure a well regimented, placidly orthodox assembly, but rather a desire for a healthy, happy, virile and active company of believers. It will involve encouragement of evident budding gift, and of desires after the things of God. Such encouragement is given as much by positive example as by precept.

Thirdly, their vigil was accomplished *by night*. It is during the short time until "the Sun of righteousness (shall) arise with healing in his wings", Mal. 4. 2, that shepherds are required for God's people. In the hours of darkness when we must walk by faith and not by sight, natural understanding, natural wisdom and the ability to organize in the natural realm are of little value in caring spiritually for the saints. Paul makes no mention of these things when he lists the qualifications of elders, 1 Tim. 3. 1–7; Titus 1. 7–9. The requirements are of a spiritual nature, such as will manifest themselves in practical living. It is at night when dangers multiply, and it is at night when natural vision is of least avail. It is during Christ's absence from this scene that shepherds, conscious of their own inability, must learn complete reliance upon, and trust in, Him who has called them to such service. Their reward is not to be sought for down here, since it is not thus promised. The lack of reward in this scene did not deter Paul, who wrote, "I will very gladly spend and be spent for you; though the more abundantly I love you, the less I be loved", 2 Cor. 12. 15. So speaks the true shepherd, since it is, above all else, the welfare of the flock that he seeks. Such an attitude is seen in divine perfection in the Lord who said, "I am the good shepherd: the good shepherd giveth his life for the sheep", John 10. 11.

If a reward is not to be sought for down here, one is certainly promised above, for "when the chief Shepherd shall appear, ye shall receive a crown of glory that fadeth not away", 1 Pet. 5. 4. This is not a fading crown of approbation or adulation from men; rather it is a glorious unfading crown from Him, for whose sake and for the sake of whose sheep, we seek to be found of Him at His coming, as those of old, "abiding in the field, keeping watch over their flock by night", Luke 2. 8.

Shepherding the Flock

by J. E. BAKER

"Where is the flock that was given thee, thy beautiful flock", Jeremiah 13. 20.

TO EVERY ASSEMBLY SHEPHERD this question must at times cause a measure of heart-searching, especially when viewed in the light of the words of the Good Shepherd, "those that thou gavest me I have kept", John 17. 12. A true shepherd must of necessity possess a shepherd's heart and a shepherd's love; only then can he gain the shepherd's crown.

First and foremost, shepherds must be men who have been raised up and equipped by the Holy Spirit. The sovereignty of God in assembly life must never be lost sight of, and it is the divine prerogative of the Holy Spirit to distribute blessing as He sees fit. Through the years their duty is clear, to be faithful to God at all times regardless of the approval or disapproval of their fellowmen. Moreover, in 1 Peter 5. 2, 3 we are warned of the sins that would render them unfit to care for the flock of God, (i) love of ease, (ii) love of money, (iii) love of power.

Over the years, the true shepherd will come to know experimentally what Paul meant when he wrote "My little children of whom I travail in birth again until Christ be formed in you", Gal. 4. 19. A progressive growth in grace as well as growth in knowledge will be a source of joy to him. He will watch the spiritual growth of the young men in the assembly. He will note their different dispositions and abilities, seeking to encourage them to function as priests before the Lord. Furthermore, he will give a word of encouragement here, a word of admonition there, maybe a warm hand clasp to help them to "run with patience the race that is set before" them.

Any evidence of unequal yoke among the flock will be a matter of deep personal concern to him, and he will endeavour by prayerful advice to turn such from this forbidden path. He will remind them that the laws of God are like the tables of stone on which they were written – inflexible. We cannot bend them to suit ourselves, and when we break the laws of God we also break ourselves upon them.

What of the awkward members of the flock, and how shall these be dealt with? One's personal desire may be to hope that they will find fresh pastures, yet, remembering that "all things work together for good to them that love God", the shepherd may realize that in the purpose of God they are there to teach him patience, to rub a few rough edges off him, and to drive him the more to his knees in order to find wisdom. As the wheels of a watch rotate in opposite directions to give correct time, so in the formation of our character; many things that we may not like are allowed by God so that we may be cast increasingly upon Him.

Furthermore, what of the feeble members of the flock, found in every assembly of God's people? Shall they be brushed aside as of no consequence? No, for these are all part of the "beautiful flock". Paul observed that those members which seem to be more feeble, are necessary, 1 Cor. 12. 22. As in the natural life, so it is in the spiritual. There are various degrees of life – some are always full of vitality, but others have to be cared for all the days of their lives. The feeble ones must be encouraged to go on with the Lord. It was written of the Good Shepherd that "a bruised reed shall he not break, and the smoking flax shall he not quench", Isa. 42. 3. We may visualize Him bending over such a one and fanning the feeble flicker into a flame. All this is part of a shepherd's responsibility. God's charge against the shepherds of Israel was that "the diseased have ye not strengthened, neither have ye healed that which was sick, neither have ye bound up that which was broken, . . . , neither have ye sought that which was lost", Ezek. 34. 4. It is in the measure in which shepherds appreciate that they were bound up by the Good Samaritan, that they will be able to bind up that which is broken. When they have been brought to that place where their only help is in God – a place perhaps of tragedy and sorrows – there it is that they discover that their God is the God of the valleys of life as well as the God of the hills. Being thus educated by God, they can be a help to the broken-hearted. Likewise, in seeking those who have gone astray, the recollections of the truancy of their own heart and mind will enable them to realize that it is only "the mind of Christ" that they have to pass on.

As the day of grace is closing and errors abound on every hand, the shepherds must ever be on their guard against the intrusion of any false doctrine. The "things which are most surely believed among us", Luke 1. 1, are our sacred trust. The deity of our beloved Lord, the preciousness of His atoning blood – these truths are woven into the warp and woof of our Christian life. There can be no compromise! When anything contrary to these is brought into the assembly, they will know at once that there is "death in the pot", 2 Kings 4. 40, but by bringing in the meal – the Word of God – they cast out the evil thing. Here, again, is another responsibility of the shepherds.

It will help them in their work for the Lord if they some-times meditate on God's ideal assembly as brought out in principle in Psalm 144. 12–15: sons as plants grown up, daughters polished, plenty of food in store, the flock in-creased, the oxen (the workers) strong to labour, no breaking in nor going out, no complaining in the streets. When they stand before the judgment seat of Christ with their lives and labours under review, how shall they answer the question, "Where is the flock that was given thee, thy beautiful flock?". Shall the under-shepherds be ashamed before Him? It would be wonderful if they could say with Him, "I have glorified thee on the earth: I have finished the work which thou gavest me to do", John 17. 4. Thus should they follow in the steps of the Good Shepherd.

Government – Overseership

by A. G. CLARKE

Introduction. In Christendom, God-appointed order is mostly supplanted by human organization, especially in the sphere of rule and ministry. Traditions gathered from writings of Greek and Latin "Church Fathers" and decisions of noted Church Councils, rather than the New Testament Scriptures, are appealed to in justification or condemnation of church doctrine and practice. Gatherings of believers endeavouring to follow the simple pattern laid down in the Word of God are often charged with repudiating leadership altogether, because no official class is in evidence. Without duly-accredited leadership, however, an assembly would soon be in confusion, like a community without government, cf. Judges 21. 25. Christ is sole Head of His Body the Church, and His sole Vicar on earth is the Holy Spirit. A visible "head" may appear to make for a smoothly-running organization, but God's order, not man's notions, must be our true guide. Recognition of Christ's Lordship involves humble submission to any rule He may establish. It is important to remember that brethren who bear responsibility are to administrate, not to legislate.

The Lord has set up two forms of leadership in His Church, "overseers" (bishops) and "ministers" (deacons), the former guiding the local assembly, the latter serving it. We must carefully distinguish "governments" from other "gifts", 1 Cor. 12. 28, i.e. administration from ministry, though they are intimately connected. Notice the order of address in Philippians 1. 1, "saints" followed by "bishops" (overseers – plural) and "deacons" (ministering brethren).

Overseers – Designation. The terms "overseers" (bishops) and "elders" (presbyters) refer to the same persons under aspects of their activities and their age (spiritual maturity), respectively; Acts 20. 17 with 28; cf. Titus 1. 5 with 7. Not all aged men are "elders", Titus 2. 2, 3 (different Greek); Job 32. 9. Eldership goes back to Old Testament times and was continued among Jews in their synagogues, Exod. 3. 16; 12. 21; 17. 5; 24. 1, etc. In early days churches followed the simple pattern of the synagogues led by "elders". Ritualists, however, have sought to model their services after the more complex pattern of the temple worship. Elders are first mentioned in connection with the Christian church at Jerusalem, Acts 11. 30, and as collaborators with the apostles, Acts 15.

Commission. It is the Holy Spirit who "makes" (sets) overseers in the local assembly, Acts 20. 28. He is the Agent on earth of Christ the Head in heaven. The Word of God knows nothing of the appointment of elders by ecclesiastical authorities, or of election by congregations or by existing elders.

Newly-planted assemblies functioned at first without elders. Missionaries, who under God had been instrumental in planting these assemblies, on a subsequent visit chose for them certain men, having spiritual and moral qualifications which indicated to their experienced eyes fitness for eldership, Acts 14. 23. In a similar way Paul instructed Titus to appoint elders in the assemblies in Crete, Titus 1. 5, but this gives no support to the idea of "apostolic succession", for the appointment conveyed no qualification to preach or to teach. Such ministry is after another order. We conclude then that the procedure was *inaugural*, and not intended to be continued once these assemblies were provided for. The writer believes we have here divine guidance for evangelists and missionaries in new spheres. Although the New Testament appears to give no specific directions for subsequent procedure, the expediency principle enunciated by Paul in 1 Corinthians would surely suggest that existing elders as spiritual guides should be on the look out for brethren having the requisite qualifications, and indicate them to the assembly. Such would then join the others in their prayers and counsels.

The appointment of a "bishop" with a "see" was an early departure from New Testament simplicity. The present system of ordination and nomination to office with the granting of "livings" by the government, by some college or corporation, even by unbelieving landowners, is certainly not of God but of the world.

Function. Eldership is strictly a local charge. It does not carry authority to "rule" in another assembly. Elders are not a board of officials set *over* an assembly but labourers *among* the saints, Acts 20. 28; 1 Pet. 5. 1, 2; cf. Luke 22. 24–26; Matt. 20. 25-28. The word "governments", be it noted, follows (not precedes) "helps" in the order of local grace-gifts, 1 Cor. 12.28, and is omitted altogether in reference to the Church universal, Eph. 4. 11. Whilst in general it may be desirable that those who attend to the business affairs of the assembly should be elders, this work partakes of a "deaconing" character.

In Scripture the work of elders is described as:

Shepherding (Greek *poimaino*). Christ Himself is Chief Shepherd of His flock, 1 Pet. 5. 4; John 10. 16, and elders as under-shepherds, 1 Pet. 5. 2, "tend"; Acts 20. 28, "feed", i.e. tend as a shepherd. Peter was an example, 1 Pet. 5. 1 with John 21. 16, 17. Paul, too, was a true shepherd as well as a pioneer missionary (see his Epistles). The only place where Christian leaders are *called* "shepherds" (pastors) is Ephesians 4. 11. Here "pastor" shows occupation with souls, "teacher" shows occupation with the Scriptures. The former's work lies chiefly in private visitation, the latter's in public instruction. The shepherd's duties, then, are to supervise (lit. to "bishop"), tend and feed the flock. Among the saints it is necessary to instruct the ignorant, visit the sick, James 5. 14, comfort the dying, console the bereaved, admonish the disorderly, encourage the faint-hearted, support the weak and restore the fallen, Gal. 6. 1, being longsuffering toward all, 1 Thess. 5. 14. Acts 20. 34, 35 also indicates giving material help where needful, either from one's own pocket or from assembly funds by arrangement. A true shepherd always pays particular attention to the lambs. False shepherds are more concerned about shearing the sheep than about serving them. Hirelings are constrained not by love, but by pay and are not prepared to take any personal risks!, John 10. 12, 13. They pasture themselves, Jude 12; cf. Ezek. 34. 2-6. Many such, alas, are found in Christendom today! Teaching for hire came in with clerisy, under which system money settles the sphere of ministry and determines doctrines to be taught or suppressed, Rev. 2. 4; Jude 11; 2 Pet. 2. 15; Hab. 1. 15, 16. As another has put it, "Pastors (shepherds) *in* assemblies are invaluable; pastors *of* churches, unscriptural".

Watching (Greek *agrupneo*, Heb. 13. 17) in the interests of souls. This is frequently linked with prayer, as in Eph. 6. 18. Adversaries are powerful, practised and persistent, 1 Pet. 5. 8; Acts 20. 29-31; 2 Cor. 11. 13-15; John 10. 12; Matt. 7. 15-20; cf. 1 Sam. 17. 34-36. Laggards and stragglers of the flock are in danger of being snapped up by the enemy; also the "sick" and feeble, Deut. 25. 18. Shepherds guard, as well as guide, the flock.

Leading (Greek *proisteemi*, to stand before, i.e. especially as examples), 1 Thess. 5. 12; 1 Tim. 5. 17; to be done with diligence, Rom. 12. 8; cf. 1 Pet. 5. 3. In Eastern lands, a shepherd is not a driver but a leader of the sheep.

Governing (Greek *heegeomai*, to preside, to rule), Heb. 13. 7, 17, 24; not as "lords", 1 Pet. 5. 3; Mark 10. 42–45; being patterns, not princes. A governor's authority is delegated, not despotic.

Steering (Greek *kuberneestees*, primarily a helmsman, Acts 27. 11), 1 Cor. 12. 28. Elders pilot the assembly, steering it clear of "rocks" upon which it might "founder".

Labouring (Greek *kopiao*, to toil; indicates wearying work as Luke 5. 5), 1 Thess. 5. 12; 1 Tim. 5. 17; Acts 20. 35 ("so" points to manual work as 34). It is not merely attending "brethren's meetings" for the discussion of assembly affairs, but working among the saints, Titus 1. 9; cf. Jude 22–23 R.V., always serving in the spirit of humility, 1 Pet. 5. 5 R.V.

Stewarding (Greek *oikonomos*, discharging a stewardship, Titus 1. 7, cf. Luke 12. 41, 42; 1 Cor. 4. 1, 2). God has entrusted elders with a responsible charge in His household, and in due time they must render account, Heb. 13. 17.

From the above it will be seen that the duties of elders are primarily connected with the *spiritual* welfare of the saints, 1 Tim. 3. 5 (same Greek in Luke 10. 34), and only secondarily, if at all, with temporal things. They should act in fullest fellowship with the rest of the assembly. Mutual confidence is essential. If some feel there has been an unjust exercise of "rule" by the elders, appeal can be made to higher authority, viz. to the Chief Shepherd and Head of the Church. Meetings of overseers should follow the Scriptural pattern, Acts 15. 6; 21. 18, 20. The very plurality of elders suggests the need to come together for prayer and consideration of assembly matters. Unity of judgment must be aimed at, for a divided oversight usually means a divided assembly. Experience and expediency both indicate the undesirability of discussing everything before the whole assembly or even before younger brethren, when, for example, private and confidential questions arise concerning the moral character of someone in fellowship and affecting possible discipline. Considerable harm to innocent parties may result by giving to the affair wider publicity than necessary especially when allegations are found untrue. Elders are surely the proper ones to investigate the case and then advise the assembly. They are to take heed to themselves first of all, then to all the flock, Acts 20. 28.

Qualification, 1 Tim. 3. 1-7; Titus 1. 5-9. Natural ability or business acumen, financial prosperity or social position neither qualify nor disqualify one for overseership. Overseers must possess moral qualities as well as spiritual capacity for the work. They should be men of the Word, men of faith and men of prayer; in short, sound in doctrine and consistent in life, Heb. 13. 7; 2 Tim. 2. 2. In ritualistic churches the personal character of an office-holder is of little account. He may be dissolute in private life yet in virtue of his office he is permitted to "administer the sacraments", even to "pronounce absolution". In true Christianity the very opposite rules. No less than eighteen different words are used to indicate the character required of God in a true overseer. Two phrases also describe his capabilities and three his circumstances.

Circumstances (a) Not a novice (recent convert), 1 Tim. 3. 6; note reason cf. 5. 22. (b) Husband of one wife, 1 Tim. 3. 2; Titus 1. 6, i.e. in a land where plurality of wives is a legal custom such a convert may be received into fellowship but is debarred from overseership. (c) Good testimony in the world, 1 Tim. 3. 7, e.g. not discredited in business; note reason.

Capabilities. (a) In effective control of his own household, 1 Tim. 3. 4; Titus 1. 6; note reason. (b) Apt-to-teach (Greek one word), 1 Tim. 3. 2; i.e. not necessarily a "platform man" but able to impart instruction at least privately to younger believers.

Character. Note the high standard to be applied and followed. Beside the general principles already mentioned, the elder is to be irreproachable in conduct, sane and impartial in judgment, self-controlled in speech and action, reasonable in attitude (not stubborn or self-willed), free from avarice, hospitable, etc.

Recognition. Overseers are recognized by the saints because they have the affections and qualifications of elders and do the work of such. Note seven exhortations:

"*Know them*", 1 Thess. 5. 12; i.e. by observation, for the Greek word is never used of a *formal* recognition. Knowledge leading perhaps to a more open acknowledgment is signified by another word found in 1 Corinthians 16. 18 with 16. Elders will obtain true recognition if they serve the saints well. Sheep will instinctively follow without appeal or coercion one they have come to know and have learned to trust.

"*Esteem them*", 1 Thess. 5. 13. Saints are to value them highly and appreciate them in love on account of their work rather than from personal liking.

"*Honour them*", 1 Tim. 5. 17; "double" honour indicates material support when necessary in addition to paying respect, 18; cf. 1 Cor. 9. 7b. Paul's example is not to be overlooked, however, Acts 20. 34, 35.

"*Trust them*", 1 Tim. 5. 19 with 1. No accusation is to be accepted against an elder except in the presence of witnesses and upon sufficient testimony, for elders are particularly exposed to misrepresentation by very reason of their work, e.g. in advising the assembly in matters of discipline. If there be ground for remonstrance, deference as to a father is to be shown, yet if sin be proved there must be public conviction, 20. Fellow-elders are not to cloak failure in one of their number.

"*Obey them*", Heb. 13. 17, i.e. in expressed injunctions, "and be submissive", J.N.D., i.e. to their known but unexpressed wishes; cf. 1 Pet. 5. 5; 1 Cor. 16. 15, 16. Loyalty to leaders is enjoined because of their grave responsibility before the Lord.

"*Remember them*", Heb. 13. 7. Here probably refers to leaders who had suffered martyrdom. Saints are to (a) consider the issue of their life (conduct), i.e. its triumphant finish; and (b) imitate their faith, i.e. faithful example. Leaders may pass away but Christ ever remains the one great Object of faith and service, v. 8. Undershepherds fall asleep but the Great Shepherd remains to raise up others, Himself exercising chief supervision, 20; cf. 1 Pet. 2. 25.

"Salute them", Heb. 13. 24; i.e. greet them with kindly wishes so as to encourage. They meet plenty of criticism! If you do not always agree with their decisions do not bear resentment. Pray for them, Heb. 13. 18; 1 Thess. 5. 25; 2 Thess. 3. 1.

Compensation. Note the wonderful promise, 1 Pet. 5. 4, to be fulfilled in the day of accounting, Heb. 13. 17; cf. 1 Thess. 2. 19; 2 John 8. What a reward for the arduous and often thankless task of an overseer!

The Future Care of Assemblies

by W. E. VINE

THE HOLY SPIRIT, by whose power and operation assemblies are formed, makes provision for their spiritual care and edification, so that the testimony, by the maintenance of the faith and by practice in conformity thereto, may be continued. The apostle Paul enjoined upon Timothy, in his closing Epistle, to commit the things which he had heard from him "to faithful men, who shall be able to teach others also", 2 Tim. 2. 2. Two qualifications were to be in evidence. The men must be faithful and competent to teach. The order is significant: first their character, then their ability to maintain doctrine. It was not a case of Timothy's mere selection. Those who were to continue the promulgation of the truth must be known from the first by their possession of the twofold requisites.

So it was in the appointment of elders in the churches, that is to say, men to act as overseers or bishops, Acts 20. 17 with 28 R.V. The men who were to fulfil these responsibilities, for instance, in the assemblies in Crete, must be men known by their godly character, conduct and competency. Such qualifications were unquestionably the effect of the operation of the indwelling Spirit of God. They were to be blameless, having a good family testimony. Each must be possessed of the following characteristics: not selfwilled, not soon angry, no brawler, no striker, not greedy of filthy lucre; given to hospitality, a lover of good, soberminded, just, holy, temperate; holding to the faithful word which is according to the teaching. Only such were to be "appointed". Only by holding to the Word of God themselves could they exhort in the sound doctrine and convict the gainsayers.

What is important to observe is that evidence of the character and conduct in the life precede any appointment or recognition. God raises up and fits men to possess these requisites apart from institutional training and ecclesiastical ordination.

Those who have already been raised up and are discharging the duties of oversight should watch the lives of young men, with a view to discerning what the Spirit of God is doing in them to prepare for the continuance of such responsibilities. And let younger men seek help from God to live and walk according to the Scriptures, in holiness and righteousness, in absolute devotion to Christ, in separation from the world, so that if the Holy Spirit should give them the privilege of continuing the testimony of an assembly and acting as overseers, they may be ready for recognition by the assembly, according to 1 Thessalonians 5. 12, 13.

We can be thankful to God for calling and preparing numbers of men for the work of the gospel in this and other lands. But it is from existing assemblies that such are commended to God, Acts 13. 1–3; 16. 1–3, and the commendation is given by those who are stewards of God, caring for the assembly life and testimony, tending the flock, Acts 20. 28. It should be borne in mind that these overseeing brethren were formerly young men whom the Lord was preparing for the carrying out of such responsibilities. Let assemblies pray for the raising up of such, especially in days of abounding error and of departure from the teaching of the Word of God. The missionary calling may be more attractive than that of an overseer in a local assembly, but those who, being exercised in heart about it, seek to respond to the call and prepare themselves accordingly, will receive present help from the Lord, and reward in the day to come.

There are evidences that here and there God is raising up young men who are manifesting qualifications for the deeply responsible work of the spiritual care of assemblies. This calls for thankfulness, for constant prayer for all such, and for the provision of others. Only thus can the testimony of assemblies on scriptural lines be really effective, through the power of the Holy Spirit.

The work of such men is called "a good work", 1 Tim. 3. 1. The word *kalos*, "good", signifies that which is honourable, goodly, noble. The character of the work is determined by the character of those who do it. It will be well therefore to observe what this chapter in 1 Timothy says in this respect in the Revised Version.

The overseer is, firstly, to be "without reproach": his life, past and present, must be entirely free from anything inconsistent with the responsibility of spiritual leadership. Secondly, his married life (if married; it does not say he must have a wife) must be exemplary. While the avoidance of polygamy was enjoined in a general condition when it was common, what is laid down involves the necessity for the strictest purity in regard to the opposite sex, and complete abstention from anything of an unholy nature in this respect. Thirdly, he must be "temperate", i.e., self-restrained; the word implies that watchfulness which guards against any kind of excess. Fourthly, "soberminded", a word which, in the original, suggests that discretion of mind which avoids mere levity on the one hand and a gravity which is characterized by moroseness on the other hand. Fifthly, "orderly", decent, not merely in outward demeanour, but in temper and spirit, avoiding that pride and self-will which make for disorder in temperament and habit.

These five have to do more especially with the inner self; the following ten relate to effects on others. Sixthly, he is to be "given to hospitality"; the word literally means love of strangers, and suggests a readiness to entertain others than friends and acquaintances, cf. Rom. 12. 13; Heb. 13. 2; 1 Tim. 5. 10. Seventhly, "apt to teach", skilled in imparting instruction; he may not have the gift of public speaking, but he must have such a knowledge of God and of the Scriptures that he is able to impart instruction to children of God, whether young in the faith or those of maturer spiritual life. Eighthly, "no brawler", the word literally means "given to wine"; as, however, that condition leads to fierce and abusive language, the overseer is to be entirely free from that kind of speech. Ninthly, "no striker"; he who is given to abuse in speech is liable to violence of act.

Tenthly, he is to be "gentle"; the word suggests that combination of forbearance and considerateness that deals with facts and deeds in a humane and kindly spirit, and does not easily take offence. The eleventh quality puts this negatively: "not contentious", i.e., free from a quarrelsome spirit, from a readiness to dispute, which so often leads to loss of temper, cf. 2 Tim. 2. 24. The twelfth is also negative: he must be "no lover of money". There are two aspects of this (which represents a single word in the original), one, that of freedom from covetousness, whether in the matter of money or anything else, the other that of generosity and liberality.

The thirteenth relates to one who has a household or family: he must be "one that ruleth well his own house, having his children in subjection with all gravity", that is, with seemliness of demeanour. This indicates that combination of authority, kindliness and benevolence which helps children to find a delight in honouring their parents. The presence of children so trained makes a true home. The character of his family has an important bearing upon his service and influence as an overseer. "If a man know not how to rule his own house, how shall he take care of the church of God?" The change of verb is significant (though "rule" is used in 5. 17 regarding the church). A well ordered house is a test of a married man's fitness to care for God's children. The fourteenth is again negative: "not a novice, lest being puffed up he fall into the condemnation of the devil"; he must have had years of experience in the things of God, in the truths relating to Christian life and to those of a local church. Otherwise there is a danger of pride and ambition and their condemnation. The fifteenth and last relates to the world, "them that are without". They are shrewdly observant of the moral life of believers, and ever ready to remark upon evil living, slackness and unreliability.

These qualifications have this in view, that the testimony of the life of those in responsibility in an assembly may be consistent with the Name of the Lord and with doctrines of the faith. All this should not deter young men from seeking the guidance of God as to the high and holy privileges of overseership and its consequent rewards.

DISCIPLINE

Discipline and the Believer

by E. L. H. OGDEN

A study on the ways of God with His people

TO DISCIPLINE HIS PEOPLE is a prerogative which God has exercised throughout the ages. Its object has always been and will continue to be His own ultimate glory, whether it be the exclusive vindication of His holiness, or the refining and development of the character of His child.

Scripture teaches much on the subject and it can best be appreciated through three avenues of study.

Paternal Discipline *affecting the* CHARACTER. Displayed through the Bible like a rod held in the hand of the all-wise, just and loving God, discipline is seen to affect the lives of those upon whom it was administered, thereby to establish them as examples from which many lessons may be learned today. It is God's purpose that all His children should live lives worthy of their godly vocation, and He would therefore have them trained in His own school of experience. In that school He fits, nurtures, teaches and trains His own, that so educated each may yield to Him the peaceable fruit of righteousness. Christ Himself is thereby formed and manifested in and through the one taught.

God administered discipline in three ways.

1. *Punitive.* The terrible end of Korah, Dathan and Abiram, together with their families, shows how fearful is the holy judgment of God. Their sin was that of pride which rejected God's authority and refused to recognize God's servants. God has no compromise with pride and there was no pardon for

those who displayed it. Although God does not dispense such discipline upon His people today, since He acts in longsuffering and grace in this dispensation, a review of this example will produce a chastened understanding of the wrath of God upon sin.

2. *Judicial*. This emphasizes God's righteousness. Moses disobeyed in striking the rock, and lost the privilege of leading the people into the promised land. Saul despised the principles of God's rule, and lost his throne. David displeased God in numbering the people, and lost seventy thousand men as well as the confidence of many. In David's case, others suffered, this being a sobering and challenging fact. In each case God's *will* had been violated; His *word* had been disobeyed; His *rule* had been rejected; His *law* had been ignored. In each case, the people saw God's just dealing and were made conscious of its rightness.

3. *Corrective*. This is the discipline of the family. It is a necessary part of the upbringing (the instruction and training) of the child. Sometimes the child must suffer loss or chastisement. The writer to the Hebrews deals with this side of discipline very explicitly, Heb. 12. 5–13. His quotation from the book of Proverbs reminds us that we are not to treat such chastening lightly, nor faint when rebuked, knowing that it is the Lord who chastens. The word for chastening (*paideia*) was used to describe the whole training and education of the child. It also speaks of the correction and curbing of passions, and includes the thought of instruction which has as its object the increase of virtue and the moulding of godlikeness in the character. It is not punishment, but a corrective measure dealing with what is displeasing to the Lord, and encouraging what is well pleasing to Him. Chastening was, and still is, a proof of God's love to the chastened one, and is the evidence of sonship. In this passage, a comparison is drawn between the character and object of the earthly father's discipline and that of the Father of our spirits, vv. 9–10. The earthly father's discipline could never be perfect because first it is for the brief period of youth, and then because human parents are fallible and are sometimes moved by anger rather than by sound

judgment. In consequence of these facts, it is possible for mistakes to be made in the discipline of the child. When our Father disciplines, it is always perfect, bringing results which can conform our lives to the image of His Son. This profound passage reminds us that "no chastening for the present seemeth to be joyous, but grievous: nevertheless afterward it yieldeth the peaceable fruit of righteousness unto them which are exercised thereby", v. 11.

It is important to emphasize that much corrective discipline is not the result of sin. When He brings us into the chastening chamber, we know that we can trust Him. He knows the purpose of the testing experience; He knows when to start and when to cease; He is too wise to make a mistake, and too loving to be unkind. His ultimate purpose is that the Lord Jesus Christ may be formed in us, and that His character may be displayed through us. The pattern must be weaved, the pottery moulded, the branch purged, the gold refined; looking back we shall sing with deeper understanding:

> With mercy and with judgment my web of time He wove,
>   And aye the dews of sorrow were lustred by His love;
> I'll bless the hand that guided, I'll bless the heart that planned,
>   When throned where glory dwelleth in Immanuel's land.

Pastoral Discipline *affecting the* COMPANY. The most precious organisms on earth today are the local churches in which the Lord is owned as Head. In a dark world they shine as lights, a thought enlarged in the description given by the apostle John in the vision on the isle of Patmos (Revelation 1). Then he saw seven golden lampstands, in the midst of which stood the Lord Himself robed in a garment which in the light of what follows is a robe of government; see Isa. 22. 21. The lampstands speak of the churches amongst which the Lord is seen as moving in chapters two and three. In the capacity of Governor or Head, He exercises the right to pass verdict upon the conditions He sees, and He rewards and disciplines as He knows best. Aaron had the responsibility of tending the lampstands in the tabernacle, a charge given him by God Himself. The local church is a lampstand ordered according to God's purpose and beautified by her Head, even Christ. Nevertheless, the Lord depends upon those whom He appoints to ensure that the light is kept undimmed. The Lord walks among His people in local church character, but delegates (as He delegated the angels of the seven churches) to make known His mind concerning the conditions He sees. In order that the assemblies shall fulfil their functions as lampstands and lights, training and discipline are necessary. To provide for this and to teach the mind of Christ, He raises up men to oversee and shepherd the flock. Such men put into practice those things which should characterize a church of God, and they seek to maintain the sovereignty of the Holy Spirit and the Headship of Christ. This is pastoral discipline, and it involves training and correction.

When exhorting the Thessalonians concerning their acknowledgement of those who are over them (as guides) in the Lord, 1 Thess. 5. 12, Paul uses the word "admonish" of their ministry, a word better rendered "train by the word" – i.e., warnings based upon instruction. Those who are guides in the Lord are entrusted with the training of the assembly. The feeding of the lambs and the tending of the sheep is their responsibility and privilege. It must not, however, be a negative training. Admonition must have as its purpose the showing of a better way, based upon the Word of God. In this way the Lord disciplines the local assembly. It should be continuous, not only by oral teaching and ministry, but by example too. Pastoral discipline sometimes assumes a corrective character which must always have restoration as its ultimate object. Upon the sad occasion when sin is discovered in the assembly it must be judged in the spirit of humility, and whatever discipline is necessary must be recognized by the whole assembly, appreciating the hand of God in the action of the elders. This will have the same wholesome effect as was the case in Corinth: "what carefulness . . . what fear, yea, what vehement desire, yea, what zeal . . . In all things ye have approved yourselves", 2 Cor. 7. 11.

As in a natural family, so in the spiritual family of the local church there is need for loving discipline in the spirit of the Lord's own character – "full of grace and truth". This is the discipline that corrects those who would walk contrary to the mind of the Lord, that seeks out the ones absent by reason of coldness of heart, that edifies, educates and encourages. This is much needed today, since an undisciplined assembly is like a family without parental control.

How is such discipline to be administered and maintained and by what manner of person? By godly men, in the spirit of meekness, spiritually equipped and mature in the holy things of God. Only by those who have known the heavy burden of souls entrusted to their care can true scriptural discipline be maintained. Only one who has himself been moulded in God's school is able to use with holy fear the rod of discipline in the local church. A company of the Lord's people will reflect the character of its elders, so the prayer of all who are jealous for the testimony of the Lord in the local church should be that God will raise up those who by example and precept shall lead His own into ever deepening experiences with Himself. Elders thus truly ordained by God will ensure that pastoral discipline with its manifold blessings may increase.

Personal Discipline *affecting the* CONDUCT. The Revised Version of 2 Timothy 1. 7 says that God has given us the spirit of "discipline". Exhortation to self-control and the discipline of the mind underlies the two letters of Paul to Timothy to whom so much had been entrusted. His writings to this young man emphasize the principle that one whom God would take up must be disciplined and strong in the grace of the Lord. We shall now review some aspects of discipline enjoined upon Timothy.

1. *The discipline of conflict:* "Fight the good fight of the faith", 1 Tim. 6. 12 R.V. The word *agonizo* as used in the context means "to contend for a prize". Whether it is a conflict or a contest, the verb implies a disciplined struggle, while the tense shows that the striving is a continuous process. The Christian life is meant to be one of victory, and for this it is necessary that we discipline ourselves. We are called to strive in the conflict and contest of the faith, which is the whole treasury of doctrine. It requires diligent control to contend earnestly, and strict discipline of mind lest we falter

in the way. In other words, the discipline of conflict demands a single eye.

2. *The discipline of separation:* "No man that warreth entangleth himself with the affairs of this life", 2 Tim. 2. 4. It should be observed that reference is made to "this life" not "this world". Paul is not concerned here with worldliness. He is concerned lest Timothy should be unduly involved in the affairs of every day living. There is nothing basically wrong with such affairs until they entangle the man and keep him from pleasing the Lord in his testimony and witness. The lesson is that there must be renunciation of anything that hinders the purpose of such testimony and witness, namely the honour and glory of the Lord Jesus Christ in the life of His followers. This is not easy; it requires discipline to live so heartily for the Lord that all else is held lightly.

3. *The discipline of suffering:* we are to "endure hardness", 2 Tim. 2. 3. The soldier character of the Christian life is again to the fore. Timothy needed to be taught the discipline of fortitude. A better rendering may be "take your share of suffering". Every believer must expect to suffer in some measure for the testimony's sake, and to stand firm at such times requires self-discipline which can only be inspired by an ever increasing appreciation of the privileges of our high calling in Christ Jesus. In 1 Corinthians, Paul wrote, "every man that striveth for the mastery is temperate in all things . . . I therefore so run, not as uncertainly; so fight I, not as one that beateth the air: but I keep under my body, and bring it into subjection: lest that by any means, when I have preached to others, I myself should be a castaway", that is, "should make shipwreck of my testimony", 9. 25–27. Here is a personal discipline exemplified: a sober outlook, a straight run, a solid fight. These demand discipline of mind and soundness of purpose. The wonderful vessels of our bodies can thus become controlled and disciplined so that they may become vehicles of power. These lessons can only be learned by personal application and determination. They cannot be learned in our own strength, but we "can do all things through Christ which strengtheneth" us, Phil. 4. 13.

May the Lord so work upon us and in us that we may be wise servants, teachable saints, and obedient sons perfected in all things for the glory of His wondrous name.

Discipline

by A. G. CLARKE

Meaning of Discipline. This word does not occur in our English Bible but the idea is there under the term "chastening" (Greek *paideia* and cognates). In a wider sense it signifies training by instruction or correction; in a narrower sense correction only is in view. We should distinguish between discipline *of* an individual believer or assembly and discipline *by* an assembly. The former is by direct action of the Lord and is His prerogative alone. The latter is His mediate action through the assembly and is its solemn duty. The one has to do with order in the "family" of God, the sphere of relationship; the other with order in the "house" of God, the sphere of responsibility. The former is illustrated by 1 Corinthians 11. 29–32, the latter by 1 Corinthians 5. 1–13. Distinguish also between God's judgments inflicted in just anger upon the ungodly world and the chastening of His own children, which is a seal of sonship and proof of the Father's love, Heb. 12. 5–13; cf. Rev. 3. 19. Discipline by direct action of the Lord is commended as a most profitable study, but our lesson is concerned rather with *discipline by the assembly*. This is a matter which is almost completely ignored in the sects of Christendom, though definitely enjoined in God's Word. Discipline is the more necessary because of the lawless spirit of the age, which has forced itself into the churches owing to the worldliness and carnality of Christians, a spirit that characterized the days of Israel's judges, Jud. 21. 25.

Three *assembly* acts are to be noted; (a) the reception of all true believers; (b) the rejection (i.e. excommunication) of all gross offenders; (c) the restoration of duly repentant offenders. The assembly may not shelve any of these responsibilities and leave matters with the Lord, 1 Cor. 5. 12, 13. The church at Corinth was sharply reproved for lack of prompt action in a flagrant case of immorality in the midst. They had adopted an easy tolerance of the evil and were even "puffed up" by the possession of many spiritual "gifts". Neglect of discipline dishonours the Lord, hinders the Holy Spirit and mars assembly testimony. Mutual concern is to be exercised on the principle of 1 Corinthians 12. 25, 26.

Discipline, then, in the sense of this paper, refers to methods adopted to deal with persons who upset godly order in the assembly.

Objects of Discipline. *Negative Aspect*—not a trial of faith but of conduct; i.e. it is not to decide whether a person is a believer or not, 2 Tim. 2. 19, nor to get rid of a troublesome brother, toward whom patience is to be shown in grace, and prayer to God made concerning him.

Positive Aspect—is (a) to *secure restoration* of the offender, 2 Cor. 2. 5–11; Gal. 6. 1; (b) to *maintain the integrity* of the assembly before God as a "temple" fit for His presence in the midst, and before men so as to remove all appearance of connivance with the evil; (c) to *furnish a warning* to all the saints lest a careless walk lead to similar lapse; (d) to *vindicate the name of the Lord* by the removal, as far as humanly possible, of the reproach brought upon it before the world. If not immediately dealt with, evil spreads like leaven, 1 Cor. 5. 6; Gal. 5. 9; cf. the law as to "leprous stones" in a house, Lev. 14. 40, 41; also Joshua 7 where Achan's sin is seen to involve in its consequences the whole congregation of Israel.

Specific Cases of Discipline. Contrary to an idea commonly prevailing, excommunication is *not* the only form of discipline. God's Word shows this is to be resorted to only as a last expedient. Seven categories of offence, some more serious than others, seem to be indicated:

1. *The Personal Offender*, Matt. 18. 15–20; Luke 17. 3, 4.
NATURE OF OFFENCE—purely an individual matter, such as evil-speaking or breach of trust.
METHOD OF PROCEDURE—note three stages; no question of excision; "shew fault"; Luke has "rebuke" (call to account:

require explanation); "hear", Luke has "repent", which implies apology and amends; note measure of forgiveness, Matt. 18. 21, 22, 35; Luke 17. 4; Eph. 4. 32; Col. 3. 13. Second stage is still of a private character; third stage if unsuccessful, results in the offender being treated by the offended one ("unto thee"—not the whole assembly) as an outsider. Until the matter is straightened out there can be no fellowship between the two. Matthew 5. 22–24 is from the offender's view-point, one who knows there is real cause for complaint against himself.

2. The Overtaken Brother, Gal. 6. 1–3.

NATURE OF OFFENCE—a temporary lapse; not pursuing an evil course but one "pursued" and overtaken by temptation; tripped up at an unguarded moment.

METHOD OF PROCEDURE—Greek signifies to re-adjust, to reduce (as a dislocated joint), to mend (as broken nets, Mark 1. 19); cf. 1 Tim. 5. 20, which though primarily of an elder conveys a general principle. The rule therefore is: private offence, private rebuke; public offence, public rebuke.

3. The Meddlesome Idler, 2 Thess. 3. 6–15; 1 Thess. 4. 11, 12.

NATURE OF OFFENCE—Walking disorderly, especially disobedience to the Word, 14; Greek lit. "out of step", indicating inco-ordination or insubordination. The form specified here is "busy-bodies" (lit. "working around"), that is, visiting the saints not for edification but for gossip, evil-speaking and "hanging-on".

METHOD OF PROCEDURE—Warning by elders, 1 Thess. 5. 14; if this proves unavailing, "withdrawal" by saints, 2 Thess. 3. 6, 14, not putting away but curtailing of fellowship, 15.

4. The Unprofitable Talker, Titus 1. 9–14; 1 Cor. 14. 26, 29.

NATURE OF OFFENCE—Wasting time of the saints in profitless "ministry", 14.

METHOD OF PROCEDURE—Warning and sharp reproof, 13 in order to silence, 10, 11. Elders are responsible to prevent such abuse of liberty, 9. Neglect is seen to lead to factions, Titus 3. 9–11; "heretical" here does not refer to denying the faith but to one who in self-will seeks to gather adherents to his opinions, especially in matters of interpretation or others not of fundamental importance. Such conduct is factious and may even end in open division, see next paragraph.

5. *The Division Maker*, Rom. 16. 17–20 R.V.; Titus 3. 9–11; Acts 20. 30.

NATURE OF OFFENCE—Causing divisions and affording occasions of stumbling to others. This includes legalists and others who distort some elements of truth, unduly swaying the saints to the fostering of a party spirit even to divisions. Differences in opinion or in judgment should *not* be allowed to lead to this.

METHOD OF PROCEDURE—In the first place reproof may be effective, Gal. 2. 11–14; 1 Tim. 5. 20. If unavailing, "mark", "turn away from", "avoid" are terms used of proper action. If this rule be followed by all the saints, division cannot result. At Corinth, though saints were professedly one, there was imminent danger of division into rival sects, 1 Cor. 1. 10–15, not an evidence of spirituality but of carnality. The devil is the instigator of this evil and the flesh is ever ready to respond, Rom. 16. 20, 18. Note the double warning to, and double responsibility of, elders, Acts 20. 28–31.

6. *The Gross Evil-doer*, 1 Cor. 5. 1–13; 6. 9, 10.

NATURE OF OFFENCE—A grave moral lapse such as listed, 11; "Fornicator" covers all cases of illicit sexual intercourse. "Covetous" covers all cases of evil desire for gain as shown in deeds; e.g. all forms of gambling, sharp practice in business, etc., cf. Eph. 5. 5; 2 Pet. 2. 14; 1 Tim. 6. 9–11. The term "idolater" includes any active association with false systems of worship (even though bearing a Christian label), sorcery and spiritualism. "Reviler" covers vilification, defamation of character and false accusations—one who is given to this. "Drunkard" suggests one guilty of the habitual sin of intemperance, not one coming under category (2). "Extortioner" would include various forms of dishonesty, e.g. misappropriation of property or funds, fraud, profiteering especially in the food of the poor, James 5. 1–6.

METHOD OF PROCEDURE—"Put away (not simply denying fellowship at the Lord's supper) from among yourselves", signifies formal rejection from the assembly fellowship to be followed by severance of all social relations, 11–13. Careful investigation of the circumstances may be called for, but in Corinth there was open sin with facts well known, hence no inquiry was needed. The offender is thus thrown back into the sphere of the world where' Satan rules and becomes fully exposed to the enemy's attacks, 5; 1 Tim. 1. 20; 2 Tim. 2. 25, 26. That the discipline in this particular case was effectual, resulting in the offender's repentance and restoration, is seen by referring to 2 Corinthians 2. 1–11; 7. 9–12.

7. *The Unsound Teacher*, 2 Pet. 2. 1–3 R.V.; 2 John 9–11; 1 Tim. 4. 1; 2 Cor. 11. 13–15.

NATURE OF OFFENCE—Propagation of evil doctrine. This points to fundamental error, not to mere differences of interpretation in non-essentials, e.g. dispensational teaching, though the latter and indeed any over-stressed doctrine unwatched may grow into "heresy". Evil doctrine can be more destructive than loose morality, for common opinion is swift to denounce the latter among Christians yet gives little heed to the former.

METHOD OF PROCEDURE—is the same as with moral evil. It is "leaven" which must be purged out, Gal. 5. 9 with 1 Cor. 5. 6, 7. Note that the apostle's action is similar in both cases— 1 Cor. 5. 5 with 2 Tim. 2. 18 and 1 Tim. 1. 20. No social intercourse is permitted, 2 John 9–11.

General Principles of Discipline. *Judicial Fairness is always to be Employed.* The Christian standard is higher, not lower, than that of world courts, 1 Cor. 6. 2, 3. Godly order suggests investigation by elders, who should reject unsupported testimony, Matt. 18. 16; 1 Tim. 5. 9. They should then furnish the assembly with a brief report of essentials only. The assembly (not simply elders) acts in "putting away" when necessary.

Partiality is to be rigidly excluded, 1 Tim. 5. 21; James 3. 17; 2. 1–4. Natural relationship or friendship must not influence judgment, Acts 15. 36–39. Extremes are to be avoided, for undue severity divides the assembly and undue lenience increases the evil. Unbalanced action destroys the confidence of the saints and dishonours God, i.e. harshness in minor matters while neglecting divine principles, Matt. 15. 1-20; 23. 23, 24; Luke 11. 42; Rom. 14. 1-3; 15. 7. Such lack of balance is to be noted in Israel, Judges chs. 17-20. There was unanimous and violent reaction against a case of immorality, yet laxity and indifference towards a case of gross idolatry which brought dishonour upon the name of the Lord.

Scripture Order is to be strictly Observed. The "cutting off" of an assembly or assemblies is quite unknown in Scripture. Carnal Corinth was not so "cut off". In Revelation chs. 2,3, though the Lord has much to reprove in several of the churches, He does not even hint at the "cutting off" of any by the other churches; it is solely the Lord's prerogative to remove the "lampstand" if He sees fit, 2. 5; 3. 16. Where grave moral or doctrinal evil is tolerated in an assembly, godly ones may have to consider withdrawal from it as from a "disorderly" person, but only after all protests have proved unavailing and other measures fail. Action must not be hasty and there should be much prayer exercise.

Assembly Decisions are to be Loyally Supported. Misplaced sympathy only encourages the offender in evil-doing and so hinders restoration. It puts the sympathizer into the class of the "unruly" as partaker of the evil, 1 Tim. 5. 22; 2 John 11, making him liable to discipline also. No believer under discipline in one assembly should readily be received by another. If, after due inquiry by elders, the first assembly is adjudged to have been over hasty or too severe, it would be well to approach that assembly with a view to reconciliation. To do otherwise would be subversive of godly order and might involve a breach of fellowship between the assemblies concerned.

Offender's Withdrawal is to be Juridically Ignored. Ceasing to attend the meetings on the part of an offender does not absolve the assembly from the duty of dealing with the case. It is essential, however, to differentiate between absence through coldness of heart, which is a matter for shepherd care, and absence to avoid discipline.

Offender's Restoration is to be Sufficiently Attested. Restoration to the Lord precedes restoration to assembly fellowship. True repentance should be manifested by departure from the evil and making restitution where necessary. Scripture does not advocate undue delay, 2 Cor. 2. 5–11. Wise discernment is here needed, coupled with true brotherly love, 1 Cor. 13. 4–8; Gal. 6. 2. The recovered one should refrain, for a time at least, from public service for God to prove his sincerity by a humble spirit and a consistent walk. There is no definite rule as to this (e.g. Peter's restoration, John 21), though it must be remembered that our Lord knew Peter's heart, whereas our knowledge is limited. Lack of commendation for some special service or disapproval for it, Acts 15. 36ff, or disqualification for overseership, 1 Tim. 3. 1–6, does not affect church fellowship.

GOD'S WORKMEN

⋘⋙⋘⋙⋘⋙

The Young Believer in the Assembly

by RICHARD D. ENGLISH

WE MAY WELL be thankful, in these days when in many of the denominational gatherings there are but a few young folk to be found, except where the attraction is some worldly activity which can never lead any to the Saviour, that in many assemblies there are active and eager groups of young believers. They are of course, the church of the future, and it is the duty of the elder brethren, not only to care for them in the nurture and admonition of the Lord, but also so to set them an example that they may say without hesitation, "This is the way, walk ye in it".

Aims of the Elder Brethren. It is unfortunate that in some assemblies the elder brethren, as regards their attitude to the young believers in their care, may be divided into two camps, neither of which can bring the results all wish to see. Firstly, there are those who are convinced that their mission is to rule the flock as despots, and who only acknowledge the presence of the tender lambs and the yearlings in occasional words of advice addressed to the "young people". Such are they who always regard any new suggestion of ways of service with the coming generation as being suspect, because it was not done in earlier days. Should the under-twenties themselves wish to carry on some activity within the assembly, there is from this band of elders much holding up of hands in would-be holy horror. "Let them come to the gospel meeting and the Bible reading; that was always good enough in our young days". On the other hand, there are those elders – often the ones who do not take kindly to advancing years (and wish

still to be recognized as being youthful, if not exactly young) –
who think the young people can do nothing wrong. However
unsuitable the scheme they suggest, it is "giving the young
people a chance to express themselves" and the assembly
premises and finances must be devoted to this cause, regardless
of what others may think. Indeed, if one so much as suggests
that there may be a wiser course, a middle way between their
attitude and the severity of the die-hards, he is at once condemned as not wanting to encourage the young people.

Fortunate, then, the assembly where some at least of the
elders are able to keep an even keel as they sail between the
Scylla and Charybdis of despotism and indiscipline in this
matter; they will be able to minister alike to old and young
as their spiritual common-sense suggests may be necessary.

This ministry takes many forms, in all of which the elder
should be blameless. Paul calls for him to be *vigilant*, 1 Tim.
3. 2. This quality will not only enable him to see the lamb
getting into difficulties and to help him back into the way; it
will also keep him vigilant as to the example he sets to those
who respect his position, and so give them cause to esteem
him highly in love for his work's sake, 1 Thess. 5. 13.

It is not sufficient that the elder should be careful of his
behaviour, in the spirit of 1 Corinthians 8. 9, lest his liberty in
some matter become a stumbling-block to them that are weak;
he must also watch his behaviour in the ordinary course of
assembly life. Perhaps the most sacred duty of those who
recognize their priestly responsibilities is in public prayer and
praise; let their words be such as express the mind of the
flock. Many a young believer has been driven from the prayer
meetings by the lengthy theological discourses of some of his
elder brethren, which in some cases can only be distinguished
from their equally unedifying ministry by the fact that when
they are praying their words are interspersed with such phrases
as "Thou knowest, Father", and "as we read in Thy Word".
Nobody, young or old, will object to a long prayer if obviously
both fervent and effective, but length without fervour never
made anyone appear a righteous man.

Again, elder brethren are, according to Paul, to be *apt to
teach*. Vigilance should be exercised in this question of aptness.
It is presuming upon the patience of the assembly – if not

downright bad-mannered – to occupy time, particularly on a Lord's Day morning, in talking for talking's sake. The young believer is probably quicker than any to recognize the brother who *must* say something for what he is – a carnally-minded self-glorifier. Equally, he who has something to say which is worth hearing, quickly has the ear of the young believer who wants to learn.

How dishonouring to our Lord it is when brethren, who should know better how men ought to behave themselves in the house of God, 1 Tim. 3. 15 R.V., allow a group of young people to get the upper hand, so that the assembly's place of meeting is turned into a place of turmoil. It is one of the signs of the times that disobedience and love of pleasure rather than of God, 2 Tim. 3, shall rule, but this should not be so among the people of God. How frequently is "chorus-singing" allowed to degenerate into a shouting-match while the youngsters have their choice – and how little is this choice guided into the right way! The elders have a considerable responsibility in the matter of the choruses and hymns which they allow to be used in the various meetings. Many choruses today suffer from having too "swingy" a tune; the sacred words might as well be abandoned, so little chance have they of making any impression on the jazz-soaked minds of the present generation. Some hymns suffer from a very different fault – they are so antiquated, their tunes so pointless and so very similar to each other, that they attract no attention at all.

An elder is required to have his children in subjection with all gravity. It is a notable fact that the "children" in the assembly enjoy far more during any meeting in which a proper standard of discipline and gravity is maintained than when the "leader" weakly submits to the demands of some rowdy minority. To be successful, meetings for young people must be brisk and full of interest, either from subject matter or change of activity. The young believers who show aptitude for it should be asked to take a controlled share in the meeting, though usually not in its arrangement – where experience is especially valuable. If this method of leading on the younger ones is employed consistently, they will learn from the older generation and at the same time learn for themselves how to apply their own talents. It can never be right to ask an untaught youngster to take a place of responsibility until he has both helped an older believer in the work and learned from the Scriptures how to serve in a God-pleasing manner.

Aims of the Young Believer. Thus far we have viewed our subject particularly from the point of view of those who are older. Let us be practical from the other approach also.

Paul's own son in the faith, Timothy, has doubtless served as an example to young belivers all down the Christian age. Certain instructions are given him in chapter 4 of the first letter, with the comment "meditate upon these things; give thyself wholly to them; that thy profiting may appear to all", I Tim. 4. 15. Now it is a very certain fact that without attention to the things of God, no young believer will ever take his (or her) place in the assembly with profit, either to himself or to others. Let us then look together at the things to which Paul drew young Timothy's attention. They will teach us how to live in the company of older believers in such a way that no man will "despise thy youth".

"Be thou an example of the believers". This, which Paul puts first, is all too often entirely forgotten in our present assembly life. The eager faith of the spiritual young believer, pure and single in purpose, as shown in the manner of his address to his elders, in his whole walk and the love which he shows to all, may often recall to some traveller in the way his own early devotion to his Lord. How precious that the life of a young believer, sanctified by constant attention to the prime necessities of spiritual life, can be an inspiration to every member of the assembly. "Much more those members of the body, which seem to be more feeble, are necessary; . . . God hath tempered the body together, having given more abundant honour to that part which lacked", I Cor. 12. 22, 24.

There is a practical out-working of this example which all young men would do well to observe. If they do not like the manner in which their elders monopolize the prayer-meeting, let them show by short and simple petitions that men are not always heard for their much speaking. If they do not like to listen to the older ones theorizing in the conversational Bible-reading, let them ask questions which by their contact with the needs of daily life will bring their older brethren to speak on a level more easily understood and more profitable to all.

Assembly government. Paul knew well that pride is the greatest breeder of failure in the Christian life. That is why in 1 Timothy 3. 6 he forbade responsibility in the assembly being taken by a novice. The young believer has no experience in this field and should not try to exalt himself into it before his turn. This is one sphere in which the famous saying of a statesman of recent years, "time is on our side", is really true. The young believer can expect his turn, in good time; for the older generation will pass away. If the younger ones think they can do better in the matter of assembly rule, their profiting will appear to all in due course. This is not to say that a young brother who is well-taught in the Scriptures may not sometimes be able to point his elders to a way of obedience which they had not seen, Job 32. 6–11. The elders in some assemblies, through lack of teaching, may perhaps be relatively ill-taught themselves, and therefore more liable to error. If they are spiritually minded they will hear God's Word, whoever explains it to them.

Paul bids the young believer

Give attention to reading. Without this no progress can possibly be made. Even in the assemblies it is unwise to accept tradition as a teacher. The Word of God must provide us in all things with the reason for the hope that is in us. Unless we are thoroughly and constantly familiar with what it teaches, we shall again and again find that we fail to please God in assembly life as well as privately. "Brethren, be not children in understanding", 1 Cor. 14. 20. "Seek that ye may excel to the edifying of the church", 1 Cor. 14. 12.

Exhortation and doctrine, referred to in 1 Timothy 4. 13, were particularly to be in the service of Timothy as he went out with the fellowship of the elders, expressed in their laying their hands on him. A similar service will come the way of any young believer with the gift, if he gives attention to reading.

How many young believers stay children spiritually, and in the assembly, because they neglect the gift that is in them?

If it is wrong for an older brother to take time in the meeting in saying things which are not edifying (and it is wrong), it is equally harmful to the meeting if a younger brother fails to give his contribution when the Spirit requires it. He may say he has never taken any previous part in public worship or service, or he may feel his knowledge of God's ways is insufficient for the occasion. If it is the former, let him no longer hesitate; if it is the latter, let him give attention to reading, let him meditate upon these things and give himself wholly to them.

If a young man wilfully neglects his gift, the whole body will suffer. He will have no profiting, no increase in his talents, and when his turn comes to take the lead in assembly life, he will then find himself for ever relegated to a spiritual back-bench, and the assembly the poorer for losing his gift. "Take heed unto thyself, and unto the doctrine", says Paul; "continue in them: for in doing this thou shalt both save thyself, and them that hear thee", 1 Tim. 4. 16.

To sum up then, the young believer must by his life and pure faith be an example to the whole church; and he must, by study and diligence, fit himself to take his place in public ministry when his turn comes. If he does not, all the church will suffer from the loss of talents which God gave him to use. It is not sufficient to say "there are others"; no other has *quite* the same gifts. God forbid that any young believer reading this should become a castaway because of neglecting the gift that is in him.

The Men God Calls

by S. EMERY

THE ACTS OF THE APOSTLES is a delightful collection of Spirit-selected incidents giving us some record of the early days of church history, and to consider this book as a development of church life and practice is calculated to yield the utmost spiritual profit. There is, however, another method of study open to us. The separate jewels of truth herein contained may be lifted out of their rare casket and individually scrutinized; for each wonderful cameo will bear the closest examination. Such a cameo is Acts 13. 1–4a.

Herein we have, described in a few weighty words, the truth concerning the Spirit's call to service which was to issue in a mighty work for God. This incident has not been recorded merely as a matter of history, supplying the initial steps in the life-service of a great apostle, but buried therein are principles applicable to the call of God's servants for all time.

The Character of the Men whom God Calls may be gathered from verse 1.

They were men who recognized their place and part "*in the church that was in Antioch*". They were not individuals who used the assembly as a convenience and boasted of being "free-lances" for God. They realized that they belonged to a local church and in its midst they lived and laboured, so that the Spirit of God, when needing men, found His instruments to hand in the assembly. Here is a much-needed lesson for all in a day when assembly truth is in danger of being lightly esteemed.

They were *men of gift*, whose gift (namely, "prophets and teachers") was already being recognized by the saints. Spiritual gifts are not manufactured by men but are dispensed to the church by a risen, victorious Lord, Eph. 4. 7–11, divided to individuals by the Holy Spirit "according as he pleases", 1 Cor. 12. 11 J.N.D. Christian work of any kind should not be entered upon merely because it is gratifying to personal desires. This has too often been the case, and that, sadly to the detriment of the testimony. How essential it is for young Christians first to seek exercise before the Lord as to the particular talent or talents He has given to them, so that the character of coming work for God may be indicated. And how equally essential for elders to watch carefully for the evidence of such gifts and to encourage their use.

Furthermore, the *gift should be patiently developed and locally exercised*. Inferentially, these five brethren were diligently giving themselves over to learning more fully the divine truth (teachers) and to discerning more fully the divine mind (prophets). Young men and women who, instead of using their time in other things, give the utmost attention

to divine matters are the most likely to be commissioned by
the Master. The spiritually industrious are to be watched and
encouraged, and, whilst every effort should be made to spur
on other young men in the things of God, we must avoid
thrusting them into ministry of any sort just for the sake of
"giving them a turn".

Then, note, these men were working in the assembly
at Antioch in the beautiful *harmony of a team-spirit*. There
was Barnabas, a Levite of Cyprus, 4. 36, a man at one time
of some financial count, already having recognition, 9. 27,
as a leader among the saints, 11. 22–24. Then there was Simeon
whose other name (Niger) may indicate that he was a coloured
man, maybe late of Africa. Lucius was there, a man hailing
from Cyrenaica. Here, too, was Manaen, foster-brother to
Herod, one having contact with the court and of no common
society; and finally Saul, the Jew yet free-born Roman, one
who had ranked high in the religious circles of Jewry. What a
rare diversity – yet what delightful harmony, each having
learned the secret of unity with his brethren. God has little
use for those who are always being a law unto themselves, but
rather seeks for those who, though so strangely different, are
diligently working together in a common yoke.

Finally, in the case of Saul, the value of *humility* seems
to be advanced for our notice. The two men chosen by the
Spirit, stand, one at the top of the list and one as a humble
tailpiece. Saul, the proud, autocratic bigot, is now satisfied
to be the "last man in"! Follow down the ensuing record and
note the order "Barnabas and Saul", vv. 2, 7 – he is still
bringing up the rear. But it is as if God says the man who is
willing to take the last place shall be His first. Consequently,
from verse 43 onwards, with but one or two exceptions, it
becomes "Paul and Barnabas", Paul eventually taking the lead
and Barnabas disappearing from the record. Truly, in the
service of God "he who exalteth himself shall be abased",
so let us be diligent to occupy without mock-modesty, the
last place, for "the last shall be first" for God. The qualities,
therefore, which are to be looked for and encouraged are:
fidelity to the house of God, a divinely bestowed and exercised
gift, harmony with others in local work and witness, and
personal humility in the service of the Lord.

A consideration of Acts 13. 2 would teach us concerning

The Conduct of the Men whom God Calls. The call of God came "as they ministered to the Lord, and fasted". They were busy for God in their own assembly, doing with their might what their hands found to do. There are young men who anticipate doing great things for God in far-off fields who sometimes fail to notice, or to be interested in, spiritual work which lies at their very doors – in their own streets and in their own halls. In this instance God called to wider service the men who were already bearing great burdens in their local assembly. Those who with purpose of heart are already giving themselves to service in their immediate vicinity, executing every labour, however menial, as a ministry "to the Lord" and doing it at personal sacrifice ("fasting"), are the men assemblies need and the men God needs, they being the most likely to be called to further work and greater responsibilities. Let young Christians manifest diligence and interest in the work and witness of their own assembly if they would earn divine and human recognition.

A further glance at verse 2 together with verse 4a would indicate something with regard to

The Spiritual Constitution of the Men whom God Calls. It is obvious that the men themselves and the assembly to which they belonged had ears tuned to catch the breathings of the Holy Spirit, and hearts obedient to His commands when known. They lived in close contact with the Spirit of God, and worked in union with Him. When the Spirit called, His voice was immediately recognized by all and His desire unquestioned. The men and women God needs today, and will most surely use, are not such as are good organizers, or those full of new ideas or who are always wanting to go about the work of the Lord with rules and regulations of man's making, but men who have cultivated Spirit-sensitiveness and always and only "move at the breathing of His will". In verse 2 the Spirit's desire is unhesitatingly received, and in verse 4 it is immediately responded to. Here are the men to observe, men whose lives are under the control of the Spirit of God.

The Consideration of the Assembly for such Men is seen in verse 3. These men who laboured amongst the saints, two of whom the Lord was shortly to thrust out, were undoubtedly those who had won the confidence of the church. This is instanced by the way in which the church immediately "fasted and prayed" on their behalf and showed such ready and heartfelt identification with them by their act of laying on of hands. Men who are likely to be most effective for God, in the assembly or further afield, are those who by their own devotion to the things of God, Christlikeness of walk and spirituality of conduct, have won a warm place in the hearts of their fellow-saints. Such are the men to be encouraged into front-line service for God.

One final word. What must be

The Attitude of the Saints to such Men whom the Lord has, in a greater or lesser degree, separated to wider service, whatever its character – men whose presence was valued and whose absence creates severe loss? We read in verse 4 that, following fasting, prayer and laying on of hands, "they let them go" J.N.D. This infers calm resignation to the divine leading, and a full agreement regarding their going. It was no doubt with many expressions of encouragement and wishes for God-speed they watched them go – their hearts were with them, their prayers for them and their interest in them. Sometimes, when a young man is called to wider service, there is a tendency to regard him as being unfaithful to home responsibilities. Let those who do this, beware lest they be found fighting against God.

In Conclusion: Is there a young man displaying a gift from God and taking every opportunity to develop it? Do we see him, with a heart for the assembly in which God has placed him, exercising his gift with diligence and humility of mind? Is he manifesting readiness of heart to work harmoniously with his brethren, not seeking to aspire to heights at their expense? And is he seen to have a deep spiritual sensitiveness, obeying implicitly the directions of the Spirit of God? Then, encourage him and be ready to observe the ways of God with him. May every young Christian (man or woman) seek so to conform to these essential principles, demonstrated in Holy Scripture, that God at all times may have His will fulfilled in them.

Commendation for Service

by W. E. VINE

THE NEW TESTAMENT RECORDS of the relationship between churches and the servants of God who went forth from them in gospel service indicate sufficiently the mind of the Lord in such matters. He might have sent His servants apart from church relationship, but this was not His will. While the first missionaries went forth in simple dependence upon Him for guidance and support without being under the control or direction of a human society, yet there remained a definite connection between them and the churches with which they had been associated. We may consider the case of

Barnabas and Saul. We are told that the church at Antioch "committed to the grace of God for the work" these two brethren, Acts 14. 26 R.V. The circumstances in which this took place are recorded in the preceding chapter. These prospective missionaries had for some time been ministering to the Lord in the church when the call of the Holy Spirit came: "Separate me Barnabas and Saul for the work whereunto I have called them", Acts 13. 2. In response to this, after a time of fasting and prayer, the elders,* representing the church, "laid hands on them" and "sent them away" (or rather, "let them go"). This gives evidence both of deep exercise of heart before God and of the great importance which the local church attached to the going forth of the Lord's servants from their midst. The question might have been raised whether there was need to fast as well as pray concerning the matter when the will of God and the guidance of the Spirit were so clear. Was there anything more required than merely to obey the command to separate those who had received the call, to hold a farewell meeting and speed them on their way? Certainly more was felt to be necessary for the fulfilment of the will of the Lord. That there was fasting demands our careful consideration. The fasting was not a perfunctory rite nor an act of formal asceticism; it was a

---

* In the context it is the prophets and teachers who laid hands on Barnabas and Saul. *Eds.*

spontaneous expression of self-humiliation before God, under a sense of the great responsibility attaching to the ministry to which He was calling His servants! The exercise of heart concerning it found a fitting accompaniment in either partial or complete abstinence from food for a time. The church took no superficial view of the sending forth of missionaries. The fact of a call from God forbade that; it laid a weight of responsibility upon the hearts of His people which demanded even more than prayer. Nor must we omit to notice the significance of the

Laying on of Hands in this passage. This was not a matter of ordination for the ministry; Barnabas and Saul had already received their divine ordination. They had for some time been prophets and teachers in the church from which they were now setting out. The act of laying on of hands bears directly upon the subject under consideration; upon the relationship between the church and those who were proceeding from it with the Gospel to regions beyond. The church, in recognition of the call and appointment by the Holy Spirit, thus gave through its elders a public expression of its identification with the servants of the Lord in the work that lay before them. Nor did the association of the labourers with the church at Antioch cease with their departure. This is clear from the fact that, upon the fulfilment of their service, they returned thither, "gathered the church together", and "rehearsed all that God had done with them", Acts 14. 27. By the same assembly Paul and Silas were commended at the outset of their second missionary journey, and thither again they returned at its close. The interval between the second and third journey was spent in the same church, and from it Paul set out for the third time. Thus throughout the greater part of his missionary activities there existed a close relationship between the servant of the Lord and the assembly from which he went. The call of God came to these servants of the Lord, and the church commended and encouraged them; the same call, summoning fresh labourers to the field, still makes itself evident in the assemblies of His people. Have they become accustomed to take a lower view of it than did the assembly at Antioch? Is missionary service regarded today with a less serious sense of responsibility than in earliest times? Is the call less divine, or the work of less importance, because of the absence of the apostolic element? Is there less claim upon us for prayer and fasting now than there was in the times of the apostles? Surely, the contrary is the case! Do not these questions deserve the serious attention of all who genuinely have the cause of Christ to heart? The Lord has called

All His Saints to take a definite part in helping forward the gospel. His command, "Go ye . . . and make disciples of all the nations, baptizing them into the name of the Father and of the Son and of the Holy Ghost: teaching them to observe all things whatsoever I commanded you", Matt. 28. 19–20 R.V., was not limited to those to whom He was immediately speaking; for He said, "and lo, I am with you alway, even unto the end of the world". Clearly His word holds good for all His followers until the age reaches its close. The commission could not imply that all were to go in person to other lands; it does, however, indicate that all have a part to fulfil in the great work. An assembly in which God calls an individual to go forth in missionary work, and gives to the saints an evidence of the call, may well rejoice in the privilege afforded of taking part in this way in the furtherance of the gospel in addition to the regular testimony in the immediate vicinity. Other assemblies in the same locality, who have had experience of the life and service of the worker now called to go forth, likewise have the claim upon them of this fellowship. Thus it was that Timothy was commended; he was "well reported of", Acts 16. 2, not only by the brethren in his own assembly in Lystra, but also by those at Iconium in the same district. The privilege of an assembly in being instrumental in sending the gospel by a representative to a remote country is no small one. At the same time, the responsibility involved in commending a worker is very great. When a labourer goes forth in simple dependence upon God for his maintenance, the assembly which commends him thereby associates itself with his conviction that God is so leading him. A commendation, therefore, carries with it the responsibility, first of assistance in any necessary preparations, and then of the continuance of fellowship, as God may enable, throughout the period of the service in which the worker is engaged. The missionary, though at work in another land, is still identified with the assembly from which he went forth. The work carried out is not merely that of the labourer abroad, it is work in which the assembly is collectively engaged. The missionary is not the servant of the assembly; all are fellow-servants of God. Was there not partnership between him and his fellow-saints in service before the call came for the labourer to go? The change of his sphere has not broken the bond of church-fellowship in service; on the contrary the sphere of the assembly has only been enlarged. Let not distance and time diminish the apprehension of the association. The fellowship should be abiding, not only in fact but in realization. The

Commendation of an Assembly should mean more than that an interest will be taken in the work of the one commended. Taking an interest in the work is a poor way of expressing it; the true view is that of fellowship and co-opera-tion. The work may be near or far away; it is, nevertheless, work undertaken by the assembly with which the labourer is identified. A recognition of this will prevent the elder brethren of the assembly from laying hands hastily on a candidate. Commendation cannot rightly be given unless there is an absolute conviction on the part of the elders, as well as of the prospective worker, that the Lord has called the latter to go; and the conviction should be based, not only upon a verbal statement as to the call, but also on the proof of the candidate's fitness, consequent upon the character of the work in which he has been already engaged. But behind this there is the necessary qualification of a good report both in the home life and in such avocation as the candidate may have been follow-ing. If incapacity has been displayed in the latter, how can it be expected that anything different will be shown in the spiritual work of the gospel? What will not do for the ordinary business of this world, cannot surely be suitable for the work of the mission field. Timothy had a good report, and this means more than a good testimony as to his capacities in gospel service. There was the character of his life behind his oral testimony. Then again, one who is going forth with the prospect of serving with fellow-labourers who have been in the country before him, should be expected to have given evidence of his ability to work harmoniously with others, and of a readiness to act in a spirit of subjection to senior workers and to listen to their counsel.

These are some of the considerations which will weigh with elder brethren, who, acting on behalf of the assembly, have before them the question of the commendation of a worker. Where such a one has been proved and approved, how happily can the saints commend their fellow-labourer to the Lord for His guidance and blessing, conscious of the smile of His approval and assured of His power in the life and work of His servant in regions beyond!

Spending and Being Spent

by J. H. LARGE

(Urging the serious re-examination of the responsibilities of those who take the lead among the people of God).

IN APOSTOLIC TIMES the spiritual care of God's people was taken as a very serious business demanding the utmost attention and vigilance, and there is an urgent need to recapture the atmosphere of those days.

With this in mind it will be profitable, if humiliating, to compare the outlook of Paul with the present-day attitude to the things of God and the life of the church, and to ask ourselves what would be the effects if we had leaders with a portion of his spirit.

It is God's normal way to raise up leaders, and people tend to become what the example and influence of their leaders make them. "The Lord stirred up the spirit of Zerubbabel . . . governor of Judah, and the spirit of Joshua . . . the high priest, and the spirit of all the remnant of the people; and they came and did work in the house of the Lord of hosts, their God", Hag. 1. 14.

Love. Think, for example, of the depth and warmth of his affections for the saints. Here was a strong character, a man of iron resolution, and yet he could remind the Ephesian elders of the tears he shed, and could tell the Philippians that he wept as he wrote of those who were the enemies of the cross of Christ. Beneath a manner often made stern by his uncompromising devotion to the cause of Christ there was a warmth of genuine feeling which evoked reciprocal affection, so that the elders wept at the idea of seeing him no more, and Timothy shed tears as the apostle left him at Ephesus. It is all very well to attribute this to the emotionalism of the Oriental – probably we feel so little because we care so little! Tears beget tears. Could the Philippians have remained unmoved by the loving exhortations of a man who, once a bigoted Pharisee and a despiser of Gentile "dogs", could now call God to witness how greatly he longed after them all in the tender compassions of Jesus Christ, who could call them his brethren dearly beloved and longed for, his joy and crown? He was gentle among the Thessalonians with the solicitude of a nursing mother toward her own children, well pleased at having been able to impart his own soul to them because they were dear to him, 1 Thess. 2. 8. So much did their spiritual well-being mean to him that intense anxiety as to the effect of persecution upon their faith, relieved by the news of their steadfastness, brought out the exclamation "Now we live, if ye stand fast in the Lord". Had the news been otherwise something would have died within him, but now he can say "What thanks can we render again to God for you, for all the joy wherewith we joy for your sakes before our God?", 1 Thess. 3. 9. When leaders love the saints like that they will wield a moral authority such as we seldom see today, and which no official position will ever impart.

But love is practical – Paul did not welter in a sea of emotion. He was prepared to spend and be spent. For three years he laboured at Ephesus, shewing and teaching publicly and from house to house, warning every one night and day. He suffered beatings, stoning, shipwreck, weariness, pain, hunger, thirst, cold and nakedness, 2 Cor. 11. 25–27; all for the elect's sake, 2 Tim. 2. 10. The partial success of false teachers in Galatia caused him such agony of soul that he travailed again until

Christ was formed in them, Gal. 4. 19. Who can enter into what Paul meant when he told the Colossians of his labouring and striving and of his great conflict on their behalf and on the behalf of others whom he had not even seen, of whose faith he had only heard?, Col 2. 1.

Prayer. But his affection led not only to patient toil – he gave himself to prayer. And what a prayer-life! If we find it difficult to pray regularly and intensely for the little group with which we are so closely associated, we may well marvel at his labours in prayer, embracing thousands of believers scattered over the wide mission-field. The care of all the churches came upon him daily, 2 Cor. 11. 28. They were ever in his prayers, he was full of praise to God on their account; he seems to have been able to remember every individual in some assemblies. He ceased not to give thanks for the Ephesians, making mention of them in his prayers. He could summon before his mind every Christian in Philippi, thank God upon every remembrance of them, always in every prayer of his making request for them *all*, not as a burdensome duty, but "with joy", Phil. 1. 3. Without ceasing he remembered the Thessalonians and prayed exceedingly night and day that he might see their face, 1 Thess. 3. 10. If he never failed to remember Timothy in his prayers night and day, 2 Tim. 1. 3, and if he always remembered his friend Philemon, v. 4, we may surely conclude that there were many others he consistently presented before the throne of grace.

It may be conceded that the apostles stood in a class by themselves, but we are not to imagine that they stood alone in this intense devotion to the interests of Christ's people. Epaphroditus longed after all his Philippian fellow-believers and was full of heaviness at the thought that news of his illness would cause them anxiety, Phil. 2. 26.

That humble Colossian, Epaphras, laboured constantly and fervently in prayer that the believers might stand perfect and complete in all the will of God, and Paul bore witness to his zeal, not only for his home-assembly but also for those in the neighbouring towns of Laodicea and Hierapolis, Col. 4. 12. In both cases Paul's particular concern for Philippi and Colosse is so strikingly reflected in the exercises of these two men that

it is difficult to resist the conclusion that Paul's very earnestness infected his colleagues. If only, like them, we had Paul's
spirit! Timothy was a young man on whom Paul could confidently rely to make the welfare of the saints his first concern,
as he genuinely cared for them, Phil. 2. 20. He worked the
work of the Lord, as Paul did, 1 Cor. 16. 10. Then there was
the household of Stephanas, addicts in the best sense –
addicting themselves to the ministry of the saints, 1 Cor.
16. 15. Or think of Priscilla and Aquila, who laid down their
necks for Christ's servant, Rom. 16. 4.

What Explains Paul's Intensity – an intensity which communicated itself to his associates? The spring of his utter
devotion to the cause of Christ and His people was Christ's
love to him, and his responsive love to Christ. Held fast in the
relentless grip of Christ's love he was irresistably impelled
along the path of His Master's will. His only object in living
at all was Christ. He counted not his life dear unto himself.
His overmastering passion was to see Christ glorified –
whether this was to be by a life of further toil or by death in
some awful form mattered nothing – what mattered was that
Christ should be magnified. He who is forgiven much loveth
much, and Paul never forgot the signal mercy shown to him.
But if we think we have been forgiven so little that we can
love Christ but feebly, we have ceased to dwell in the shadow
of the cross, where we perceive our guiltiness because our
ransom was so great.

It is inevitable that such a man would long to know what was
Christ's supreme interest. Christ loved the church and gave
Himself for it! Very well – he would love Christ in loving
Christ's church, he would give himself for Christ in giving
himself for Christ's church. He could even rejoice in his
sufferings as he filled up that which was still wanting in the
afflictions he must endure for "his body's sake, which is the
church", Col. 1. 24.

He had been given a vision of what the church was to Christ
and henceforth he saw the church through the eyes of Christ.
If the Ephesian Epistle gives us an insight of the glorious
vision he had been given of the church as the body and the
bride of Christ, and the temple of God, his Epistles to the

Corinthians show how, jealous for God's honour, he laboured to see produced in local companies some true reflections of those same features. "Know ye not that ye are a temple of God?" "Now are ye a body of Christ." "I have espoused you as a chaste virgin to Christ." *Vision*! Is that lacking today? Oh for men who have had a vision from God, to whom an assembly is much more than an organized group of Christians, even an organism instinct with the life of Christ, and who under the thraldom of that vision will feel that they can give no better proof of their love to Christ than by their devotion to the flock committed, at least in part, to their care.

Self-interest. The sad fact is that the spirit of this material-istic age has infected the souls even of God's people until one would almost think that the necessity of "getting on" in the world is part of their creed. It ought to be quite needless to point out how utterly alien this outlook is to the New Testament conception of life, where the uniform emphasis is on the subservience of all else to the supreme claim of Christ to all we have and are.

What is involved? It will be apparent from what Paul and Peter say to elders, that the spiritual care of an assembly is a much more serious task than is generally realized. Those who will meditate upon such expressions as: Take heed to your-selves and to all the flock of God; Tend the church of God; Therefore watch; Let us wait on our ministry; Comfort the faint-hearted, support the weak; Be vigilant; Given to hos-pitality; Rule well; Labour in word and doctrine; Holding fast the faithful word; Able by sound doctrine both to exhort and to convince the gainsayers; They watch for your souls as they that must give account; those who meditate upon these expressions will have it borne upon them that the shepherding of a flock is not a service which can be attended to casually in intervals between outside activities. Certainly a father must attend to his family, a business man to his business and an employee to his job, but a real overseer will find enough in the assembly to engage his full attention when those other responsibilities have been faithfully discharged.

Reflections. We believe there is a need for earnest young men to consider whether God would have them addict themselves to the ministry of the saints in its many and varied aspects, so that they might begin by prayer and study to prepare themselves for this high task. The call is for men who will be ready to forego the worldly prizes their abilities could win and be content with a modest sphere in life so as to be free to give priority to all that shepherd-work will involve. We do not for a moment forget that God wishes to have servants in every honourable sphere, and no doubt some are definitely called to find their vocation in some profession where they must concentrate their energies if they are to be a credit to their Christian calling. Here they can adorn the doctrine of God and serve Christ in a special way, but we would nevertheless stress the need for men like the humble but great Carey, who regarded the service of God as his vocation and "cobbled to pay expenses".

Such will be prepared to take to heart the exhortation to Timothy, "Meditate upon these things; give thyself wholly to them", 1 Tim. 4. 15. The sacrifices involved will be considerable but the compensations will be more than adequate.

Realism demands that we recognize the practical difficulties in the complex economic set-up of this specialist age and we can think of many reasons and excuses which may be urged against the practicability of this suggestion. It is an interesting sidelight on the subtle genius of language that we say "Make excuses" and "Give reasons". We will add no more than this. It would surely be well for us to make sure that objections we raise will be found valid at the Judgment-Seat of Christ.

GOSPEL WORK

The Lord of the Harvest

by WILLIAM JACKMAN

TO THOSE OF US who through the years have spent much time in the harvest-field, the Lord's use of the title "The Lord of the harvest" suggests a striking conception of God's great interest in the work of gathering souls to Christ. Boaz, as he walks among his reapers, taking interest in all who are in his fields, noting all that is going on, and speaking of "my harvest", becomes a faint picture of God's close connection with all that is going on in the spiritual harvest-field. This surely warrants our seeking to learn what this title implies, by considering our own experiences in the natural harvest for which we give God thanks.

The Farmer Plans the Harvest. Far from being a haphazard affair, the farmer has to give careful thought to his cropping plans before he sets to work in the field – it is then, in the farmer's mind, that the first step is taken that will result, he hopes, in fields of golden grain.

The day is coming when a harvest will be reaped which will fill the granaries of heaven – fill them to the delight of God's heart, for it will be after the kind of the original seed, the Lord Jesus Christ, the corn of wheat which fell into the ground and died, bringing forth much fruit. But this will not be the result of an after-thought on God's part – it will be but the fruition of a plan formed in a past eternity. Great changes must take place to turn prairies into wheat-fields, but vaster changes are needed to turn sinful men into the "many sons" who will be brought to glory. The field is the world, and we cannot cease to marvel at the grace which chose such an unpromising field for the fulfilment of His eternal purpose.

> Surely the thought was Thine,
> And only Thine could be,
> Fruit of the wisdom, love divine,
> Peculiar unto Thee.

The Farmer Bears the Cost of the Harvest. Months before he can hope to reap, the farmer's expenses begin – the field has to be paid for, the seed has to be purchased, the workmen's wages have to be found and expensive equipment provided in order to carry out the necessary ploughing, cultivating, fertilizing and sowing. He can forecast with a fair degree of accuracy most of the expense likely to be incurred, but what can be said about the infinite cost of the spiritual harvest?

Although it is unlikely that we shall ever be able to comprehend what it involved, we must remember that God knew the heavy cost to Himself, if any return from this sin-cursed earth was ever to be obtained. The husbandman cannot forecast just what the harvest will be – he ploughs in hope and waits with patience, relying upon God's promise to Noah long ago. Nevertheless results vary a great deal, and so the joy of harvest is relative – it does sometimes happen, though rarely, that a farmer finds he has laboured to some extent in vain. Yet, infinite though the cost of God's harvest, the Saviour who gave His life for its success shall see of the travail of His soul and shall be satisfied. His joy shall be complete.

The Farmer Welcomes Help in the Harvest. There are busy days in harvest when the farmer presses everybody he can into service – there is work for all who are willing to help. Not only are the men busy in the fields but the spirit of harvest imbues all the personnel of the farm, and even the members of the household. There is so much to be done while the opportunity lasts, that a task can be found for any person who will help. There are meals to be sent out, as well as corn to be carried, and the one is as necessary as the other – the duties may be many and varied, but the harvest is one.

Similarly in God's harvest-field there is something each of us can do. The need in the harvest is for "labourers", and this word is connected with various spiritual activities. There are those who *labour* in word and doctrine; we read of those who *labour* in prayer, and of others whose service was a *labour* of love. Can any Christian say that he cannot, at least in some small way, contribute to one of these spheres of service? At the end of his letter to the Romans, Paul was glad to acknowledge by name a number of men and women, whose contribution to the furtherance of the gospel he valued highly, though their actual work might have been judged by some as relatively unimportant.

The Farmer Directs his Men. Despite the efficiency of the average farm-worker, the harvest would not proceed very satisfactorily if every man did that which was right in his own eyes. It is the farmer who sees the harvest as a whole, and it is he who must plan each day's work. Even so he does it very imperfectly, for the simple reason that he never knows what a day may bring forth.

Our "Lord of the harvest" has no such limitations – He knows the end from the beginning, and the very best ways to accomplish His ends. When He gives "to every man his work" He makes no mistake, either as to our qualifications or the course that events will take. Just as the men come to the farmer each morning for instructions as to the day's work, so it is our responsibility to get our orders direct from the Lord. A farmer cannot very well direct a man who doesn't turn up!

In actual practice a farmer is always pleased to receive suggestions from his men – to say the very least it is evidence of interest in their work, and this makes all the difference to the relations between the men and the master. Our Master encourages our co-operation – is there not a hint of this in the call to pray the Lord of the harvest to thrust out more labourers? Such a prayer would be evidence of concern over the need – it would prove they had the work at heart.

The Farmer Equips his Men. In these days it would be impossible to perform the many tasks involved in gathering a harvest, without all sorts of complicated machines, in

addition to the simpler and old-fashioned tools. The farmer
has to decide who will use the various implements. One man
will be entrusted with a tractor, another may operate a
binder – some will just work with their hands. Each is part
of a team, and the harvest depends on the faithfulness of each –
many a grand day's work is done with a humble pitchfork.
Whatever the job, it is faithfulness the farmer appreciates –
the task and the tool are the farmer's choice; he is the best
judge of each man's suitability.

God's servants are variously equipped ("dividing to
every man severally as he will") and it is foolish for us to
envy the seemingly better gifts of others. After all, the tractor
belongs to the farmer and not to the man entrusted with it.
The most costly and up-to-date tractor and its accompanying
trailer needs some sturdy labourer to pitch up the sheaves.
To the operator of a complicated machine one might say, as
Paul said to a highly-gifted church, "What hast thou, that
thou didst not receive?".

The Farmer Encourages his Men. A wise master
will encourage his men – a good man values appreciation
and will make an extra effort to give of his best.

Our wise and gracious Master never fails to encourage
His faithful servants – but He does more; He empowers
them. A farmer may appoint a man his task, may provide
him with all the necessary equipment, may encourage him
in every way, but he can never give the man the energy
upon which everything else depends. In the spiritual field
the energy of the human servant is of no avail – without the
imparted power of the Holy Spirit, nothing will be accomplished. God must work in and through His servant. A
spiritual gift is one thing – the power to use it effectively is
quite another thing. The tractor and the pitchfork are
equally useless unless there is the energy to use them. Physical
strength and mental endowments can do much in human
fields of endeavour, but the most gifted and energetic of our
brethren accomplish nothing, save as the Holy Spirit empowers them.

The Farmer Works with his Men. The presence and help of the farmer on the field makes a great difference to the work of the harvest, and no farmer likes to be away from home in harvest-time. It is a common thing to read in reports of markets, sales and other farmers' gatherings that "harvest operations affected the attendance". God not only works through His servants, but with them.

The idea of an indifferent God, far remote and detached, is a flat contradiction of what has been revealed of Him. When the complacent Pharisees found fault with the Lord for His tireless works of mercy, healing even on the Sabbath day, He could appeal to the example of His Father – "My Father worketh hitherto, and I work". Those who were associated with Him realized what a great worker He was. If the farmer has to rise up early to get a full day of harvest, let us remember that the prophet uses a similar expression of God, in order to convey to our little minds some impression of God's earnestness. When Christ sent His apostles "into all the world" He added, "Lo, I am with you alway". Paul embraced his co-workers in the expression "workers-together" but he added "with God". The presence of the loved and respected Boaz moving amongst his harvesters exerted an influence on his men and maidens – how much more the presence of the Lord of the harvest with us in our labours for Him.

The Farmer Pays his Men. In every field of labour some reward for effort is sought, and wages and profits are perennial topics. In James' day there seemed to be some who defrauded men of their right and proper remuneration, but the Lord of the harvest will never fail. "He that reapeth receiveth wages" is the abiding law – indeed God saw to it that the very oxen who trod out the corn were allowed their reward as they followed their weary round. The reward of the servant of Christ will be far more satisfying than ever pounds, shillings and pence succeed in being. Sower and reaper shall rejoice together.

A farmer generally pays according to time worked, even though on occasions the work done one day may be undone by weather the next day. The men are not blamed for that –

they did their best. We are told that "each man will receive according to his own labour". Faithfulness and zeal in the use of such opportunities as we have, willingness to put our gifts to the best use, submission to the directions of the Lord, encouraged by His presence and empowered by His Spirit, will guarantee to the humblest labourer the supreme reward of his Master's "Well done".

Making Known the Eternal Purpose

by R. V. COURT

All quotations are from the Revised Version

AN EXAMINATION OF PAUL'S LETTERS makes it clear that he regarded the commission to preach the Gospel which had been given to him as an immeasurable privilege. This is not to say that the weight of responsibility in relation to it did not rest heavily upon him. In one place he says, "Woe is unto me, if I preach not the gospel", 1 Cor. 9. 16, but this sense of responsibility did not rob him of the thrill of knowing that in the sovereign counsel of God he had been chosen to bring to men a message which had originated in eternity, a message which revealed God's thoughts of grace, a message which brought that grace into the ambit of man's experience.

When writing to Titus he drew attention to the fact that eternal life was something that God "who cannot lie, promised before times eternal", 1. 2. God's purpose for this universe included the determination that men should be brought into relationship with Himself, sharing His own life, and this by implication brings the cross into the centre of the eternal counsel. When consideration is given to 1 Peter 1. 18–20 and the reference to the Lamb "foreknown indeed before the foundation of the world" is noted, it is impossible to avoid the conclusion that these two things are very closely linked; "before times eternal" life was promised, "before the foundation of the world" a Lamb was foreknown. God knew that to give life to men was going to cost Him His Son, the most

costly gift that He could give, and it was going to cost His
Son His life and the unutterable agony and shame of the
cross. We can only bow in worship at such love and grace.

> We bless Thee, O our Father
> For Thine electing grace,
> Before the world's foundation
> Thy purposes we trace –
> That Thou wouldst have a people
> Redeemed by precious blood,
> To dwell with Thee in glory
> Beloved as sons of God.

But, when in the fulness of time the cross had become a
fact of history, how could these purposes be made known to
men? Had they remained shut up in the heart of God, they
would have continued to be secrets hidden from the knowledge
of those who were to be blessed through them, and this
ignorance of the purposes of God and the true meaning of
the cross would have kept men in the darkness and slavery of
sin. God must find a way to bring the knowledge of His
eternal purposes to those who are involved in them and Paul
exulted in the fact that, in His sovereignty, God had chosen
men to be the vehicles for the conveyance of this knowledge.
If Titus 1. 2 takes us back to eternity, verse 3 brings us into
this present time and we see that God has "in his own seasons
manifested his word in the message". As Paul wrote these
words he realized afresh, with deep gratitude, that this word
had been committed to him "according to the commandment
of God our Saviour". He understood, by the teaching of the
Holy Spirit, that it was God in His character as Saviour who
had commanded that the "mystery" should be revealed and
he rejoiced that God had chosen him to do this.

When the apostle wrote to the church at Thessalonica
at a much earlier date, he linked the eternal purpose with the
Gospel which he had been privileged to preach to them,
2 Thess. 2. 13–14. He gave thanks to God for those whom he
could describe as "brethren beloved of the Lord" because they
had been from the beginning chosen to salvation and this "in
sanctification of the Spirit and belief of the truth". The

divine purpose is seen in this choice unto salvation, but "belief of the truth" is recognized as a vital link in the chain of blessing presented, says Paul, by "our gospel".

Ephesians 1 also emphasizes the link between the "determinate counsel and foreknowledge of God" and the Gospel by which this counsel is made known. Verse 4 indicates that God has chosen "us in him (Christ) before the foundation of the world, that we should be holy and without blemish before him". This was "according to the good pleasure of his will", v. 5. Verse 9 speaks of God "having made known unto us the mystery of his will" and the passage goes on to speak of God's intention to "sum up all things in Christ" and links the believer with Christ in relation to all this, vv. 10–12. The question naturally arises, how were these mysteries of His will made known to the men of Ephesus – how did they come to understand their place in the purpose of Him "who worketh all things after the counsel of his will"? Paul answers this question by saying "in whom ye also, having heard the word of the truth, the gospel of your salvation – in whom, having also believed, ye were sealed with the Holy Spirit of promise", v. 13. They heard the message, they believed it, they were incorporated in Christ and sealed. They would for ever be grateful that God had sent human messengers to make known His purpose for them.

There were those who challenged Paul's message and denied its divine origin, and from time to time he deemed it necessary to emphasize that God was responsible for it. Galatians 1. 11–12 is very plain in this matter: "For I make known to you, brethren, as touching the gospel which was preached by me, that it is not after man. For neither did I receive it from man, nor was I taught it, but it came to me through revelation of Jesus Christ". He continues the thought in verses 15–16 of the same chapter, "But when it was the good pleasure of God, who separated me, even from my mother's womb, and called me through his grace, to reveal his Son in me, that I might preach him among the Gentiles".

Notwithstanding the opposition of false teachers, the insidious workings of the powers of darkness and the growing hostility of those in authority, this conviction of the divine origin of salvation and the divine choice of men to convey the truth to those who were to be the objects of the divine love never left the apostle. A consideration of 2 Timothy 1. 9–11 (his last letter) will show that the wonder of it was still with him. He reminded Timothy that Christians have been called "with a holy calling, not according to our works, but according to his own purpose and grace, which was given us in Christ Jesus before times eternal". He then told Timothy how in the fulness of time this purpose and grace was "manifested by the appearing of our Saviour Christ Jesus, who abolished death, and brought life and incorruption to light through the gospel". As he contemplated the majestic movement of Deity from eternity into the "now" of the manifestation of Jesus Christ, he ignored the fact that he was a prisoner with a severe limitation placed upon his activities, and exulted in his link with the divine purpose, "I was appointed a preacher, and an apostle, and a teacher".

Brethren, have those of us who preach today lost the thrill that came to the apostle and the other early preachers of the Gospel? Have we forgotten the high privilege that is ours in being chosen as God's messengers to bring to men a knowledge of His eternal purpose in Christ? Perhaps we have become so accustomed to preaching it that the wonder of the message does not grip us as once it did, and maybe because of its lack of impact upon us it is having little impact on those who hear us. Possibly a consideration of Ephesians 3. 7–9 will revive this sense of privilege; such is the gospel of which "I was made a minister, according to the gift of that grace of God which was given me according to the working of his power. Unto me, who am less than the least of all saints, was this grace given, to preach unto the Gentiles the unsearchable riches of Christ; and to make all men see what is the dispensation of the mystery which from all ages hath been hid in God".

By divine grace the privilege conferred upon Paul is also conferred on us. May the wonder of it grip us anew!

Gospel Preaching:
the Message, Motive and Method

by E. W. Rogers

THE FIRST GOSPEL PREACHERS were men with a **message.** It was not second hand, but one which they had obtained direct from their Lord. It was, therefore, His word to the people with which they were sent. It was received as the result of immediate contact with Him. While it is true that, as apostles, they stood in a unique position and possessed unique authority, yet the principle is the same today. There is no reason why the preacher of the gospel should not now also have immediate contact with the Lord Jesus and receive his message direct from Him. He speaks now in the written Word which is living and abiding, and is capable of adaptation to the varied modern needs and conditions met with among men and women. The message given to the apostles was vocal; that given to us is written but, in each case, the source is the same and its vital nature is identical. The first essential then to effective preaching is that the preacher should be in touch with the Lord. There should be "nothing between". His life should be so ordered that it should be free from witting indulgence in all that is contrary to the mind of the Lord. Sin separates from God; it breaks communion; it destroys contact; and puts the ear out of tune so that it cannot receive the word from His lips.

Perhaps the next thing in importance is that

The Preacher's Motives should be able to bear the test of divine examination. "As of sincerity, as of God, in the sight of God", is how he should speak in the cause of Christ, 2 Cor. 2. 17. God, Himself, must be known as One of his audience; He not only listens to the words of the preacher but He reads his heart and motives. There must be no tickling of the ears. There must be no trimming the sails to the public whim. There must be no mere platitudes which soothe but do not disturb. The message received must be the message transmitted without addition or subtraction. It must not be alloyed for any reason whatsoever. By no means must other considerations be allowed to influence the preacher. How many messages have been distorted because the preacher has endeavoured to save, as he thinks, his reputation or to please his audience, or has had his eye on money. This latter is the bane of organized Christendom and the servant of the Lord is not immune from this danger.

The Method Adopted is simple: it is as old as Enoch: it will bear no improvement. It is "preaching" or "heralding". Who could imagine Enoch entertaining his audience so as to make his message more attractive! A band of sympathetic helpers is most useful, as Peter found when he "stood up with the eleven"; if eleven are not available one other fellow-worker is a source of comfort and strength as Paul often found. "Preaching" is itself no foolish thing, (1 Corinthians 1. 21 refers to the thing preached, not to the method). The prophets of old and the Lord Himself employed this method of reaching the people. It is admittedly old-fashioned, but it is in every way best. No better vault can be found than that which has the sky as its ceiling. No better place can be found than the market square, or the public park, or the equivalent of a Mars' Hill, or the usual public rendezvous. The preacher himself is a living witness of the truth of his message. He is one of like passions with his audience from whom any of them may expect a sympathetic understanding. There is nothing to be compared with the living voice of the person who comes into immediate contact with the people. Other methods of approach are altogether inferior; they lack so much that the good which is left is seriously handicapped. Not that they are altogether useless – by no means – but they are not the best. There is nothing to excel the preaching of a saved sinner who has received a message from the Lord. No wonder he bursts out singing thus:

I've a message from the Lord, Hallelujah.

The preacher thus stands between God and the people and has dealings with both. From God he first receives the message. To men he thereafter gives it.

If anything should be permitted to prevent the reception

by the preacher of the word of the Lord what can result but barren talking? As the audience changes from time to time so it is necessary for the message to be suitable to the particular people for whom it is intended. It is only by constant and unbroken fellowship with God, who knows the hearts of all men, that the preacher can learn from Him in what manner to clothe each message which, at heart, is always the same, in that it has to do with God's Son and the cross.

Recall to Reality

by A. G. ANSTICE

AMONG THE FAMILIAR TEXTS of Holy Scripture perhaps few are better known or more popular than Romans 1. 16, "For I am not ashamed of the gospel of Christ: for it is the power of God unto salvation to everyone that believeth; to the Jew first, and also to the Greek". It is quoted repeatedly in our prayer-meetings and it is almost certain that every gospel preacher has at some time or another taken it as the text for his message. Yes – but do we really believe it? If we do – how can we excuse the lack of concern at the comparative ineffectiveness of much of our preaching?

The gospel is the power that God uses in the salvation of men, and if we are not experiencing this manifestation of power, the failure is obviously with ourselves. Yet when the lack of power has been recognized it has too often been the tendency to resort to innovation instead of self-examination. Enterprise, of course, is not to be despised but innovations cannot make the gospel more effective – it has ever pleased God by the foolishness of the thing preached to save them that believe, 1 Cor. 1. 21 R.V. marg. Instead of finding plausible excuses for our failure we would be wiser to face the fact that, as it cannot be in the gospel, it must be in us as the channels through which the gospel comes.

Surely it is evident that certain conditions are indispensable if our preaching is to be effective – we venture to suggest at least three – *Preparation, Power, Passion*. Ere the Lord ascended up into heaven He said to His disciples, "but tarry ye in the city of Jerusalem, until ye be endued with power from on high", Luke 24. 49. This tarrying period was not time wasted; on the contrary it was time profitably spent, for we read that they "were continually in the temple, praising and blessing God", v. 53. Again, "when the day of Pentecost was fully come, they were all with one accord in one place", Acts 2. 1.

Preparation. Life is so full and active today, and especially so for the servant of the Lord, that it is necessary at times for him to "tarry a while". What gracious thought and provision are revealed in the Lord's words to His disciples, "Come ye yourselves apart and rest a while", when many were coming and going and they had no leisure so much as to eat, Mark 6. 31. It is generally recognized today, in every sphere of life, that a period of rest and change is necessary at times so that vitality may be renewed and the body braced up, to face again the varied demands of life. This being undoubtedly true in the spiritual realm, it may be the Lord will call us to "tarry a while" so that, in the resting period, we shall receive fresh endurement and be enabled to go forth in the anointing and power of the Holy Spirit.

Also in this "tarrying" it will be our blessed privilege to sit down under His shadow, and great will be our delight as He unfolds to us the riches of His grace, enriching us in the knowledge of Himself, and in wisdom and understanding, so necessary to all who would serve the Lord effectively. We shall then be ready for the final stage of our preparation. Renewed in heart and spirit, the love of Christ constraining us, 2 Cor. 5. 14, and the power of Christ resting upon us, 12. 9, we shall be energized to go forth again in His Name.

May we know this preparation that brings to us spiritual refreshment, change of strength, and a going forth in the energy and power of the Spirit of God.

An excellent illustration of, and instructive lesson in, "preparation" is given us in 2 Chronicles chs. 34, 35.

34. 31 "And the king (Josiah) stood in his place, and made a covenant before the Lord". The result?

35. 4 "Prepare yourselves"
    6 "Prepare your brethren"
   10 "So the service was prepared"
   16 "So the service of the Lord was prepared *the same day*".

Power. We all desire to see the evidence of God's power in the gospel-meeting, but whilst it is possible to be in such a healthy spiritual condition that we can experience it, on the other hand it is solemnly possible to limit God's power. In Acts 2, we find a company in united fellowship, and as Peter lifts up his voice he has the full support of the other apostles. Can you wonder that three thousand souls were saved? Genuine conversions too! for "they continued stedfastly". You say "But that was Pentecost". Listen again to the inspired word: the gospel of Christ *is* "the power of God unto salvation to every one that believeth". Two things seem linked together in connection with divine power. They are *prayer* and *praise*. How they prayed! How much the apostle Paul coveted the prayers of the saints! Effective and fervent prayer. How the Lord notices the praying soul! "Behold, he prayeth", Acts 9. 11.

Reference has already been made to those who were continually in the temple praising and blessing God, but in Acts 16. 25 we find two men doing the same in a dismal prison. They have endured ignominy, shame and physical suffering sufficient to break the stoutest heart; but not so these two men, for we read *"and at midnight* Paul and Silas prayed, and sang praises unto God". Something was bound to happen and it did! A jailor and all his family were saved that night and knew it. What rejoicing in heaven and on earth! Again we find prayer and praise linked together in Philippians 4. 6, where we read "Be careful for nothing; but in everything by prayer and supplication with thanksgiving let your requests be made known unto God". We have everything to praise God for, and in such a manner that others may see and know our joy in the Lord. Long centuries have passed since the Psalmist wrote, "And he hath put a new song in my mouth, even praise unto our God: many shall see it, and fear, and shall trust in the Lord", Psa. 40. 3. We too, have a new song to sing, and it is to Him who loved us and gave Himself for us. Praise gives wings to prayer.

But a third and essential link is necessary if we are to experience the divine power in our midst. There must be the Lord's *presence*. In Matthew 10. 1, it is written, "He gave them power". In this particular case it was the power to work miracles, but that same power is needed if the miracle of salvation is to be performed. How blessed then to read His own words, and to remember that they were spoken as He gave the great commission to His disciples "All power is given unto me . . . Go ye into all the world, and preach the gospel to every creature . . . and lo, I am with you alway, even unto the end of the world", Matt. 28. 18, 20; Mark 16. 15.

May we know much of this spirit of earnest *prayer*, fervent *praise* and the *presence*, in power, of the Lord.

Passion. We think of this word in the sense of "strong emotion". "Ah!" says someone, "that is of the flesh, it must be kept under; it must be crucified". Before you take this drastic step and bury it out of your sight as something very terrible, consider a few Scriptural illustrations which show what is meant by the words "strong emotion".

Lamentations 3. 51: "Mine eye affecteth mine heart". What was this? Acts 17. 16: "Now while Paul waited for them at Athens, his spirit was stirred in him, when he saw the city given wholly to idolatry". What was this? Revelation 5. 4: John says, "And I wept much". What was this? Who can read the Gospels and not be profoundly impressed as they consider the infinite compassion of the Lord Jesus? It is recorded of Him that when He saw the multitudes as sheep without a shepherd, He was moved with compassion towards them. Consider again the journey into Jerusalem as mentioned in Luke 19: "And when he was come near, he beheld the city, and wept over it", v. 41. And yet again at the grave of Lazarus, "Jesus wept". These are but a few of the Scriptures that reveal to us the depth of divine feeling for men in their great need.

He who created us made us so that we may be reached and touched, and, in turn, may reach and touch others, but it may be that we require a *renewed vision* to save us from apathy in the presence of appalling need. We need to see the Lord in the glory He had with the Father before the world was; to see Him as He comes "The Lord from heaven" and is made in the likeness of men; to see Him as He humbles Himself and becomes obedient unto death, *even* the death of the cross. To see Him now exalted at the Father's right hand, and made a Prince and a Saviour. To see the fields as He saw them "white already to harvest". And with such a vision to be deeply moved and constrained to yield ourselves unreservedly as labourers in His "harvest field".

With such a vision and with renewed consecration we shall surely *rise to the opportunities* that are ours in making known this wondrous message, which is the power of God in the salvation of men. How we long to see once again men, women and children, deeply wrought upon by the Holy Spirit, brought to an end of themselves and gladly opening their hearts and lives to the Lord Jesus, confessing Him as Saviour and Lord, and in "newness of life" giving evidence of the reality of their salvation.

If we rise to the opportunities set before us we shall certainly *reap the harvest*. For it is written, "He that goeth forth and weepeth, bearing precious seed, shall doubtless come again rejoicing, bringing his sheaves with him", Psa. 126. 6. Yes, the gospel of Christ *is* the power of God unto salvation to every one that believeth. Having been refreshed and strengthened, may we go forth with a burning desire to proclaim this soul-saving message.

> Oh, for a passionate passion for souls!
> Oh, for a spirit that yearns!
> Oh, for a love that loves unto death!
> Oh, for a fire that burns!
> Oh, for a prayer-power that prevails!
> That pours itself out for the lost!
> Victorious prayer in the Conqueror's Name!
> Oh, for a Pentecost!

The Preparation for a Gospel Message

by E. L. LOVERING

THERE ARE THREE ESSENTIALS for every would-be preacher of the Gospel.

1. **Seek the Mind of God.** This is both the preacher's motive and incentive. He must know, if he is to make known, the mind of God; he must see men and things as God sees them. Above all men he must emulate God's pity and compassion for the lost and perishing. Thus it was with our Lord: "when he saw the multitudes, he was moved with compassion on them, because they fainted, and were scattered abroad, as sheep having no shepherd", Matt. 9. 36. In the synagogue on the Sabbath day He said: "The Spirit of the Lord is upon me, because he hath anointed me to preach the gospel to the poor; he hath sent me to heal the broken-hearted, to preach deliverance to the captives, and recovering of sight to the blind, to set at liberty them that are bruised", Luke 4. 18. We learn from this that our Lord had, first, *a vision of men*. He saw them "as sheep having no shepherd"; He saw them "poor", "broken-hearted", "captives", "blind and bruised". This is how the preacher must see men, for "where there is no vision, the people perish", Prov. 29. 18. Second, our Lord had *a passion for men*. He "was moved with compassion on them". The measure of our power with men will be determined by the measure of our pity and compassion for them. Third, our Lord had *a mission to men*. He was anointed to preach the gospel to the poor. Preacher, "Let this mind be in you, which was also in Christ Jesus", all God's messengers must have a vision, a passion and a mission. It is by the "foolishness of preaching" in contrast to the "wisdom of men" that God is saving souls, and for the preacher the compelling, controlling and constraining power is the love of Christ.

2. **Search the Word of God.** This is the subject and basis of the preacher's message. He must know, if he is to make known, the Word of God. If he is to preach the Word

he must be familiar with it. In the words of Solomon: "because the preacher was wise, he still taught the people knowledge; yea, he gave good heed, and sought out, and set in order many proverbs. The preacher sought to find out acceptable words: and that which was written was upright, even words of truth", Eccles. 12. 9–10. We note here, first, *the selection of the subject*. The preacher "sought to find out acceptable words", "even words of truth". The facts of the gospel as stated by the apostle Paul are these: "For I delivered unto you first of all that which I also received, how that Christ died for our sins according to the scriptures; and that he was buried, and that he rose again the third day according to the scriptures", 1 Cor. 15. 3–4. The preacher must present with no uncertainty the facts and the faith of the gospel. The gospel must be asserted, delivered and preached, for "it *is* the power of God unto salvation to every one that believeth", Rom. 1. 16. It is not our commendation or proof of it, but the gospel itself which is the power of God. Individual salvation does not come about by human persuasion but by divine power. Secondly, consider *the suitability of the subject*. The preacher weighed with discrimination the nature of his subject, choosing words and expressions most suitable to his hearers and pertinent to the matter in hand. He "gave good heed, and sought out, and set in order many proverbs". For the preacher, this will need careful thought and thorough preparation. He will need to be "a workman that needeth not to be ashamed, rightly dividing the word of truth", 2 Tim. 2. 15. The sermons of our Lord were never haphazard but pointed and plain. Never let your hearers be lost in a maze; set before them a straight path. Mark *the aim of the subject*. This is not merely to impart knowledge but to stir the soul. To quote Solomon again: "the words of the wise are as goads, and as nails", Eccles. 12. 11. True preaching will hurt before it heals, it will convict before it converts.

3. Speak the Truth of God. This is the object and character of the preacher's message. He must know, if he is to make known, the truth of God. He must speak the truth of God *lovingly;* he must speak the truth and speak it in love. The preacher must avoid criticism of others or other groups of Christians. To entice a hungry dog from a bone offer him more meat. We must speak the truth of God *sincerely*. This should characterize every gospel message. A careful use of hands, voice and eyes can be helpful here. The apostle Paul made good use of these on more than one occasion. At Jerusalem when facing a hostile crowd he "beckoned with the hand unto the people", Acts 21. 40; when he began his noble defence in the court of Festus he "stretched forth the hand" to Agrippa, Acts 26. 1; at Lystra he rent his garments and "fixed his eyes on the man". While there is no need to remain static, there is no reason to become a windmill. We must speak the truth of God *simply*. The most powerful words and expressions are often the simple ones. This does not mean that sermons must be childish, for no one likes to be "talked down to". Avoid vague and long-sounding words and expressions; why say: "We would suggest or commend to your consideration" when "I have something to say" would do; or why use "felicity" for "happiness" or "subsequently" for "afterwards". It is the quality that matters, not the quantity. Someone has said that the Lord offered "strong prayers" not "long prayers". Try to make things simple by suitable illustrations, anecdotes and parables. What a wonderful use our Lord made of these! Lastly, we must speak the truth of God *reverently*. Reverence always becomes the things of God, and lightness in preaching the greatest message known to man is to be strongly deprecated and avoided. Let your hymns be relevant to your subject and the music suitable to the theme. Finally, however successful you may become as a preacher, remember that the power is in the seed and not in the sower.

The Teacher –
a Servant and Soul-winner

WORDS OF COUNSEL TO SUNDAY SCHOOL TEACHERS

by FRANK MCCONNEL

TEACHING IN THE SUNDAY SCHOOL is no easy task. The work is of a complex nature, and takes in a variety of duties. It is necessary that there should be Sunday School teachers. It would be wrong, however, for any to enter upon the work in a careless and light-hearted fashion; as if the only thing that mattered was getting the work done as quickly, and with as little trouble, as possible.

The need for Sunday School teachers bespeaks the importance of the work. There are probably more of them required than for any other form of service. Because there are so many teachers needed, we must not assume that the work is lacking in importance or that it can be taken up by anyone who feels so inclined. It is a work which requires special fitness and clearly-defined qualifications. As in every other form of service, there must be a knowledge of what is involved in the work, and of what is needed to carry it through successfully.

In speaking thus we do not wish to scare anyone away from the work as being too difficult to undertake, but rather that those who are already teachers and those who contemplate taking up the work should view their task seriously, being conscious of the dignity which ought to characterize what is done.

We must face the fact then that in becoming Sunday School teachers we are undertaking a work for God which, if we are going to be successful therein, will make great demands upon us. It will require us to regulate our life in its various departments, in order that each section of the work may make its contribution to the success of the whole.

Having these things in view we propose to consider the teacher and the necessity for the regulation of the life in relation to the various duties involved. We have indicated something of this in our title, but we wish to make our consideration three-fold and insert between the Servant and the

Soul-winner another designation, that of the Student. So then we are to consider:

1. The Teacher in relation to the *Lord* – A Servant.
2. The Teacher in relation to the *Scriptures* – A Student.
3. The Teacher in relation to the *Child* – A Soul-winner.

These are by no means comprehensive, but will at least help us to appreciate what is involved in the work from three different points of view.

1. The Servant. What we have to say will probably apply to service generally but can be taken as being of particular importance to Sunday School teaching.

First of all, we must realize that *sonship comes before service*. In 2 Timothy 2, Paul speaks of the servant of the Lord in several ways but he opens the chapter with the thought of *sonship*. "Thou therefore, my son, be strong in the grace that is in Christ Jesus". Timothy was Paul's son in the faith. He had been the means of his conversion. But Paul could only claim him as his son, because Timothy was a son of God. The inference is clear. We cannot serve God in any capacity whatever unless, and until, we have become the children of God through faith in Jesus Christ. Conversion to God is an absolute necessity if we are to serve Him. Like the Thessalonians of old, we must turn to God from idols, to serve the living and true God, 1 Thess. 1. 9.

We must realize also that *surrender comes before service*. One of the reasons why so much service is ineffective is because it has not been preceded by whole-hearted surrender. Even with the Lord Jesus there was first of all surrender to the will of God, then the undertaking of service. "Lo I come to do thy will, O God", Heb. 10. 9. "The Son of man came not to be served, but to serve", Mark 10. 45. We are to give ourselves to the Lord, before we offer to Him our service. What we are before the Lord is of far more importance than what we do for Him, and doing cannot be made the substitute of being. No amount of service can ever make up for the lack of surrender. Conversion must be followed by consecration.

What then is involved in becoming a servant of the Lord in a particular sphere such as the Sunday School? We may notice the following:

We must be Called. It goes without saying that the need for Sunday School teachers is great. Superintendents are constantly on the look-out for fresh helpers. At the same time we must remember that the need alone does not constitute the call. This must come from the Lord. It may come through a wise and discerning superintendent and be coupled with the existence of the need. But there must be the strong conviction within that the Lord Himself is calling us to the work. It is a fallacy to think that Sunday School work can be successfully undertaken without such a call.

We must be Controlled. When the Lord calls us to His work He does not leave us to our own devices, to carry it out as we think fit. He is in control and from Him we must take our orders. This means that we shall be constantly reporting for duty, always at His disposal, ready to do His bidding. It will help us to realize the value of prayer if we remember that not only must we speak to the Lord, we must also give Him the opportunity of speaking to us. Christ-controlled service means fruitful service and is the only service which really counts.

We must bear in mind however that this control may be expressed through those of His servants who are mainly responsible for the work in which we share. This is specially true of Sunday School work. We should always be ready to receive advice and guidance from the superintendent and from other teachers who are older and more experienced than ourselves.

We must be Consistent. Need we say that if our work goes only in fits and starts it is worse than useless? We all know those who are full of zeal and enthusiasm one day and then who are lagging behind, and dragging their feet, the next. If the work has been commenced as a definite commission from the Lord, we shall not feel like giving up the first time we come up against difficulties and discouragements. The work of God demands patient plodding on and a consistent continuity in all that we do for Him.

We must be Considerate. Whilst the call to the work is individual, the work itself is usually carried out in a collective capacity. We work with others and what we do should fit in with what others are doing. The Sunday School is not the sphere for one who cannot get on with others. There is a wonderful opportunity for the development of the team-spirit. A team can only operate successfully as each member subordinates his personal interests to the interests of the team as a whole. "In lowliness of mind, let each esteem other better than themselves", Phil. 2. 3.

2. The Student. The main object of all Sunday School work is to win the child for Jesus Christ. We must remember, however, that conversion is the work of the Holy Spirit and is not brought about by the mere persuasiveness of the teacher. In order to provide material which the Holy Spirit can use, it is the responsibility of the teacher to instruct and to impart to the mind of the child a knowledge of the Word of God. To be able to teach, we ourselves must be taught. The ability to impart knowledge is of no use unless there is an intimate acquaintance with the subject in hand. Therefore the teacher must of necessity be a student of the Scriptures. A Sunday School teacher without a knowledge of the Scriptures is like a warrior who does not know how to use his sword, or a workman who cannot handle aright his tool. This knowledge is not easily acquired. It demands patient and painstaking application to the study of God's Word, but it is infinitely worth while.

Our Attitude to the Scriptures. The Bible is the divinely inspired record of the revelation of God. We must be quite clear about this. The Book will never yield its treasure to the one who doubts its truth. It was divinely originated and has been providentially preserved. More than this, it has been accurately transcribed. The Bible we possess in our mother-tongue is in the main a reliable translation of the original documents.

(i) Our attitude to the Book must be marked by *simplicity*. God has hid these things from the wise and prudent and has revealed them unto babes, Matt. 11. 25. We are to be as little children: not childish, but childlike.

(ii) It must also be marked by *sympathy*. The Bible refuses to disclose its meaning to anyone who regards it from a critical point of view. It becomes a closed book to such. If Jesus Christ is our Saviour, then at once there is a bond of sympathy with all that the Bible reveals.

(iii) In addition there must be the mark of *surrender*. It is not scholarship which is required to be a successful Bible student. There must first and foremost be a willingness to surrender ourselves to all that we learn. We must be prepared to obey the precepts of the Bible and to live the kind of life which is in keeping with its teachings. We must forsake the sins which it condemns. It has been well said that sin soon separates from the Bible those whom the Bible does not separate from sin.

Our Approach to the Scriptures. It is impossible to over-stress the fact that acquaintance with the Scriptures involves actual Bible-study. The value of such an acquaintance will soon become obvious. We shall find intellectual profit in its information and instruction, we shall find moral profit in its guidance and warnings, and we shall find spiritual profit in its doctrinal and experimental truth. It will result in peace in our hearts, purity in our lives, and power in our service.

With such study there must be some kind of method. With many Christians, their knowledge of the Bible is confined to its beauty-spots. Some of the choice narratives of the Old Testament, the story of Joseph, some of the Psalms, samples of Isaiah's eloquence. In the New Testament, the parables, and maybe, a few of Paul's outstanding passages. Sylvester Horne said years ago, "Today the territory of Scripture is like a modern continent, extreme and unhealthy congestion at certain well-known centres and vast tracts of country uncultivated and unknown". Whilst such knowledge of the Scriptures is not to be despised, it is far from ideal and the only remedy is methodical study.

It is not our purpose to discuss methods of Bible-study, but we would stress the importance of looking at the Bible as a whole, as well as in detail. The quickest way to begin the study of geography is to take a good look at a globe, or an atlas of the world. We see at a glance the proportion of sea to land, the outlines of the continents, and the relative sizes of the various countries. So it is with the Bible. By looking at the whole before studying a part, we shall be able to relate each part to the rest and determine its relative importance.

We shall become acquainted with the diversity of the Bible as well as its unity. We shall see how God has superintended the growth of this divine Library, until out of sixty-six books, some large, some small, there has been produced one complete Book. Like a living organism, no part of the Bible can be taken away without maiming the rest. Each part is necessary to the whole.

Above all, we shall come to know that the chief purpose of the written Word is to reveal the Living Word, and shall cultivate the habit of looking for Christ in all the Scriptures.

3. The Soul-winner. Such study as we have indicated will provide us with abundant material for the preparation of our lessons, especially as we come to the more detailed study of the Scriptures.

Preparation. Alongside of our general studies there must of course be the preparation of our lessons with the needs of our children especially before us. This cannot be dispensed with if we are going to be successful teachers. We must study the child as well as the Book, in order to co-relate the one to the other. Regarding evangelism it has been said, "The man who merely studies the Book will be unpractical, the man who merely studies the soul will be unfurnished, the man who duly studies both will be a good minister of Jesus Christ", C. H. M.

There must be variety in our messages. It is our responsibility to teach the children the difference between right and wrong. We can do this by making full use of the law of Moses and especially the ten commandments. Let us not be afraid of taking our children to Mount Sinai, as well as to Mount Calvary, thereby making them conscious of the need of salvation.

Practice. As in everything else, practice makes perfect. The best way to learn how to do a job is actually to do it. This is essential in the work of soul-winning. God may bestow the gift, but that gift has to be developed. The constant use of our gift will undoubtedly enhance its value. On the other hand if we do not use it, we shall in all probability lose it. We must welcome every opportunity afforded in this direction, whether in the Sunday School or outside it. It will help us in practising the divine art of soul-winning if we take note of the methods of other soul-winners, especially those who have been successful among children.

There is a peculiar fitness in the way the Lord Jesus likened soul-winning to fishing. Maybe it was one of the reasons why among His first followers He chose fishermen and changed them into fishers of men. A fisherman must be watchful, always on the alert; he must be persistent, always keeping at it; he must be courageous, deep-sea fishing involves great risk of life; he must be tactful, wisdom is needed; and he must be forgetful of self, he must keep himself out of sight. All this the soul-winner must be. Always on the alert, always on the job, courageous and tactful, and always seeking to hide self in order to display Christ.

Perseverance. It sometimes takes a long time for a seed to germinate and burst into life. If we patiently sow the seed and wait for God to own our labours, the results will surely come. It is easy to press a child into decision, but what we want are true conversions and these are worth waiting for. Decisions are human, conversions are divine.

We must not be afraid of discouragements. Children can be so trying at times. Often we shall be tempted to think that we are utter failures. It is then that, above all else, we must cast ourselves upon the Lord and seek grace to persevere, and carry on with the work. At such times we need to remind ourselves of the great possibilities which are inherent in the work we are doing. When a child is won for Christ it is a double salvation. A soul saved and a life saved. The life thus saved may turn out to be of great use for God. Many Sunday School teachers have had the joy of seeing children whom they have taught and won taking their places in the front line of the battle in the cause of Christ, becoming in turn mighty soul-winners. We cannot all be Peters, winning the crowds for Christ; but we can be Andrews, and perhaps lead a Peter to Christ. Would it not be right to say that if there were more Andrews there would be more Peters?

Moreover, the Sunday School, and young people's work, is usually the most fruitful section of the whole field of evangelism. There are far more conversions before the age of twenty-one than there are afterwards. It has been stated that the peak age for conversions is thirteen. What a responsibility and yet a privilege to have children around this age under our care. How we should watch them carefully and rejoice if we are allowed to reap where others have sown.

Taking the long view, we shall be assured of much encouragement. We shall be ready to admit that the work we are doing brings with it much happiness and is the cause of much joy and rejoicing which we would otherwise miss. More than this, we may rest assured that faithful Sunday School teachers will be well in the forefront when the servants of the Lord appear before their Master's Bema to hear His "well done" and to receive His reward. This surely will be more than a sufficient recompense.

Open-air Effort

by ERNEST BARKER

THERE ARE MULTITUDES who never enter a building to hear the gospel. How are these people to be reached? They can be reached to a great extent through open-air effort. It is, however, essential that open-air meetings be conducted in a way which *commends* the gospel.

There are numerous examples of open-air preaching in both Old and New Testaments, and a rapid glance at a few of these examples would be worth while, seeing that they are not only interesting, but also suggestive and instructive.

The Pattern. The Lord Jesus frequently took advantage of the open air for the proclamation of that gospel which He came to make possible by His vicarious sacrifice and triumphant resurrection. His incomparable Sermon on the Mount was preached in the open air; also the parable of the sower, with others of the parables mentioned in Matthew 13. Similarly His grand invitation "Come unto me" was given in the open-air, also His notable Bible-reading to the disciples on their way to Emmaus. Our Lord was the *perfect* open-air preacher, as He was the *perfect* teacher, the *perfect* exhorter, and the *perfect* expositor. He "spake with authority", and not as the unprincipled scribes who interpreted the law to suit their convenience. It was for this reason that the people were "astonished at his doctrine". Having the Word of God in our hands, it is our privilege to speak with the same divine authority.

Be Scriptural. An historical open-air meeting was held in Nehemiah's day, when Ezra the scribe stood upon a pulpit of wood (which had been constructed for that purpose). He then opened the book in the sight of all the people (for he was above the people), and read in the law of the Lord *distinctly*, and gave the sense, so that the people understood what was read. It might be wiser before an unsaved audience to quote appropriate Scriptures with earnestness, as very few men can hold an open-air audience when reading. If Scripture is read it is of first-rate importance that it be read intelligently, and brethren should aspire to become as proficient as possible in this sacred art.

Be Clear. If we ought to be distinct in our reading, we ought to be clear in our preaching. To many people the Bible is practically a sealed Book. They therefore need a lucid explanation. The answer which the Ethiopian gave to the question raised by Philip, "Understandest thou what thou readest?" was significant: "How can I, except some man should guide me?". The same is true of those who need the gospel. They want it explained to them.

Be Pointed. A further example of open-air preaching is recorded in Jonah 3. For one whole day Jonah preached in the streets of Nineveh. His message was short – "Yet forty days and Nineveh shall be overthrown". This suggests a splendid principle for open-air preachers – not to be too long, otherwise they may find themselves to be "moving" speakers in the wrong sense! Jonah's message was one of judgment, and in this respect it differs from the message which we are called upon to deliver in our day and generation.

Be Appealing. The gospel which has been entrusted to us is a gospel of grace, peace, and joy, as indicated by the declaration of the heavenly messenger at the birth of our Lord; "Behold, I bring you *good tidings of great joy,* which shall be to all people", Luke 2. 10. It is a mistake to preach nothing but judgment. Our message is one of *love,* and we do well to bear in mind that the Lord Jesus told Nicodemus in plain language that the Son of man came not "to condemn the world, but that the world through him might be saved". It is, of course, necessary to preach judgment as occasion demands, though even then its certainty and necessity should be mentioned with fear and trembling. Incidentally, the results of Jonah's preaching were greater than the prophet anticipated.

Be a Voice. John the Baptist was one of the greatest and most courageous open-air preachers the world has ever known. He was willing to be "a voice . . . in the wilderness": a voice – *anything for God;* in the wilderness – *anywhere for God.* He was a man of character; a man of purpose; *a man of God.* "He was a burning and a shining light". His testimony was both effective and far-reaching. He was "a voice of one *crying* in the wilderness". That does not imply shouting, or howling. The way some speakers shout in the open air makes one wonder they do not injure their pharynx!

Be Adaptable. The apostle Paul's open-air discourse at Mars' Hill, recorded in Acts 17, was masterly. Taking for his text the words, "TO THE UNKNOWN GOD", he impressed upon his hearers the great truth that God "dwelleth not in temples made with hands, neither is worshipped with men's hands, as though he needed any thing (i.e. such spectacular performances), seeing he giveth to all life, and breath, and all things": that "in him we live, and move, and have our being". The preacher confirmed this by quoting certain of their own poets who had said, "For we are also his offspring". This was a master-stroke. The Greeks well-nigh idolized their poets, and assumed that what they said was the last word.

Some friends have been inclined to find fault with the Mars' Hill discourse because the clear message of the gospel appears to be wanting; but such criticism is unjustified. Paul had already encountered his audience in the market-place, where he had preached "Jesus and the resurrection". He had therefore already proclaimed Christ as Saviour, and his address at Mars' Hill was a continuation of his discourses in the market-place.

Be Discreet. It is sometimes profitable in open-air gatherings for two brethren to engage in a dialogue in matters relating to sin, righteousness, salvation, assurance, and other subjects, though this should be done discreetly, and the plan of campaign very carefully considered beforehand.

If a stranger should ask questions, endeavour to answer him as far as possible from the Scriptures. If the question is beyond you, do not attempt to answer it. Endeavouring to manufacture an answer on the spot is often a sad business. There are certain questions which no man can answer, just as there are difficulties which the wisest man in Europe is unable to solve.

Personal Contact. One of the greatest and most useful gifts which God has granted is the gift of personal work. Although the exercise of this gift implies a combination of qualities such as wisdom, patience, and grace – plus personality and winsomeness – surely the grace of God is sufficient to grant these to any of His children who are willing to place themselves at His disposal?

The Voice. Let me at this juncture give a few suggestions regarding the manipulation of the voice. By discreet usage the voice should be *strengthened* by open-air preaching. Voice is *vocalized breath*: therefore by deep and regular breathing you may be heard clearly in a large gathering. It is very easy to over-strain the voice by exercising it unnaturally. It is also of the utmost importance to bear in mind that the back of the throat should never be unduly taxed. Many years ago I was advised by an expert in voice-production to concentrate on three essentials for clear enunciation; namely, the lips, the teeth, and the tip of the tongue. By practice this can be accomplished quite easily, and, together with correct breathing, the result may prove an inestimable blessing both to speaker and hearers. Regular gargling with a suitable preparation will be found beneficial.

Endeavour to avoid speaking against the wind, otherwise your efforts may be disappointing, and even futile. Also, if possible, avoid speaking in places where the voice might be drowned by traffic and other inconveniences.

Be Punctual and Reverent. Strive to be present when the meeting begins and, if possible, stay until it ends. If you must leave before the close, do so without being observed. Also, during the progress of the meeting, refrain from conversations with your fellow-workers.

Be Prayerful. I fancy I hear my readers say, "I cannot speak, and I feel that I am utterly helpless". But stay! You can help in many ways: by your presence, your singing, your quiet inaudible supplications, and by manifesting an intense interest when God's servant is delivering the message.

Be Prepared. A word of encouragement to my younger brethren. If you have never attempted to speak in the open-air, why not make the attempt? Although it calls for the best workers, yet it is often a splendid training-ground for young soldiers of Christ. Take time to prepare carefully, thoughtfully, and prayerfully, a short message which will last five or ten minutes. In your preaching do not hesitate to make it clear that salvation is a *personal* matter, just as the Bible is a *personal* book. Tell the people plainly that Christ Jesus came into the world *to save sinners,* and show how the apostle Paul included himself in this category, even placing himself at the head of the list when he said, "of whom I am chief". Follow this up by emphasizing Paul's personal interest in Christ in such words as, "The Son of God . . . loved *me,* and gave himself for *me*". Seek to avoid unnecessary arguments but, at all cost, in every place, and at all times, give the people what they so desperately need, namely, the Word of the living God. Whatever you do for your Lord and Master, do it thoroughly. Give your very best to Him who gave His very best for you. Exercise whatever gift God has entrusted to you, and thus seek to fulfil your Lord's command, "Go ye into *all the world,* and preach the gospel to *every creature*".

A Guide to Personal Work

by a PERSONAL WORKER

SOUL WINNING is a great work, and personal work is one of the best ways of accomplishing this. But many find it hard to do, and therefore leave it undone. If every Christian became a personal worker, we believe the face of the world would soon be changed. There are thousands who would gladly do this if they only had a better grasp of how to proceed, while many who are doing it would do it far better if they had clearer guidance, and this, it is the writer's desire to give.

There was a time when he found it to be one of the hardest things of his life, but after making a study of the work and following certain principles, he found it a great joy, and therefore, wishes to pass on to others some of his experience.

First, do not make a point of speaking to everyone, or it will soon become a burden and you will find yourself avoided by those you meet; be Spirit guided. Even here there is a danger of waiting until God so lays it on one's heart that one cannot refrain. This often means it is not done at all. Let us practice responding to the inward promptings of the Spirit at once, and soon we shall learn His voice.

A friend once told me that he had it much laid on his heart to speak to a certain man who was standing nearby, but he deliberately refused, saying to himself, "I know too much about him, he will only abuse me". Then he had a long conversation with a young man who was anxious, but having grieved the Holy Spirit, he was powerless to help him. The next day when only a few feet from the man to whom he had refused to speak, he had the unpleasant experience of hearing him fall to the ground; on reaching him he found the man was dead, and he had the task of helping to carry away his body. The same evening he was led to cross the street to speak to a well-dressed gentleman and, remembering his experience of the previous night, he ventured to obey, and to his joy found him in deep soul trouble, and was able to lead him into peace.

It is also extremely important to be *courteous;* nothing will be gained otherwise, because we shall be disobeying the commandment of God–"Be courteous"–and thereby grieve the Spirit. It will also annoy rather than win the hearer. This covers much ground and it is advisable not to speak to such except in a natural way, that is, bring the spiritual into the ordinary conversation, as the Lord constantly did. Again, better do so with the person alone, people do not care to open up in front of others. Seek to gain people's confidence first by acts of kindness or words of sympathy; the world is full of sorrow and kindly words are never out of place. Finally, do not assume a superior position. Above all, do not sit in judgment. The writer has found it to be far wiser to assume, for purposes of conversation, that the one to whom he is speaking is a Christian. It gives confidence and hearts are opened which would otherwise be closed.

Often the mistake is made by *saying too much*. One word kindly and fitly spoken is worth far more than much talk.

A young lady, after being baptized, said to the writer, "I was brought to the Lord simply by your saying to me, 'I am praying for you'. I there and then decided if that were so, it was time I prayed for myself, and I did".

To waste time *arguing is useless*; better give them the Word of God and let Him drive it home. A man who was arguing with a Roman Catholic, at last gave up in despair. Another quietly said, "Look, God's Word says, 'He that hath the Son hath life', now, have you the Son?". The Roman Catholic replied, "No, I have not, but I wish I had". Then said the other, "Get on your knees then and tell Him so"; he did there and then, and was saved.

The aim should always be to find the state of the person to whom we speak, and it is imperative to *start with conviction of sin*; if this is lacking, the whole structure will fall because there is no foundation. Then repentance, which is a change of mind, leading to a change of affection, that manifests itself in a change of action, and it is not until the exceeding sinfulness of sin and the goodness of God is realized that repentance will lay the foundation for faith. As long as they refuse to repent they will not believe, Matt. 21. 32.

To *press people is fatal*. Let the Word of God do its work; there must be sowing before reaping. Pressure only tends to place people on a false foundation, whereas a steady going on with God will be rewarded by Him, and we shall not be disappointed by unreal cases, such as is inevitable when undue pressure is brought to bear.

How many of us would have acted as our Lord did in the case of the rich young ruler. He allowed him to leave while under the conviction of sin. He did not even present "faith" to him, but only "law", then left him to learn his utter helplessness to get eternal life by works. How wise He was!

We cannot do better than close with an illustration from the life of the Lord in John 4. How did He do this piece of personal work? First, He honoured the woman at the well by appealing to her generosity – "Give me to drink". Then, to her curiosity – "If thou knewest". Next, to her soul's deep longing – "Shall never thirst". Now, her conscience – "Go call thy husband". Finally, He leads her to Himself – "I that speak unto thee am he". How great His wisdom and how perfect His example! May He help us to do likewise.

Establishing a New Work

by L. WILSON

TO ESTABLISH AN ASSEMBLY YOU NEED:

Prayer. Before you go to the place: while you are there and after you leave.

Patience, 2 Cor. 12. 12; Rom. 5. 4. Patience to wait God's time, and patience with converts. In Isaiah 42. 19 we read "Who is blind, but my servant? or deaf, as my messenger that I sent? Who is blind as he that is perfect and blind as the Lord's servant?".

In new work it is often necessary to close your eyes and ears to a lot of things; not sin of course, but mannerisms, actions, certain expressions, and phraseology new to us and our background, and not altogether scriptural, nor in some cases unscriptural.

One must be patient and let the Word of God and the Spirit of God adjust these things. One may cause offence in trying to do it personally. When we try to force growth we often hinder it, like forcing open the petals of a rose or seeking to help a butterfly out of its silken tomb. Much patience is required until some people unlearn a lot and then learn "the more excellent way". Some good brethren were once rough diamonds; patience saw them polished. Other Christians with possibilities were stumbled because of impatience on the part of the older brethren.

Perseverance. There will be bitter with the sweet; rough with smooth. The main thing that enables one to persevere is knowing one is in the will of God; to have God's assurance that He has "much people in this place". Paul says in 2 Timothy 2. 10, "Therefore I endure all things for the elect's sake, that they may also obtain the salvation which is in Christ Jesus with eternal glory". When Paul entered a city he knew some of the elect were there and he preached and endured until the material for an assembly was gathered.

Power of the Spirit of God. This is the most important of all. "And I, brethren, when I came to you, came not with excellency of speech or of wisdom, declaring unto you the testimony of God. For I determined not to know anything among you, save Jesus Christ and him crucified. And I was with you in weakness, and in fear, and in much trembling. And my speech and my preaching was not with enticing words of man's wisdom, but in demonstration of the Spirit and of power; that your faith should not stand in the wisdom of men, but in the power of God", 1 Cor. 2. 1–5; "For our gospel came not unto you in word only, but also in power, and in the Holy Ghost, and in much assurance; as ye know what manner of men we were among you for your sake", 1 Thess. 1. 5. No doubt these verses refer to Paul's pioneer effort. Note the emphasis on the power of the Spirit.

Personality. A sanctified, a strong spiritual personality. One has said that "personality is the kind of person you are". "The outward expression of the inner life which influences other people favourably or unfavourably". "A strong positive personality is the magnetic outward expression of the inner life, dominated by positive and pleasing qualities, such as courtesy, courage, graciousness and truthfulness, thus attracting people and influencing their lives. It makes a man a leader in the affairs of life instead of a follower, for the greatest and most vital power in influencing life is a sanctified personality." Some have personality without spirituality and power; others may have spirituality and power without personality. The latter certainly is preferable of the two, but when both are combined you have a power for God.

Fellowship is your grip on God; personality, your grip on man.

Your work will likely correspond with the amount of each of the things listed above; little of them will produce a small work, much will produce a large one. The field may qualify somewhat this remark.

Persistence. "According to the grace of God which is given unto me, as a wise masterbuilder, I have laid the foundation, and another buildeth thereon. But let every man take heed how he buildeth thereupon", 1 Cor. 3. 10.

We often have been foolish learners trying to build, instead of wise masterbuilders. The one who plants an assembly lays the foundation; presents and instructs in foundation truths, such as the gospel, salvation by grace, assurance, law and grace, the two natures, soul-winning, the Lord's supper, baptism, the Lord's coming. The man or men who follow build upon that foundation.

The superstructure may mean such truths as the ones in the foundation more fully developed; also the one Body, the Spirit and His work, the priesthood of Christ and of all believers, could be included in the superstructure.

Sometimes the pioneer or the one who lays the foundation has to remain long enough to build the framework of the superstructure before leaving it. The framework of course is not too solid or secure; much filling in and much hard work remains for the follow-up man or men before the building or assembly can be termed solid and stable; in a building the filling-in or finishing work takes longest and is the most tedious. Elders and overseers are not produced overnight, are not to be novices, but often take from ten to fifteen years to develop; they must first be proved. Many a work that had a good start faltered because it was left to local or inexperienced men too soon.

FINANCING GOD'S WORK

◕◕◕◕◕◕

What Shall I Give?

by ARTHUR T. SHEARMAN

ONE OF THE MOST striking pictures, painted in words by
the writers of the Gospels, is that of the Lord Jesus sitting
over against the treasury, watching those who gave of their
wealth. This incident took place near to the end of His public
ministry and perhaps its appeal is all the more forceful in the
light of the self-emptying devotion of the cross. Mark records
in one brief phrase the object of His watching: He "beheld how
the people cast money into the treasury", 12. 41. Luke says
that He "saw the rich men casting their gifts into the treasury", 21. 1. Mark comments "many that were rich cast in
much", 12. 41. But we are bound to feel that the actual amount
cast in that day mattered little to the Saviour. If this had been
the prime consideration, the poor widow around whom the
story is built would have had no place. He "beheld how they
gave" – this turns our minds from the *riches* cast in to the
manner of the giving, which is a prime factor in all Christian
giving. In what manner do we dispose of goods and possessions
for the Lord? Is it without sacrifice being involved, out of our
abundance? Remember, David would not give to the Lord
that which had cost him nothing, 2 Sam. 24. 24.

Early in Christian experience, the question of rightly
balanced giving is bound to arise in our minds. One thing is
certain. None can evade the *challenge* of the lavishness of God's
giving. He "giveth to all men liberally, and upbraideth not",
James 1. 5; He "giveth us richly all things to enjoy", 1 Tim.
6. 17. These, among many other Scriptures, tell of a God who
delights continually to give. Generosity is a Christian grace

and it is true, in a largely selfish world, that liberality brings its own recompence. It is also sadly true that the work of God suffers in many ways when there is a lack of concern regarding the "grace of giving". To give is to be God-like; the measure of giving should be as He has given to us.

We can consider four features linked with the meaning of the Christian's giving.

1. Giving must be the Expression of Living. The way we give *to* God is invariably the expression of the way we live *for* God. Notice the order in Paul's commendation of the liberality of the churches of Macedonia; they "first gave their own selves to the Lord, and unto us by the will of God", 2 Cor. 8. 5. How wonderful this is and how important. For all sanctified giving to the Lord must spring from the devotedness of sanctified and surrendered lives. As we value God's giving to us, we must realise that the *Giver* is much more important than the *gift*. We know, with deep thankfulness, that because we have the *Giver*, the *gifts* are ours to an unlimited extent. It is none the less true that, unless God has our lives first, He will not receive that for which He is looking. Let us surrender our lives to Him, putting them at His disposal, and then our giving will be directed aright.

2. Giving is the Undeniable Expression of Loving. "God so loved . . . that he gave", John 3. 16. This wonderful truth lies at the very heart of the gospel and must inevitably colour all our thinking in relation to giving. When God looks at our response to His great giving, we can be sure that He looks beyond the *hand* that gives to the *heart* that lies behind it. As the Saviour witnessed the giving of the widow at the treasury, His commendation gave evidence of His appreciation of the thoughts of her heart. The grace of giving is therefore more than a duty. Cold duty sets its limits and calculates the extents of giving. Devotion sets no limits but is prodigal, giving out of a full heart. Thus of the Macedonians Paul said, "according to their power, I bear witness, yea and beyond their power, they gave of their own accord", 2 Cor. 8. 3 R.V. Dutiful giving is so often linked with philanthropy and acts of charity, but God does not ask for charity to support His work.

He desires gifts that are the result of loving, sympathetic hearts responding to His own love. Let us make sure that our giving is inspired by an irresistible response to the unbounded love of our God.

3. Giving is an Intelligent Exercise through Learning of Need.

All fruitful Christian giving must be controlled by a right understanding of need. It is easy to be satisfied with putting a few coins in "the collection", without considering the relationship it has to possessions or needs. It is so often asked "How shall we know how much to give?". Systematic giving is an essential. The whole tenor of the New Testament teaching on giving indicates that there must be a part of personal possessions set apart exclusively for the Lord, 1 Cor. 16. 2. This must be His – for His servants – for His work. Tithing is a good exercise and leads to good strong giving habits, but it is well to recall that the tenth was God's portion. If it was withheld, the people "robbed God". It was what they freely gave in addition to the tenth that was accepted as true giving by God.

We must also learn to give sympathetically, with a true knowledge of the needs existing. There is a great danger in giving vaguely, hoping that it meets the right need. We must prayerfully seek God's guidance, asking Him to show us the various areas of need. How many wonderful stories can rewarded faith tell of assistance received at the time of desperate need. Behind these stories there lies the power of guided giving – generosity controlled by an intelligent, spiritual mind. Let us then study to give systematically and sympathetically, learning the extent of our power to give and also of the needs to be met.

4. Giving is the Result of Longing to Share.

Earnestness and sincerity result in useful giving. "God loveth a cheerful (joyous) giver", 2 Cor. 9. 7. It is possible to give a large gift with a niggardly, grudging spirit. It is also possible to give a small gift with a large-hearted generosity so that unmeasured wealth seems to be there. God takes account of that which is left as well as that which is given. Let us never forget that heaven was emptied in order that God might prove His longing to bless, to share His love with men. God literally could give no more. Of the widow the Saviour said, "She . . . did cast in all that she had, even all her living". Behind the gift given, there must be the depth of a self-sacrificing spirit. Liberality must be inspired by deep and fervent love, 1 Pet. 4. 7–10. And thus out of the *grace of giving* there will ascend *gratitude that glorifies* the great Giver Himself. Thus the end is achieved, lasting glory to God.

Church Finance

by A. G. CLARKE

Introduction. The question of finance, which often presents such problems to the churches of Christendom, is really simple if the Scriptural pattern be followed. Nowhere in the New Testament is there the slightest hint that the world is to be appealed to for funds to carry on the Lord's work. Those who do it are dishonouring Him. Giving to God is a privilege belonging to His people, whose offerings alone, spiritual and material, are acceptable to Him. As to others, God asks them to receive, not to give. It is particularly reprehensible to take up a collection at gospel meetings, indoors or out. In sending out His preachers the Lord Jesus said, "Freely (gratuitously) ye received, freely give. Get you no gold, nor silver, nor brass (copper) in your purses", Matt. 10. 8, 9 R.V. Paul was careful to adopt this divine policy, 2 Cor. 11. 7, labouring with his own hands rather than be chargeable to his hearers at Corinth and elsewhere, Acts 18. 3; cf. 3 John 7. God's salvation is "without money and without price", Isa. 55. 1; cf. Eph. 2. 8, 9. On the other hand it is inadvisable to announce "No collection", as this sounds like advertising generosity and may be deemed a reflection upon the pockets of those who wish to attend.

There will be abundant supply for all needs in the Lord's work if Christians recognize their privilege and rise to their responsibility according to the precepts of God's Word.

Importunate solicitation, burdensome exactions, worldly expedients and elaborate financial organization, all will then be unnecessary. Such methods call down the just reproach of the world upon the church as a money-making concern.

Provision of Funds. It is a fundamental principle that all a believer has belongs to the Lord. He himself is not his own, and all his possessions are held in trust as a steward of God, 1 Cor. 6. 19, 20; Rom. 12. 1; Luke 16. 9–13; 2 Cor. 8. 5. Under the Mosaic economy, God claimed back from Israel a certain portion of their possessions on the same principle, namely, that all they had was first given to them by Him. The first-born males of man and beast were His, though the offspring of man and ass could be redeemed by a lamb as a substitutionary sacrifice, Exod. 13. 1, 2, 11–15. The first-fruits from the land were His, Exod. 22. 29, 30. The tithe (tenth of all) belonged to Him, and this He gave back to the tribe of Levi in lieu of a common share in the division of the land of Canaan among the tribes. Tithing was observed by Abraham before the giving of the law, Gen. 14. 20; Heb. 7. 4–10. Withholding any part of the tithe was robbing God, Mal. 3. 8–10. Then certain sacrifices and parts of sacrifices were the Lord's. All these were obligatory as a rendering up of that which was not Israel's. Giving to God in the true sense began after these obligations had been met and is regulated under the term "free-will offerings" which, as the name indicates, were wholly voluntary. First mention of a free-will offering is in connection with the materials and work for the tabernacle of Jehovah, Exod. chs. 35, 36. As to sacrifices, see Lev. 22. 17–25; 23. 38; Deut. 23. 21–23, etc. These passages all contain valuable instruction that may be applied to Christian giving. Further examples may be noted in connection with the building of the first temple, 1 Chron. 29, and the second one, Ezra 2. 7.

Under grace, giving is wholly voluntary but the standard should hardly be less than that under the law, even as the privileges Christians enjoy are far superior to those of Israel. Five times in the New Testament giving is called a "grace" as being that which, in the Christian, is responsive to the revealed grace of God.

1. *Means of Giving.* As we have seen, these lie with each individual believer, and instructions are found chiefly in 1 Cor. 16. 1–3; 2 Cor. 8 and 9, which passages should be carefully studied. Note "each one of you", well-to-do or otherwise, though the former have greater opportunity, 1 Tim. 6. 17–19. The churches of Macedonia gave out of their poverty, 2 Cor. 8. 2–4, the first principle of giving being stated, v. 5. Women, too, manifested this grace, Luke 8. 3, and the Lord accepted the ministry of their gifts. Brethren wholly engaged in the Lord's work are not exempted, for they are like the Levites of old, Num. 18. 25–32.

2. *Measure of Giving.* This is to be according to a person's ability, 2 Cor. 8. 11, 12; Acts 11. 29; "as he may prosper", 1 Cor. 16. 2. Liberty rules, not law, 2 Cor. 9. 5, but inasmuch as God is a liberal giver, James 1. 5; John 3. 15; Rom. 8. 32, etc.; His children should be like Him. Our Lord impoverished Himself to make us rich, 2 Cor. 8. 9. Such superlative grace is an incentive to all; cf. Rom. 12. 8, marg.; 2 Cor. 8. 2; 9. 11, 13. Note the Lord's estimate of measure, Mark 12. 41–44; Luke 21. 1–4; and the Lord's promise, Luke 6. 38; cf. 2 Cor. 9. 6; Prov. 11. 24, 25; 22. 9; Mal. 3. 10.

3. *Motive of Giving. Negative* – not for the admiration and applause of men, Matt. 6. 1–4, therefore our giving should be done unostentatiously and, as far as possible, privately. It is the world's way to publish lists of charitable gifts, placing the names of those who contribute the largest sums at the top, contrast Luke 21. 1–4. *Positive* – love to God and man, 1 Cor. 13. 3; 2 Cor. 8. 8; 1 John 3. 17, 18; Gal. 6. 10; constrained by divine love not by human appeals, 2 Cor. 5. 14; seeking the glory of God, 1 Cor. 10. 31.

4. *Manner of Giving.* Willingly, 2 Cor. 8. 3, 11, 12; and cheerfully, without grudging, 2 Cor. 9. 7; Acts 20. 35. Christians are to give honestly, by which is meant that they give only what is rightly theirs. Debts to tradesmen and others, for instance, and prior family obligations must be discharged first, Rom. 12. 8; Mark 7. 11–13; 1 Tim. 5. 8; 2 Cor. 8. 20, 21. Also necessary is a clear conscience in relation to brethren for gifts to be acceptable to the Lord, Matt. 5. 23, 24.

5. *Method of Giving*. The Word of God teaches us to give systematically not haphazardly, 1 Cor. 16. 1, 2. This is done by: (a) *Laying up a store* proportionately to income, setting aside with purpose as before the Lord. Some have a special box at home for this. Well-to-do brethren often have a separate bank-account. Others simply make a book-keeping entry. It is from such a store that gifts are made to various objects as exercised by the Spirit of God, and thus the embarrassment of a sudden call is avoided, 2 Cor. 9. 5. (b) *Regularly putting by*, 1 Cor. 16. 2, linking it thus with worship and the remembrance feast of the Lord's Day. (This was also the day of the presentation of the first-fruits in Israel, (a) the wave sheaf, Lev. 23. 9–14, and (b) the wave loaves, Lev. 23. 15–21, typical of our Lord's resurrection, 1 Cor. 15. 20, 23 and Pentecost, Acts 2, respectively.)

Collection of Funds. Collective gifts are indicated in Acts 11. 29, 30; Rom. 15. 25, 26; 1 Cor. 16. 1; Phil. 4. 15, 16; individual gifts, 2 John 5–7; Gal. 6. 6; Heb. 13. 16; 1 Tim. 6. 18; Acts 4. 36, 37. Contributions for many local church expenses can scarcely be regarded as giving to the Lord. Rent, furnishing, light and heat, caretaking, etc., are necessary to secure the comfort and convenience of the saints themselves. Sharing such expenses is a matter of obligation, a debt rather than a "free-will offering".

Administration of Funds should be in the hands of more than one brother, Acts 6. 3–6; 1 Cor. 16. 3, 4; 2 Cor. 8. 18–21; 9. 3–5. This wise arrangement leaves no room for unkind suspicions, increases the confidence of saints, and spreads the burden of responsibility. Though such brethren minister in temporalities, their moral and spiritual qualifications are to be high, Acts 6. 3; 1 Tim. 3. 8–13. Obviously they must also possess business capability. From these passages it would appear to be a principle with the Lord, that those who contribute funds should have a voice in the selection of persons to take charge thereof. Other than the possession of the necessary qualifications no indication is given of the method of choice, so that elders as leaders in the assembly would seem free to judge the most expedient way of discovering the mind of the saints. Accounts should be rendered at regular intervals, again on the principle of 1 Cor. 14. 40.

Distribution of Funds. In the New Testament we see four main avenues for the disbursement of gifts.

1. *Needy Widows,* Acts 6. 1–6; 1 Tim. 5. 4–16. Not all widows in the assembly are qualified for such aid. They must be (a) really destitute, having no family able to support; (b) at least sixty years of age; (c) a woman of prayer and trust in God; (d) one bearing a character approved for godly living and activity.

2. *Poor Saints,* Rom. 12. 13; 15. 23–27; Gal. 2. 9, 10; Acts 11. 29, 30; 24. 17; 2. 44, 45; 1 Cor. 16. 1–3; 2 Cor. chs. 8, 9; Prov. 19. 17. There is no lack of opportunity, Mark 14. 7. This does not include the indolent and thriftless, 2 Thess. 3. 10. Compare the charge to Israel, Deut. 15. 7–11.

3. *God's Servants,* Phil. 4. 15–19; (a) the evangelist, 1 Cor. 9. 4–14; (b) the teacher, Gal. 6. 6; (c) the elder who labours in the Word, 1 Tim. 5. 17, 18 – in cases where secular employment has been relinquished for the sake of serving the Lord. Apostolic example should not be forgotten, however, Acts 18. 3 with 20. 34. Questions of expediency may arise – (a) to make the gospel without charge, 1 Cor. 9. 15–18, so removing all ground for suspicion of mercenary motives, 2 Cor. 11.7–12; (b) to be an example in the matter of Christian giving, Acts 20. 33–35; (c) to avoid being burdensome to saints both poor and suffering persecution, 1 Thess. 2. 9; 2 Thess. 3. 7–9.

4. *Philanthropic Efforts,* Gal. 6. 10; 1 Thess. 5. 15. The household of faith has prior claim upon the gifts of God's people but not an exclusive claim.

The Effects of Giving are seven:
1. It is well-pleasing to the Lord, 1 Cor. 9. 7; cf. Heb. 13. 16; Phil. 4. 18.
2. It brings relief to necessitous saints, 2 Cor. 9. 12.
3. It stimulates others to like effort, 2 Cor. 8. 1, 2; 9. 2.

4. It promotes thanksgiving in grateful recipients, 2 Cor. 9. 11–14.
5. It evokes prayer for the kind-hearted givers, 2 Cor. 9. 14.
6. It increases capacity for further giving, 2 Cor. 9. 8–10; Prov. 11. 24; Luke 19. 24–26. Note the divine principle here.
7. It produces fruit to the donor's account, Phil. 4. 17; 2 Cor. 9. 10.

The Rewards for Giving. Giving after the divine pattern brings a present reward in the joyful knowledge of doing the will of the Lord, and in the pleasure of assisting others in need; Prov. 11. 24, 25; Luke 6. 38. Nevertheless, God is pleased to indicate further means of approval in a coming day, faithful stewardship ranking high in His gracious estimation, Matt. 6. 19–21; 25. 14–30; Luke 16. 9–13; 19. 11–27; 2 Cor. 9. 6. Note the principle, Matt. 25. 40; 10. 42. A "well done" from the Lord is assured, and a "welcome (well come)" from many friends in the eternal tabernacles, Luke 16. 9.

Summary. Christians, then, should give (1) devotedly (Godward); (2) lovingly (manward); (3) willingly (with cheerfulness); (4) liberally (abounding in this grace); (5) methodically (purpose – preparation – proportion); (6) unostentatiously (no self-display); (7) honestly (only what is truly theirs).

Extra Note. It is hardly becoming in servants of the Lord to advertize personal needs. Paul and other apostles did not do so, though they did make known the needs of distressed saints. Information is often desirable but solicitation never. Servants of Christ look to their Master alone for due support. He it is who moves the hearts of His people in right directions to meet His servants' requirements. Gifts for personal service may be acknowledged by word or letter, but account of stewardship should be given for the disbursement of all entrusted funds.

WARNINGS AND EXHORTATIONS

<><><><><><>

The History of
the Assembly at Ephesus

by P. James Poole

Ephesus is unique among the assemblies mentioned in Scripture in that it is possible to trace its history over a comparatively long period, from purely Scriptural sources. Its nucleus consisted of the small number of disciples, about twelve, mentioned in Acts 19. 7, whom Paul found there on his second visit to the city. His first visit, recorded in chapter 18, had been a very short one, and we have no record of any converts made on that occasion. In the meantime Apollos had been in Ephesus, and it is possible that these twelve were the fruit of his labours. There is no proof, but their ignorance of the truth of believers' baptism, as distinct from that of John, would seem to indicate that they had received what teaching they had enjoyed from Apollos. Paul expounded the truth to them more perfectly, and they were baptized and received the Holy Ghost, speaking with tongues and prophesying.

After Paul had preached three months in the synagogue opposition arose, and he withdrew with the disciples, "disputing daily in the school of Tyrannus" for the space of two years. His preaching was accompanied by miracles, and "all they who dwelt in Asia heard the word of the Lord Jesus, both Jews and Greeks". The tumult organized by Demetrius, Acts 19, gives an indication of the great blessing that had attended the preaching of the gospel. After the tumult Paul departed into Macedonia, Acts 20. 1, and from that time, as far as Scripture tells, he did not revisit Ephesus. *En route* to

Jerusalem, however, 20. 16, he sent for the elders of the Ephesian assembly to come to him at Miletus, to whom he discoursed as recorded in Acts 20. 18–35.

From the discourse we learn that from the very first day of his being in Asia he had been active in the work of the gospel, in ministering the Word to the believers, preaching the kingdom of God, declaring *all* the counsel of God, and keeping back *nothing* that was profitable. He had also mingled warnings with the teaching. From this we can see that the Ephesian believers had enjoyed a rich and searching ministry during the three years in which the apostle was among them, Acts 20. 31.

Our next link is the Epistle to the Ephesians. (That the Epistle which we know by this title *was* written to Ephesus, and from Rome, is the verdict of competent investigators.) It confirms one's impressions of richness and fulness, as the didactic contents of the Epistle reach almost, if not quite, the very peak of divine revelation. It does not, however, contain much material to enable us to form an idea of the internal state of the assembly at the time it was written. We may perhaps feel that the apostle would hardly have opened such a wealth of truth to an assembly that was not, in general at least, worthy of it. He refers to them as the faithful in Christ Jesus, 1. 1; he thanks God for their faith and love to all the saints, 1. 15, 16, and closes with a benediction on all who love the Lord in sincerity. On the negative or sinister side, 4. 14 might indicate that some in the assembly were trying to introduce false doctrine, and 5. 6 might be a hint that some were even minimizing the seriousness of unclean practices. The Epistle's general exhortations are such as are applicable to all churches in all ages.

Returning now briefly to the discourse in Acts 20 (which antedates the Epistle), we find that he not only reminds them of the past, but warns them of the future, and of developments which would ensue if the elders were not watchful. Grievous wolves would beset them from without, while from within subversive elements would be manifested. The preventive of this was "God, and the word of his grace", v. 32. As we have seen, up to the date of the Epistle to the Ephesians these sinister developments appear not to have shown themselves to any degree that we can be positive about.

The two Epistles to Timothy are the next link in this chain of history. They were written not long after the Epistle to the Ephesians. Authorities vary, but the interval was probably not more than 'five years or so, at the most. Timothy had been left behind in Ephesus by Paul when the latter went on a journey. (Incidentally, the statement of 1 Timothy 1. 3 must be accepted as fact; there is no trace of this event in the Acts.) These Epistles show that the deterioration foretold in Acts 20 had set in. Whether Timothy was left at Ephesus to repair the damage done by the local elders, or to strengthen their hands is, I think, indeterminate, though probably the latter would be the correct view. In the assembly there had begun to appear false teachers and unprofitable talkers, 1 Tim. 1. 3, 4, Judaisers and their "vain jangling", vv. 6, 7. There is a hint of "profane and old wives' fables" in 4. 7, and the "oppositions of science falsely so called" in 6. 20, 21. Some had unfortunately been drawn away by this last form of error, v. 21. These all are definite indications of the downward trend, being amplified by a further reference in 2 Timothy 2. 14–16. In addition, and most sinister and grievous, though not perhaps to be specifically applied to Ephesus, is the remark in 2 Timothy 1. 15 that to Timothy's own knowledge "all in Asia" had turned away from the apostle.

The two Epistles to Timothy are invaluable from every point of view. Their foretellings of the state of things in the religious world in the "last days" have been only too fully justified by events. We today see all round us the very developments of which they warn us. But the infant church also was beset by every kind of enemy, and it is probable that Paul saw the beginnings of these sinister conditions in his own day. If so, 1 Timothy 4. 1–11; 2 Timothy 3. 1–17; 4. 1–4 are further indications that all was not well with Ephesus.

Between these two Epistles and Revelation 2, our last link, there is a gap of about thirty years. The non-scriptural histories of the early church say that the apostle John spent some years in Ephesus after Paul's death, and himself died there. If that was so we may be sure that Ephesus had the benefit of yet further years of faithful ministry from that venerable servant of Christ. Be that as it may, we are on quite safe and firm ground in Revelation 2, where we find in some senses a considerable improvement in the situation. False teachers and practisers of evil deeds had alike been repudiated, and expelled from the church or prevented from entering it. Instead of a partial heterodoxy we have strict orthodoxy; all doctrinally correct and satisfactory. In addition, "for my name's sake thou hast laboured and hast not fainted". But for all that, the church had *fallen*, in that she had left her first love. Her state therefore was *orthodoxy plus formality*; a sort of automatic activity, which lacked the only element that made the rest worth anything in the eyes of the Lord Jesus, namely, a true and vital love to Himself. She is threatened with removal unless she repents; a severe penalty indeed, which appears to have been imposed in the end, though Scripture is silent as to her later course. It is well known that for many centuries there has been no church in Ephesus; indeed no Ephesus itself. Whether repentance and restoration did ensue from the Lord's words to her is not known, but this ancient assembly stands as a warning to all assemblies from then to now, and in every place, your assembly and my assembly included.

Formality. How often does this really deadly paralysis set in in the assemblies of God's people! We may rejoice (with trembling) that false teachers and evil-doers are not a present disease of the assemblies at large, but who can deny that formality characterizes them in too many instances? The remedy is that all the saints should be living in godliness and true holiness, and that all the *men* in the assemblies should be continually exercised that their contributions to the active life of the assemblies are the outcome of the inworking of the Spirit. Whatever we do frequently is bound to beget the *habit* of doing it, and *habit*, as such, is a deadly foe to spiritual efficiency. In the very nature of the assemblies' life and activities, the same things are being done at very frequent intervals. The greater therefore is the need that we take warning from Ephesus, that ancient church, whose fault in the eyes of the Lord was that she had left her first love.

Disagreement

by R. PENNEY

ONE PROBLEM FOR CHRISTIANS is how to put into practice the scriptural injunction "be ye all of one mind", 1 Pet. 3. 8; Phil. 2. 2. The painful fact is that we are often far from this; we quarrel, we fall out, we separate ourselves, and worst of all, assemblies may be split. The testimony of our Lord Jesus Christ is thereby brought into disrepute and the witness of individual believers and of assemblies is vitiated.

The Root of the Problem lies in the fact that we are human and living in bodies of flesh. It is true that we have new natures, born of God, that do not sin, 1 John 3. 9, and if we allowed at all times this new nature to control, being guided by the Spirit of God, we should never disagree one with another. But the flesh, ever striving against the Spirit, intrudes and trouble is the result. Since there will be no such intrusion when we are in heaven, then heavenly people on earth should strive now for agreement amongst themselves.

Our Use of and our Attitude to Scripture provides one solution to the problem. We need carefully to "prove all things", 1 Thess. 5. 21, and not follow easily-formed traditions. We may do something or hold an opinion convinced that it is scriptural, yet under close examination it turns out to be human tradition, fleshly bias or conformity to the herd instinct. Motives may be governed by a combination of these, and may be cunningly rationalized as obedience to the will of God. Well may Scripture warn, "Thou shalt not follow a multitude to do evil; neither shalt thou speak in a cause to decline after many to wrest judgment", Exod. 23. 2. Scripture is indeed the supreme arbiter in every case, "To the law and to the testimony: if they speak not according to this word, it is because there is no light in them", Isa. 8. 20. But the Holy Spirit leads us into all truth, John 16. 13. Moreover, if our wills are subject to God and if we desire to do His will, then we "shall know of the teaching", John 7. 17 R.V. Here again the flesh may intrude, and we find different "interpretations".

Sometimes these differences are made the excuse either for not studying Scripture at all or for acting in disobedience to Scripture. This problem would cause despair, but God has left us with guidance as to what is to be done when disagreements have to be resolved.

The Lord's Provision. The Lord Jesus taught, "Moreover if thy brother shall trespass against thee, go and tell him his fault between thee and him alone: if he shall hear thee, thou hast gained thy brother. But if he will not hear thee, then take with thee one or two more, that in the mouth of two or three witnesses every word may be established. And if he neglect to hear them, tell it unto the church: but if he neglect to hear the church, let him be unto thee as an heathen man and a publican", Matt. 18. 15–17. Christians are responsible to settle, amicably and justly, any matter that may arise between them. If this cannot be done between individuals, the aid of others is sought, and then if the disagreement persists it becomes a matter for the whole church to deal with. Today, this procedure is seldom practised. Brethren and sisters harbour grievances against one another, but never bring them into the open. These grievances become a source of bitterness as they are cherished within the heart, leading to a narrowing of outlook and a stunting of spiritual growth. The Christian joy and witness of such a soul are non-existent because of failure to take heed to the words of the Lord Jesus Christ. This may also be the state of some local assemblies, leading to a vitiated and worldly testimony. It is frequently the sin of pride that helps to bring about this state, so that sin added to sin makes things worse. Pride may prevent us humbling ourselves before a brother or sister to admit a fault.

The Holy Spirit Restricted. Another reason why the procedure given by the Lord in Matthew 18 is not followed may be because it is not taught. The public ministry of the Word of God in local assemblies may be adversely affected by tradition. There is nothing wrong with the procedure whereby ministry is given by invited gifted and accredited brethren, but this may tend to become a system that shuts out the free operation of the Holy Spirit. Ministry may become a talk by a diplomatic and tactful brother who will keep well away from thorny problems. This may be easy and pleasant but it can also be enervating, since thorny and difficult problems make us seek the Lord and search the Scriptures. Today there are many such problems among the Lord's people, but how seldom are these touched upon in ministry meetings.

Teaching is, perhaps, too often thought of as a one-way process, where the invited brother expounds the Word of God to the local assembly. Paul indicates one of the principles governing such ministry, "let the prophets speak by two or three, and let the others discern", 1 Cor. 14. 29 R.V. This suggests that there is room for ministry to be of a more free and open nature, with room for discussion and the interchange of ideas. This is not a one-man ministry and it is certainly not an any-man ministry. It is rather the situation where the Holy Spirit is able to direct the teaching in the local assembly through all those to whom He has given the gift of teaching.

As we have said, the real solution to the problem of disagreement is a familiarity with the Word of God and submission to it. Hence the restriction in any way of the activity of the Holy Spirit merely papers over the cracks and does not do anything about the real problem. The application of the real remedy is prevented. But "the word of God is quick, and powerful, and sharper than any two-edged sword, piercing even to the dividing asunder of soul and spirit . . . and is a discerner of the thoughts and intents of the heart", Heb. 4. 12. On occasions when the "two-edged sword" should be applied we may merely get diplomatic homilies. Where disagreement defaces the ministry of the Word, the answer is an earnest searching of Scripture and for the "others (that is, other prophets) to discern".

The Work of the True Pastor. In 2 Timothy 2. 24, 25 we read, "the servant of the Lord must not strive; but be gentle unto all men, apt to teach, patient, in meekness instructing those that oppose themselves; if God peradventure will give them repentance to the acknowledging of the truth". Here is the application of the Word by a true pastor. Such a person has no need of external marks of authority, or of human props to dignity. The man who is "apt to teach" and who can handle the Word of God should be able to deal with situations that may arise. As God showed Jeremiah, His Word possesses its own authority which needs no human patronage, and which condemns all that originates from any other source. "What is the chaff to the wheat? saith the Lord. Is not my word like as a fire? . . . and like a hammer that breaketh the rock in pieces?", Jer. 23. 28, 29. Where an assembly has overseers who are "apt to teach" and where the Holy Spirit is allowed to have His way in the teaching, this will minimize the amount of local quarrelling. There may be plenty of discussion and even disagreement, but this will not lead to scenes that deface the testimony. To be able to disagree with one's brother and not fall out with him is a sign of spiritual maturity.

The Gregariousness of Believers. Because human beings are naturally gregarious, Christians often submit to prevailing opinions, or, if they cannot make themselves agree they just keep quiet and try not to disagree. In either case, being denied proper expression because of the subtle, and sometimes not so subtle, psychological pressures brought to bear upon them, such people become inactive and passive as far as Christian work is concerned. These pressures to conform may cause terrible mental distress and inner conflict, with the result that spiritual life is vitiated. The Lord alone looks on the human heart, man only looks on the outward appearance, 1 Sam. 16. 7. In the light of this fact, we should all ask ourselves whether or not, in the cause of what we deem to be truth, we are not in fact bringing very cruel and unkind pressures to bear upon a dear brother or sister, thereby retarding and warping spiritual growth.

Likemindedness. The absence of this is reflected in many ways. Some may change their opinions whenever they move house, merely showing the desire to conform. Others may leave a local assembly to meet elsewhere. Others may travel past a local assembly's hall in order to find fellowship with another assembly. There may be nothing wrong in the person concerned, but if an assembly holds ideas and follows practices that prevent a saint enjoying its fellowship then something is wrong somewhere.

But Scripture exhorts us to be likeminded. This does not imply a legality to toe the party line; rather the scriptural way for saints to achieve likemindedness is by growing "in grace, and in the knowledge of our Lord and Saviour Jesus Christ", 2 Pet. 3. 18. The more we are conformed to His image, the more we shall find agreement together and the less we shall differ because "we have the mind of Christ", 1 Cor. 2. 16. We may achieve this by holy discussion together in an atmosphere where the Word of God is honoured and ministered by godly and gifted men. Conformity merely for the sake of an outward show of agreement is a sign of serious spiritual defect in an assembly. Where Scripture is grasped, understood and applied, an atmosphere of liberty and confidence will be generated in which the Holy Spirit can lead believers into all truth thus to glorify our Lord Jesus Christ, John 16. 13, 14.

Formalism

by J. H. LARGE

WE FEEL IT WILL SERVE a very useful purpose if we devote space to the examination of an objection that is made from time to time. The objection amounts to this – New Testament principles have been held in a cold and formal way and it is supposed that our advocacy of them will tend to encourage this attitude. On this point we have three things to say.

(1) If it is true that what are called "assembly truths" have sometimes been held in a rigid and lifeless way it is deplorable, but the neglect of principles on the mere ground that they have been abused is a precarious proceeding, which, if generally adopted in life, would quickly reduce everything to chaos. The abandonment of the principles offers no remedy, as is clearly proved by the fact that greater formalism is often found where there is not the slightest pretence of following them. Formalism is no by-product of the principles for which we stand – it is the negation of them. It is simply another instance of the weakness of human nature, about which none of us need have any illusions, and it is here we must place the blame. Of course, we are not so foolish as to suppose that a Pharisaical adherence to certain views will miraculously compensate for those spiritual qualities which only genuine fellowship with God and with one another can produce, and

without which assembly life must degenerate into a religious existence. In fact, it is one of the many practical advantages of the New Testament pattern that it will function properly only in the right conditions. We maintain that, granted these conditions, adherence to the Scriptural order will conduce to the assembly's maximum effectiveness for God.

(2) Furthermore, it is fatally easy to give exaggerated emphasis to isolated cases, and so fall into the common error of basing sweeping condemnation on the strength of individual cases of failure. We think that a careful examination of the situation as a whole will satisfy the unprejudiced observer, that in the overwhelming majority of cases, the spiritual tone and vigour of assemblies, large and small, testify to the practical value of the principles on which they were founded and by which their development has been regulated.

(3) But to come to the crux of the matter. Are these principles in accord with the Word of God? That is the question. If they are, it behoves us, in spite of instances of human failure, to work them out by the grace of Christ, the love of God, and the power of the Holy Spirit, in living warmth and reality. We earnestly hope the ministry reprinted in these pages will encourage this attitude of mind and heart in those whose objection we have been considering. We are convinced the result will be a complete answer to their fears.

Let Every Man Take Heed

I CORINTHIANS 3. 5–17

by J. H. LARGE

THE POPULAR INTERPRETATION which makes Paul's words about building gold, silver and precious stones refer to the individual believer's responsibility to cultivate in his personal life those qualities which please God, obscures an essential but much neglected line of teaching as to responsibility in the local assembly.

Earlier in the chapter the apostle has been telling the Corinthians that he and Apollos were ministers by whom they believed, v. 5. In this they were "labourers together with God", and the Corinthian believers as a company ("ye" – plural) were God's husbandry, v. 9. Turning from this agricultural metaphor to architecture he adds, "ye are God's building" and the special character of that building is indicated in verse 16, "ye are the temple of God". Certainly, later in the Epistle, 6. 19, he touches on the truth that the *individual* believer's body is the temple of the *Holy Spirit*, and upon this truth bases his argument for personal sanctification, but here he is speaking of the believers as a community – it is the *assembly* which is the temple of *God*. With the building of the believer's body as a temple of the Holy Spirit Paul obviously had no part, but in connection with the building of the local assembly at Corinth as the temple of God he claims that as a wise master builder he had laid the foundation. In other words, during the eighteen months he had been preaching the Word of God among them, Acts 18. 11, he was laying the foundation upon which the growing assembly was to rest.

When Paul departed from Syria, the responsibility of continuing the work he had commenced fell on the shoulders of other men who must build on the foundation he had laid – "another buildeth thereon", v. 10. Since every assembly similarly owes its foundation to some servant or servants of God, and its progress to the labours of those who succeeded, this message of Paul's should be taken to heart by all upon whom rests, or will one day rest, the responsibility of caring for the wellbeing of an assembly. Any attempt to build for God on a foundation different from that which Paul laid for Corinth will be futile – "other foundation can no man lay" – but even on such a solid foundation each must take heed *how* he builds. Furthermore he must be careful as to the material which he builds into the structure because "every man's work shall be made manifest, for the day shall declare it, because it shall be revealed by fire, and the fire shall try every man's work, of what sort it is", v. 13. The words "made manifest", "declare", "revealed", "try", invest this test with a peculiar solemnity and may suggest a searching scrutiny which penetrates even to the hidden motives.

Perhaps it will be helpful (adopting the style of verse 10) if we consider Paul's exhortations as four cautions, i.e.:

(1) Let every man take heed, *where* he builds, ("Other foundation can no man lay", v. 11).

(2) Let every man take heed *how* he builds, ("Let every man take heed how he buildeth", v. 10).

(3) Let every man take heed *what* he builds, ("If any man build . . . gold, silver, precious stones, etc., v. 12).

(4) Let every man take heed *why* he builds, ("Every man's work shall be made manifest", v. 13).

Although all four cautions are thus suggested by the passage we have been considering, it is useful to look upon them as corresponding with the first four chapters of the Epistle.

1. The Foundation. Where we Build. READ CHAPTER ONE. God recognizes only one foundation for an assembly, for "other foundation can no man lay than that which is laid, which is *Jesus Christ*". We take this to mean that unless our work is carried on in practical subjection to the acknowledged Lordship of Christ, we are not building for God. The assembly is His, and His will must be supreme at all times and in every situation. There is no place for self-will and it is a solemn thing for any man to thrust himself forward with a view to having his own way. How much havoc this has often caused – yet the solemn warning stands, If any man mar the temple of God, him will God mar, 3. 17.

Christendom affords examples of communities which rest upon some humanly devised constitution, and it would be perversity to deny that in many cases they have been strong and vigorous in their early stages, but the foundation has been unsatisfactory and it is instructive to notice that when in such circumstances decline or departure sets in, the process is usually irreversible, so that we have today the warning spectacle of communities which once made a valiant stand for gospel truth, being hopelessly riddled with modernism. On the other hand, where a company rests solidly on the Lordship of Christ, so that His will is sovereign, there is a constant ground of appeal adapted to every situation, and it is always possible to rebuild.

Hence it is that when Paul was led to write to the Corinthians with a view to remedying the serious abuses which had crept in, he first stresses the Lordship of Christ, evidently realizing that the success of his appeals would depend upon the Corinthians' willingness to accept this fundamental ground in all the questions which had arisen. As they listened to the Epistle being read, could they have failed to notice how the full title of Jesus Christ as Lord, ran like a refrain through the opening sentences, occurring no less than six times in various impressive and significant connections?

> Call upon the name of Jesus Christ our *Lord*.
> Grace and peace from . . . the *Lord* Jesus Christ.
> The coming of our *Lord* Jesus Christ.
> The day of our *Lord* Jesus Christ.
> The fellowship of His Son, Jesus Christ our *Lord*.
> I beseech you by the name of our *Lord* Jesus Christ.

They would notice, too, how before he commences to speak of the means by which his work in Corinth was done, he winds up (what we call) chapter one with, "He that glorieth, let him glory in the *Lord*". In keeping with such an introduction the title "Lord" is constantly mingled with his appeals, occurring over sixty times in the Epistle.

2. The Means. How we Build. READ CHAPTER TWO. Here Paul elaborates the means by which his work at Corinth was accomplished – no confidence in the flesh, in natural ability, but utter reliance on the Holy Spirit, who is frequently mentioned in this second chapter.

Paul's natural gifts and qualifications would have enabled him to appeal to the Corinthians' love of "wisdom"; he could have charmed them with excellency of speech and enticing words of man's wisdom and obtained an enthusiastic following – for a while, until some new philosophic fashion took the field. Against this temptation he resolutely set his face, in the conviction that results obtained by such means would be transient – the work would not "abide". He knew full well that not only does the natural man not receive the things of the Spirit of God, but that they are foolishness unto him, v. 14, and it could not have come easy to a man of Paul's temperament to rest his whole appeal on a Christ who not only appeared weak and foolish to the worldly wise, but the crown of whose work involved a death of unspeakable disgrace. It was not only "Jesus Christ", but "him crucified", v. 2. To preach Jesus Christ was an offence – to preach a crucified Christ was an insult. We to whom the cross has become the symbol of the triumph of divine power and wisdom, 1. 24, cannot hope to understand how abject seemed the preaching of One as Saviour, the ground of whose saving power was that He had meekly submitted to a degrading death. Jew and Gentile joined in hurling at Christians such scornful and scathing jibes as Lucien's, "A gibbeted Christ!".

The Athenian's contempt for such a message, even when very carefully presented, Acts 17. 18, 32, made quite clear what kind of reception Paul could expect at Corinth, and he confesses that he was with them, "in weakness and in fear, and in much trembling", v. 3. Nevertheless allied to human weakness was "the demonstration of the Spirit and of power", v. 4. What a contrast to the self-confidence and the brave show with which much of spiritual (? religious) work is conducted today, which can neither be said to be in weakness and in fear and in much trembling – nor, alas, in demonstration of the Spirit and of power. If we saw less of the self-sufficiency of man, we might see more of the adequacy of the Spirit's power, 2 Cor. 3. 5. Any genuine concern at the low ebb to which the tide of spiritual blessing has receded, is cause for deep thankfulness, but unfortunately consideration of the remedy is too often confined to exploring the possibilities of *new methods*. It would surely be a mistake to discourage enterprise, but the crucial need is not new methods, but the *old power*. The most elaborate machinery is useless without the power to drive it. Probably there never was a time when religious work was better organized than it is today – the machine is wellnigh perfect, but organizers, valuable as they can be, will accomplish nothing in the absence of agonizers.

There is an ever present danger of substituting activity for spirituality – indeed there may be willingness to be self-deceived because activity demands far less of us than does spirituality. It is easy to assume that because an assembly is alert and enterprizing, and its affairs are conducted with business-like efficiency, that it is necessarily healthy. It is in such an atmosphere that the intellectual, the organizer and the business man, take the place of the spiritual man. It is no credit to any assembly if its affairs are conducted in any but an efficient manner, but this is no guarantee of spiritual prosperity, which after all, is what matters.

Of the various translations proposed as an improvement on the Authorised Version in verse 13, "comparing spiritual things with spiritual", the one most appropriate to the context seems to be, "imparting spiritual things by spiritual means". In other words only spiritual power can procure spiritual effects. There are various kinds of power and each secures results only in its own realm. Physical power can accomplish physical results – and physical results only. Much that goes for spiritual ministry may be merely the outcome of intellectual power – the ability to grasp and to impart to others certain truth. Clear and accurate exposition of the Scripture is not to be despised, but if it is simply intellectual it is merely a case of mind imparting to mind. If it ends there, no work for God is done – it is in word only, 1 Thess. 1. 5. Some can discern what is merely intellectual, who nevertheless fail to make another and equally important distinction between soulish (psychic) power and spiritual power. Men with certain gifts of soul have the ability to influence the emotions of others – soul imparts to soul. These sensations are mistaken for spiritual operations, but soul power produces only soulish results and the effects soon evaporate. This is not to say that God does not use the intellectual or soul powers of His servants – we simply contend that if the work goes no deeper, nothing of abiding spiritual value is achieved. Spiritual power, which is characterized by the Holy Spirit's operations upon the spirits of men, results in enlightenment, whereby convictions are formed and wills are moulded to the will of God. No doubt this is usually preceded or accompanied by intellectual processes or emotional experiences, or both, but these are secondary – the crucial thing is the application of spiritual power to men's spirits. This was the only thing in which Paul placed confidence – "that your faith should not stand in the wisdom of men, but in the power of God", v. 5.

Not one of us will dispute that only what is wrought by the Spirit's power is acceptable to God, but how many of us have paused to apply this disconcerting test to all that we fondly regard as service for Christ? Yet apply it we must if we are to escape the humiliation of seeing our work burned up. Only the work which "abides" will count – permanence is the criterion, not the spasmodic appearance of success.

3. The Material. What we Build. READ CHAPTER THREE.
Here our thoughts are directed to the materials to be built into the spiritual structure of the assembly – the character of the work done. Gold, silver and precious stones refer to those many forms of ministry which contribute to the consolidation and adornment of assembly life and witness. Space does not allow of a detailed study of the many suggestive lessons to be learned from a comparison of the two classes of materials, one so inflammable, the other so indestructible – we must be content to notice that the keynote is *quality*, not quantity. God is not so much concerned with the apparent *size* of our work – the fire shall try every man's work of what *sort* it is. How slow we are to learn this lesson, and how easily we are deceived into thinking that the value of our service is proportionate to the amount of work we attempt – not infrequently the reverse may be the case.

Wood, hay and stubble may make an imposing pile and yet be worth only a fraction of an apparently insignificant amount of gold, silver and precious stones. Similarly a man whose work looms large in the public eye, whose natural gifts enable him to occupy sphere upon sphere with acceptance and every appearance of success, may actually be accomplishing less for God than an obscure saint who is content to fill a little sphere – but a sphere to which God has called him – and to fill it with prayerful and devoted subjection to the guidance and empowering of the Spirit of God. His contribution to the spiritual structure of the assembly may be overlooked, or, at the best, under-rated, and it may be the other man who is regarded as the assembly's chief ornament and support. But "today" must soon give place to "the day" when so many of earth's verdicts will be reversed.

We may well ask ourselves whether we are allowing our natural eagerness to do as much as possible, to be misused by the devil to trap us into occupying so many spheres that we can bring to none of them that spiritual depth and reality which alone can hope for true success. Maybe many a true servant of Christ would accomplish more if he were content to attempt less, because his *real* work for God would then be of a better quality. Alas, the trouble is that he often finds the decision very hard to make – he would gladly do less if so many of his brethren were not so content to do nothing. On the other hand, his attitude may be excusing if not encouraging their idleness.

4. The Motive. Why we Build. READ CHAPTER FOUR.

Do these verses give us to see what fire it is which reveals every man's work – is it the searching scrutiny of our Master's all-seeing eyes, which John describes as a flame of fire?, Rev. 1. 14. Those eyes in examining our work will try not only the quality of the materials (what sort it is) but will also bring to light the hidden things of darkness, and will make manifest the counsels of the hearts, v. 5. Then will be seen not merely *what* we really did build, but *why* we built it. Not merely the materials but the motives. Unless we are very watchful we easily become swayed by mixed motives, when the glory of Christ ought to be the main-spring of our service. How the human heart covets the prominent place and the praise of men. If we go in for these things we shall probably get them – in that case we have had our reward – and need not expect to get in addition, the reward we never valued until too late – the praise of God, Matt. 6. 2. What we shall get is the exposure of our real motives.

"Then shall every man have praise of God", v. 5, can hardly mean that all will be praised. If this be the meaning, how are we to explain the contemplated case of a man's work being burned up and his being saved, yet so as by fire?, 3. 15. Will he have praise of God? Does it not rather mean that whereas now the praise of men may count for much in the eyes of some, then the praise of men will have no place – any praise which is given will come from the only One whose praise has any real value.

In the full realization of this, Paul (whilst never indifferent to his brethren's genuine convictions, or scornful of their commendation) thought man's estimate of him, favourable or unfavourable, a matter of very little consequence – "with me it is a very small thing that I should be judged of you, or of man's judgment", v. 3. Indeed, he did not presume to assess the value of his own work – "yea, I judge not mine own self". Certainly he judged himself in the sense that he was careful to keep a clear conscience, and this priceless boon he enjoyed, for having judged himself in this sense, he "knew nothing by (against) himself", v. 4. Nevertheless he realized that his knowledge of himself was very imperfect – his honest verdict on his own service was no guarantee of his Lord's final approval – "He that judgeth me is the Lord". He must be content to wait for the Judgment Seat of Christ.

In like manner we are to "judge nothing before the time, until the Lord come", v. 5. Certainly we are to examine ourselves and to judge and put away what we see to be contrary to the mind of God, but we are competent neither to assess the value of our work, nor to guarantee the purity of our motives. Similarly, though we are justified in bringing the teaching of the Scripture to bear upon the service of others, for our guidance, we must resist the temptation to pass judgment on the quality of their work, and most certainly we are not to be so impertinent as to dare to pronounce on their motives. "Who art thou . . .?", Rom. 14. 4. Enough for us, that we have to answer for ourselves.

Paul reminds us that "it is required in stewards, that a man be found faithful", v. 2. If we honestly strive to be faithful and yet are not allowed to enjoy very much apparent success, it should certainly call for exercise of heart, but not for despondency – it may be a mercy which would keep us from its pitfalls. At any rate, we cannot command success – but we can be faithful, and that in the last analysis will prove to have been true success.

Happy is the assembly whose leaders are *builders*, who recognize only one Lord, and His Word as the one ground of appeal, who have no confidence in the flesh but rely utterly on the Holy Spirit, who know and are content with the sphere of God's appointing, and there render service characterized by spiritual quality, and whose master-motive is not the glory of self, but the glory of Christ. They are the builders whose work will "abide".

Finally, Brethren . . .

by C. E. HOCKING*

MANY ASPECTS of "Church truth" have been dealt with in this book. One proof of the importance of this theme is shown by the many different facets of the truth which are presented in the New Testament. The divine emphasis given to Church doctrine and practice is reflected in the 69 chapters preceding this one. Not that the subject has been treated exhaustively. There are still many paths to discover, and many fruitful fields await the reaper. Sufficient has been said, however, to encourage a re-examination of these things, and to safeguard against unthinking and unscriptural winds of change.

A Changing World. We live in a constantly changing world. The new developments introduced by man's ingenuity and resourcefulness increase with the days. Sometimes the change in policy or practice is for the better. More generally, however, the new scheme, or the new technique, only tends to accelerate the departure from God and His ways. The conditions abroad in our generation cause many a heart to faint for fear. Where will it all end?

The spirit of any given generation tends to affect the attitude of God's people living in it. If men and women living in the world ignore, or dismiss, the lessons of the past in their desire to be different or "with it", little time elapses before numbers of God's people are looking for something new, a change from the "outdated and outmoded" attitudes and activities of an earlier generation. In some cases, the changes purposed and introduced prove to be good, because they are based upon a fresh examination and application of God's Word. In many other cases, however, the desire for change does not spring from such exercise over the Scriptures before the Lord. It may be fruit of little more than wanting to mimic the conditions abroad in the world, whether secular or religious. Such changes undermine a spiritual work, and can only tend to disaster.

*This article has been specially written for this book.

Many a Christian, squarely facing both the need of the times and the condition of things in the Church, tends to despair. Yet however great the need, and however strong the winds of change, our God is the same; He does not change. Our Lord Jesus Christ is the same yesterday and today, yea, and forever. We must add to these stabilizing and heart warming facts the unchanging character of the counsel of the Word of God.

> How firm a foundation, ye saints of the Lord,
> Is laid for your faith in His excellent Word!

Paul, well aware of the problems which would develop in the assembly at Ephesus, confidently commended the assembly elders to *God and the Word* of His grace, Acts 20. 32. Peter, when many went back and departed from the Lord Jesus during His earthly ministry, freely admitted the divine resources upon which he was depending in the words, "Lord, to whom shall we go? *thou hast the words* of eternal life", John 6. 68. Can we do better in our day than draw upon the illimitable resources available to us in our unchanging God, in our unchanging Lord, and in the unchanging Word of God?

Our Unchanging God. There are numerous passages of Scripture which emphasize this truth. One in particular is peculiarly appropriate to our own day. Malachi's times were set at the end of a phase of God's dealings with His people. The times were in many ways dark and discouraging, not least in the work of God. There were religious leaders but they seemed totally ignorant of God's requirements, Mal. 1, 6, 7, 12; they paid deference to men while denying God the honour due to Him, 1. 8; they served for money rather than out of a ready mind, 1. 10, 13; they did not teach the Scriptures to the people and by their own bad example stumbled many, 2. 8. Little wonder that the professing people of God as a whole were far from pleasing to Him. There was not that separation from the world with its pleasures and passions which should distinguish the godly of every age, 2. 10–16. Every exhortation was challenged with such retorts as "Wherein hast thou loved us?", "Wherein have we wearied

him?", "Wherein have we robbed thee?", 1. 2; 2. 17; 3. 8.
These were times when there was much form, but so little
reality; the power was missing.

Yet all was not lost. "Then", says Malachi, when there was
so much departure from the Word of God, and truth was
challenged with every breath, *then* "they that feared the Lord
spake often one to another . . . and . . . thought upon his
name", 3. 16. This minority was occupied with the Lord, and
through their common attraction to Him they experienced the
joy of fellowship with one another. Though they saw change
and decay in all around them, their lives were enriched individually and collectively by a sense of the interest and
presence of *the Lord who changed not*, 3. 6.

The Unchanging Christ. How the New Testament
emphasizes this truth for *our* encouragement as well as for its
original readers. Those addressed in the Epistle to the
Hebrews had their problems. The Lord's way with them,
and the pressures and persecutions of unsympathetic "religious" compatriots, were proving to be very trying to them.
Their early enthusiasm had cooled; their preparedness to be
made a gazingstock by reproaches and afflictions, and to
accept joyfully the confiscation of their goods and property,
had waned, Heb. 10. 33–34. In the writer's treatment of their
problems, do we not detect a living message for ourselves?
We should surely imitate those who through faith and patience
inherit the promises, 6. 11–12. We ought not to forsake the
assembling of ourselves together as some do, 10. 25. We should
remember those of an older generation who had the rule over
us, who spoke the Word of God to us – men who had bought
the truth and would not sell it, 13. 7. Whatever the changes
proposed or introduced in the "religious" scene of those
Hebrews, or for that matter in our own times, the people
of God are encouraged to imitate the faith of yesterday's
generation. They had the same unchanging Lord available to
them as we have today, and as He was more than sufficient for
the problems of yesterday, so we will find Him more than
sufficient for the problems of our little today. The truth stands,
"*Jesus Christ the same* yesterday, and to day, and for ever",
13. 8.

The Unchanging Word. We have yet another resource in a changing world. It is the unalterable Word of God. Without it, we would be exposed to the danger of following every whim and fancy proposed by men. The Lord, by revealing His mind and will in the Scriptures, has safeguarded us from this. Whether it be some novel line of teaching or the claims of some long standing tradition, we should seek to ascertain what the Scriptures say about the matter. If it is something affecting our conduct and we would know what the Lord requires of us, then "He hath shewed thee, O man, what is good". It is not the Lord's intention that we should remain in ignorance of His purposes and requirements. An understanding of God's will in the Scriptures is an effective safeguard against being tossed to and fro, and carried about with every wind of doctrine.

As the world church schemes of men develop, and as much of Christendom pursues a path alien to the simplicity which is in Christ and contrary to the teaching of God's Word, we must pay the more earnest heed to what "the Spirit saith to the churches" in the Scriptures. Not least, we need to rediscover, return to, and to reaffirm the principles and precepts of God's unchanging Word in connection with the subject of the Church. One of the most cheering effects of Ecumenical pressures upon the Lord's people is the fresh impetus they have given to the study of the Biblical doctrine of the Church. In the light of the half truths and errors being propagated under the auspices of furthering "church unity", many "evangelicals" of different denominational persuasions have been forced to consider what the Bible says on this subject. Nothing but good can result from such fresh examinations of God's Word if followed by a desire to do His will. We hope that this book will have stimulated the reader to a similar deepening interest in Church doctrine, and also to a desire to put this into practice.

INDEX OF SCRIPTURE REFERENCES

Pages are denoted by numbers in bold type